The Slaughterhouse Cases

LANDMARK LAW CASES

AMERICAN SOCIETY

Peter Charles Hoffer
N. E. H. Hull
Series Editors

RONALD M. LABBÉ
JONATHAN LURIE

The Slaughterhouse Cases

Regulation, Reconstruction, and

the Fourteenth Amendment

ABRIDGED EDITION

UNIVERSITY PRESS OF KANSAS

© 2005 by the University Press of Kansas

Published by the University Press of Kansas (Lawrence, Kansas 66049), which was
organized by the Kansas Board of Regents and is operated and funded by Emporia
State University, Fort Hays State University, Kansas State University, Pittsburg State
University, the University of Kansas, and Wichita State University

Library of Congress Cataloging-in-Publication Data

Labbe, Ronald M., 1933-
The slaughterhouse cases : regulation, Reconstruction, and the
Fourteenth Amendment / Ronald M. Labbe, Jonathan Lurie. — Abridged ed.
p.   cm. — (Landmark law cases & American society)
Includes bibliographical references and index.
ISBN 0-7006-1409-5 (pbk. : alk. paper)
1. Slaughtering and slaughter-houses—Law and
legislation — Louisiana — History — 19th century.   2. Civil rights — United
States — History — 19th century.   3. Monopolies — United
States — History — 19th century.   1. Lurie, Jonathan, 1939-   11. Title.
111. Series.
KF228.S545L33 2005
344.7304'2—dc22   2005011127

British Library Cataloguing-in-Publication Data is available.

Printed in the United States of America

10 9 8 7 6 5 4 3 2 1

The paper used in this publication meets the minimum requirements of the
American National Standard for Permanence of Paper for Printed Library Materials
z39.48–1984.

Again, for Dolores and Mac, and for our grandsons Dominic, Alex, and Zachary

*"The Law . . . cannot be dealt with as
if it contained only the axioms
and corollaries of a book of
mathematics. In order to know what
it is, we must know what it has
been, and what it tends to become."*

—Holmes, "The Common Law"

*"It is carrying fiction too far to say that the
Courts must always know how the law will be."*

—Lord Abbinger

CONTENTS

A quick look at law reviews published in the first half of the first decade of the new millennium reveals that the *Slaughterhouse Cases* were discussed in 133 articles. Some of the citations were pro forma, but others involved a close rereading of the majority and minority opinions and varying degrees of analysis of their application to current issues in law. Unlike some famous constitutional contests, these cases were landmarks from their inception and remain so, closely watched for their outcome because they addressed the meaning of congressional Reconstruction, the fate of the reconstructed Southern state governments after the Civil War, and, most important, the application of the equal protection, due process, and privileges and immunities clauses of the newly ratified Fourteenth Amendment to the U.S. Constitution. Whether that amendment was meant to fundamentally change the relationship between federal and state governments and create a wide range of rights defensible in the federal courts, or whether it was intended to protect the newly freed men and women from unreconstructed racists and former slaveholders, the high court would decide. But that decision, as is always the case in systems like ours, would be subject to periodic review and revision by later courts.

In law scholarship, evidently, revision is essential. Whether we believe in the doctrinal orthodoxy of originalism (constitutional provisions must be interpreted in light of the framers' purposes) or in the necessity of a living constitution that changes with the times, legal scholars will always revisit the meaning of landmark cases. In history, too, revision is a good thing — it keeps the blood flowing within the body of scholarship. Brilliant revision — revision based on newly uncovered sources, newly interpreted texts, and innovative ways of reading — is rare, but Ronald M. Labbé and Jonathan Lurie have done just that. To the *Slaughterhouse Cases* they have brought the keen eye of a political scientist well versed in Louisiana politics and public health issues and a legal historian whose verve and insight are already well displayed in print. Together, they revise what we have long assumed about these critical challenges to federal jurisprudence and state regulatory authority.

Although the 1869 Louisiana law that limited the slaughter of animals to a regulated and clean facility was then and has since been reviled as a product of scalawag and carpetbag corruption, the authors reveal how the ordinance also addressed long-standing and compelling health needs in the city of New Orleans. Though the law was denounced as a particularly censurable exercise of Reconstruction tyranny in the South, the authors recenter the cases in terms of the revolution in cattle and other livestock handling that occurred after the Civil War all over the country. Despite the hint of stock fraud in the new company's creation, opponents of the Crescent City Company were eager to get their hands on its stock, and the whole country was undergoing an orgy of shady stock and bond deals. Nor was the battle in the lower courts waged between butchers seeking their rights under a free-market ideology and a corrupt company fronted by monopolistic legislative henchmen. Instead, as the authors trace out in detail, it was a struggle between economic interests using the law to further themselves.

The story involves lawyers, including a former U.S. Supreme Court justice who resigned to serve the Confederacy; a governor who wanted the great experiment in Reconstruction to succeed but could not free himself from the toils of party politics and private interests; local judges hurling injunctions in all directions; and, finally, a Supreme Court whose members' experiences and ideologies were ill fitted to the brave new world of the Fourteenth Amendment they had to interpret.

Questions of fact—Was there bribery and fraud? Was the statute and the company it created the best way to ensure public safety? Did the monopoly deny the butchers of the city their right to practice their trade?—blended into questions of law that were as inscrutable as they were novel. What did the amendment's language mean? Could it be applied to questions of restraint of trade? How far did the state's power to regulate the economy in the name of public health and welfare extend into everyday matters such as the slaughter of cattle and hogs?

Over all the deliberations, arguments, briefs, and opinions lay the brooding omnipresence of a Reconstruction regime under attack, of increasing violence against the newly freed men and women, and of the Republican party, already split into radical, moderate, and conservative factions, having to decide whether the courts could do what the Congress and the occupation forces could not. If the state courts could not sort out these issues, then appeal to the federal courts might, and that is what the losing butchers did in 1870.

{ *The Slaughterhouse Cases* }

The authors recount the next three years of legal and political maneuvering, bringing the cases to the Supreme Court with such clarity that it is hard to conceive that this account will ever be superseded. The narrative is filled with sudden twists, such as Justice Joseph Bradley's ruling, on circuit, that the privileges and immunities clause barred monopoly-creating legislation such as Louisiana's, whatever its merits for public health or the rightful police powers of the state. For conservative members of the Court, who opposed the extension of federal authority (in particular, the authority of the federal judicial system), the cases posed a problem — the acts of the Reconstruction state government could be overturned only by federal authority of an open-ended sort based on a loose construction of the privileges and immunities clause. Such a construction might then be applied to any police or health-based state regulation of the economy, an invitation to an active and interventionist federal government. Defenders of the federal program of Reconstruction, by contrast, would have to narrow the reach of the Fourteenth Amendment, and with it the federal courts, to protect the actions of reconstructed state governments.

How the Court shook out on these questions, the nature of the legal reasoning of the majority and minority, and the subsequent impact of the decisions merit a persuasive and elegant presentation, and that is what they receive here. In a series of chapters on the case in the high court, the authors untangle the opinions and explain how the legal ideas inherent in them grew out of the Civil War and then had to adapt to the novelties of the industrial nation the Civil War had midwifed. In this combat of ideas, there would be a great casualty, but this preface will not reveal that final twist to the story. You will have to read the book — a most enjoyable prospect.

PREFACE AND ACKNOWLEDGMENTS

The *Slaughterhouse Cases* decided by the U.S. Supreme Court in 1873 required the high court to decide whether an act of the Louisiana legislature regulating the slaughterhouse industry in New Orleans was prohibited by the terms of the newly adopted Fourteenth Amendment. The act was an exercise of the state's well-settled power to regulate persons and property on behalf of the health, safety, and well-being of the public. It led to a dramatic confrontation in the New Orleans courts and to a historic decision by the Supreme Court.

The Fourteenth Amendment occupies a place of unique importance in the Constitution. It was proposed by Congress as a means of writing into the fundamental law of the land the Union's victory in the Civil War. It contains sweeping provisions aimed at protecting civil rights from state action. In the *Slaughterhouse Cases*, the Supreme Court gave the new amendment a controversial and apparently much more restricted meaning than many of its supporters had hoped for. Yet in the course of arguing and deciding the case, positions were taken and new legal doctrines suggested by counsel and justices alike that had enormous influence on the future development of American constitutional law.

This book is an abridged edition of our book of the same title published by this press in 2003. It differs from the original in that it is shorter, the footnotes have been omitted, and the lengthy bibliography has been replaced with a bibliographical essay of noteworthy sources. Like in the original edition, however, every effort has been made to recapture the *Slaughterhouse* controversy, from its colorful beginning in New Orleans during Reconstruction to its final resolution in the Supreme Court.

A study of one of the Supreme Court's great constitutional cases involves more than an analysis of the decision and the several opinions of the justices. A great deal needs to be said about the political, economic, and social background out of which the case arose. The first chapters of the book are devoted to these matters. They establish a powerful rationale for the regulatory statute that led to the case, and they help explain why the controversy provoked so much interest and generated so much heat. Much also needs to be said about the identity of the parties to the case and about the lawyers who converted the parties' interests into legal arguments. Given the large number of cases involved in the *Slaughterhouse* controversy, marked attention must be given to how the dispute was handled in the lower courts, the resulting decisions, and the questions that were preserved for appeal. In a concluding chapter we discuss the aftermath of the *Slaughterhouse* decision and briefly trace the future course of the legal doctrines involved in it.

Over the years that it took to research and write this book, quite a few debts have been incurred. We are indebted to the late David Fellman and to Harold Hyman, who each suggested the need for this book. Judge Albert Tate Jr., late of the U.S. Court of Appeals for the Fifth Circuit and formerly a member of the Louisiana Supreme Court, befriended this project in its early stages. We are also grateful to Jean Kiesel and Alvin Bethard, directors of the Louisiana and Microform Collections, respectively, at the Dupré Library at the University of Louisiana at Lafayette, and Susan Daigle and her staff at the university's Department of Printing Services; Leon C. Miller, Joan G. Caldwell, Kenneth Owen, and other members of the staff in the Special Collections Division of Tulane's Howard-Tilton Memorial Library; David Combe, director of Tulane's law library, and Patsy Copeland at Tulane's Rudolph Matas Medical Library; Collin B. Hamer Jr. and Wayne Everard in the Louisiana Division of the New Orleans Public Library; Sally S. Stassi at the Williams Research Center of the Historic New Orleans Collection; Wilba Swearingen and Pauline Fulda at the library of the Louisiana State University Health Sciences Center in New Orleans; Sally K. Reeves and Ann Wakefield at the New Orleans Notarial Archives; Kathryn Page, curator at the Louisiana State Museum library; Marie Windell at the Supreme Court's archives at the Earl K. Long Library at the University of New Orleans; and, in a special way, Donn M. Kurtz II, Janet E. Frantz, Thomas Ferrell, and Mathé Allain, colleagues at the University of Louisiana at Lafayette, who each contributed in his or her own way. Thanks are also due to the donors and administrators of the Bernard and Kaye L. Crocker Professorship of Political Science at the University of Louisiana at Lafayette.

We enjoyed the open-door policies of the libraries mentioned above and of the library at the Paul M. Hebert Law Center and the Louisiana

Collection of the Middleton Library at Louisiana State University in Baton Rouge; the Louisiana Supreme Court's Law Library of Louisiana; both the main library and the Moritz Law Library at the Ohio State University; the Library of Congress and its legal division; the Southern Historical Collection at the University of North Carolina library; the Barker Texas History Center, University of Texas; and the United States Supreme Court Historical Society.

This book was funded from time to time by grants from the National Endowment for the Humanities, a grant from the American Philosophical Society, and research awards from the University of Louisiana at Lafayette and the Rutgers University Research Council.

We are deeply indebted to Michael Briggs, editor in chief of the University Press of Kansas, for his persistent inquiries about the state of our manuscript and for his very bright idea of bringing the two of us together, and to Paul Kens and Phillip Paludan for their careful examination of our manuscript. We also wish to acknowledge with deep appreciation the Scribes Award bestowed by the American Society of Writers on Legal Subjects on our book as the "best book on law published in 2003."

Again, we thank our wives, Dolores Egger Labbé and Maxine N. Lurie. Scholars in their own right, they deserve more credit than can be stated here. Finally, we would like to acknowledge our debt to each other. This work is the result of a close collaboration that took place over six years, with never a quibble. "What, *never?*"

"Well, hardly ever."

CHAPTER I

Beef from the Pork Barrel?

Introduction and Overview

You never know. Historical events intended for one purpose sometimes result in the unintended, and American history is not immune to this tendency. Thus the Civil War — first considered by Lincoln as nothing more than an attempt to prevent Southern secession — ultimately went far beyond an effort to preserve the Union, far beyond ending American Negro slavery, far beyond even ensuring continued western expansion. By 1866, the war had wrought changes in the relationship between the federal government and the states, the federal government and its people, and the states and their citizenry. Although these changes may well have been unintended, and their extent unclear, these transformations doomed the Union to continue as it had been — producing instead a new connection between the American people and their legal order that is still evolving. One manifestation of such change was the Fourteenth Amendment, adopted by Congress in 1866 and ratified by the states as part of the Constitution in 1868. Five years later, the Supreme Court first considered its meaning and scope, and there lies a story rich in irony.

Intended to facilitate a changed relationship between the ex-slave and white America, the new amendment was first presented to the Court on behalf of some white butchers arguing with other white butchers and livestock dealers over a Louisiana statute enacted in 1869. Their lawyer — a former Supreme Court justice who had resigned his seat when his state (Alabama) seceded — now called for a new level of federal supremacy and state subordination diametrically opposed to both his own long-held views and past American history. Finally, the high court, whose function was and remains the reconciliation of law with ongoing change, could not agree on the extent of constitutional alteration mandated by the amendment.

In this the justices were not alone. Uncertainty about what the new provision meant, as well as its application and scope, characterized both congressional debates and contemporary commentary. In April 1873, by a five-to-four vote, the Court first interpreted the Fourteenth Amendment and offered its own assessment — one that remains a landmark in American legal history. Speaking for a five-member majority, Justice Samuel F. Miller sustained the Louisiana statute regulating slaughterhouses and held that with the exception of the ex-slave, the new addition to the Constitution had not altered in any significant fashion the traditional pattern of federalism. Although at least two later members of his Court endorsed this analysis, more frequently Miller's opinion has been rebutted, denounced, and condemned.

Indeed, a cacophony of criticism has enveloped his decision ever since it was announced. Miller's decision, according to the *Cincinnati Enquirer* in April 1873, reflected the "degeneracy of the Court" in sustaining a statute enacted by those "elected by the bayonet and through the agency of the most degraded and ignorant portion of the population." A recent comment by the late Yale law professor Charles Black described Miller's opinion as "probably the worst holding, in its effect on human rights, ever uttered by the Supreme Court." According to Harvard law professor Lawrence Tribe, "there is considerable consensus among constitutional thinkers that the Supreme Court made a scandalously wrong decision in this case." Yet Miller's decision has not been overruled. Moreover, it did not prevent his Court, sometimes with his concurrence, from finding awesome breadth and depth in the amendment — a process that accelerated after his death and especially during the mid- and late twentieth century.

Given such long-standing criticism, why has the Court retained *Slaughterhouse*? Why this veneration for stare decisis in the face of sustained denunciation? We know that when it so desires, the Court can overrule itself, sometimes within a brief span of years. The *Legal Tender Cases, Betts v. Brady,* or *Brown v. Board of Education* immediately come to mind, and more recent examples can readily be cited. Perhaps one answer is simply that the justices, for whatever reason, do not wish to overrule the 1873 holding. And here again, we may ask, why? A possible answer may be found in a careful reexamination of (1) the background of the case, (2) the context in which it arose, (3) exactly what

Miller's majority believed it had decided, and (4) what the dissenters insisted were the real issues involved in the litigation.

For reasons that follow, this study looks anew at *Slaughterhouse*, including what seems to have become the standard negative interpretation. The purpose of our book, however, is one of reinterpretation rather than refutation. Given the varied ways in which the Fourteenth Amendment was perceived, the lack of certainty as to its intent, the existing tradition of federalism, the potency of the police power as a constitutional doctrine, and the unusual background of sanitation reform efforts in New Orleans, it is far from clear that in 1873 Miller's opinion was "scandalously wrong."

Turning first to the question of legislative intent and the Fourteenth Amendment, its adoption *must* be seen in the context of federalism and the police power as understood during the mid-nineteenth century. Moreover, the conservative nature of the new enactment — specifically Section 1 — should be noted. The terms *equality, freedom,* and *civil rights* do not appear; nor is there any hint of suffrage for the ex-slave. Scholarly emphasis on its conservative character is not new. More than twenty-five years ago, Michael Les Benedict pointed out that the amendment's framers intentionally left most Southern rebels with the vote and Southern blacks without it. He argues that the amendment "in no way challenged the tradition that states had primary jurisdiction over citizens in matters of police regulation, the regulation of conduct for the protection of the community."

More recently, William Nelson concluded that "confusion and contradiction abound" concerning the Fourteenth Amendment's adoption. He infers, however, that the new enactment had meaning for its proponents. Nelson sees it as an effort to resolve the tension between equality and individualism, as well as between federalism and majoritarianism. The method was to employ vague language, leaving the precise accommodation between these principles to be resolved later. The framers, Nelson implies, dealt with conflict not by resolving it but by bequeathing it to the future. Nelson notes further that the Republicans remained committed both to completing the unfinished wartime work of emancipation and to retaining the "traditional values of federalism." The new provision may well be seen as satisfying both commitments. He writes that its framers sought to reaffirm a long-standing "commitment to general principles of equality, individual rights, and local self rule."

Finally, Nelson emphasizes how quick the Republicans were to reject the claim that their amendment "would give Congress power to legislate about matters previously reserved to the states and thereby result in a consolidation of power and the destruction of the federal system as America had known it." John Bingham, the primary author of Section 1 and a speaker not always distinguished for his clearness of thought, had no difficulty making this point. His wording, he insisted, "took from no State any right that ever pertained to it."

A search of the congressional debates for insights concerning the scope of Section 1 leaves us with some ambiguity and uncertainty. A variety of views concerning its intended coverage were offered, but the words employed "made so many promises to so many persons." For our purposes, the most important point is that when the Court interpreted the new amendment, Miller could have reasonably concluded that the congressional debates furnished no clear guidance as to intent in general and certainly no specific mandate that federalism was to undergo a major transformation.

Besides the intentions of the Fourteenth Amendment's framers, attention must also be focused on the historical and political context in which the 1869 Louisiana statute was adopted. There can be no doubt that for New Orleans in particular, the slaughtering of cattle and hogs represented a long-standing health problem of impressive dimensions. For more than sixty years, the controversy over it had festered, and the search for a solution presented an ongoing challenge to effective public policy. Time and again, attention had been called to the appalling state of public health in the Crescent City.

As will be seen in the chapters that follow, efforts by city officials to remove slaughtering operations from the city date from 1804. They had virtually no effect, however, because as the city grew, so did the number and political strength of the butchers and stock dealers. By the Civil War era, more than 300,000 animals were slaughtered within New Orleans and adjacent Jefferson City each year. New Orleans lacked a public sewer system; therefore, wastes were either dumped in uninhabited areas of the city, such as the broad levee of the Mississippi River, or simply emptied into open gutters, as was the practice of the large hotels. Similarly, the offal from the slaughterhouses was thrown either into the river or onto city streets. The humidity and swampy environment of New Orleans contributed to these deplorable conditions. Leading physicians branded it the dirtiest and most unhealthy city in the country.

It is certain, then, that the regulation of slaughterhouses had concerned New Orleans long before 1869, as the following chapters explore in some detail. But the statute at issue must be seen in another context, besides the matter of public health, for it was the controversial product of a controversial legislature. In 1868, under federal protection, a convention created a new constitution for Louisiana. Never before had the South seen a major elective body with a majority of black members. The new charter contained a remarkable embodiment of Reconstruction goals. It provided for desegregated public schools. It prohibited discrimination in public places and withheld the vote from disloyal voters. The new document outlawed the black codes, and it was the first Louisiana constitution to contain a bill of rights. Later constitutions were modeled after it.

The first Louisiana legislature elected under this new constitution was a truly integrated body. Thirty-five of the 101 members of the house were black, all of them Republicans. Seven of the 36 members of the senate were black and Republican. It enacted several very controversial measures in 1868–1869. The Slaughterhouse Act was one of them. Others included an act that mandated that public schools be open to all races and one that made it a criminal offense to deny African Americans access to certain facilities serving the public, such as hotels, steamboats, and railroad cars. Such enactments from an integrated legislature outraged local white voters, and they were in no mood to distinguish between different statutes with different motives for passage.

In spite of all the controversy caused by the Slaughterhouse Act, the practice of centralizing slaughtering in an urban area was not new. Centralized abattoirs had already been established in European and other American cities, and more than one effort had been made to implement this arrangement in New Orleans, though without success. But the act was the product of a highly conflicted context, and its passage raised a number of issues — all directly applicable to our story. These include concerns about legislative motivation, bribery and corruption, the scope and function of the police power, the place of public health regulations, the question of monopolies, the actual provisions and implementation of the 1869 statute, the adequacy of the facility it established, the costs to those affected by it, and legitimate doubts concerning the constitutionality of the statute and the role of the courts — both state and federal — in its enforcement.

It will be noted that absent from these concerns is the matter of race. Of course, there can be no doubt that issues of race were involved in Louisiana politics after 1865. But apart from the fact that the act was the product of a legislature that was despised partly because of its racial makeup, it is our contention that race is one of the less important factors in the *Slaughterhouse* story. To argue that the *Slaughterhouse Cases* must be seen primarily in the context of racial Reconstruction is to miss the point that had there been no blacks in the legislature, opposition to the statute still would have been profound. This is not to say, however, that issues of race did not figure indirectly in the *judicial* resolution of the dispute. It was based, after all, on the Fourteenth Amendment, and in 1873, no one could doubt that race had been a factor in bringing about *its* enactment and ratification. How the justices used the issue of race as they wrote the several opinions that make up the case is also explored in later chapters.

Another part of the traditional account of *Slaughterhouse* must also be considered: that the statute was the result of a corrupt group of carpetbaggers with no legitimate reason to support the new law, other than their own financial interests. Accusations of misconduct in the passage of the act were widely reported in the conservative New Orleans press and achieved a level of credibility, given the popular antipathy toward the legislature. Similarly, the claim of legislative collusion in granting the favored butchers a monopoly should be reexamined. There is no doubt that the statute granted one company the exclusive right to build and operate a slaughterhouse in New Orleans. But any butcher who wished to do so could either slaughter his beef at that site or have it slaughtered for him subject to a fee that was stipulated in the statute. Further, as Miller later emphasized in his opinion, the slaughterhouse faced substantial penalties if it denied any butcher access to its facility. In a real sense — and lawyers for the favored group were quick to make this point — far from restricting it, the statute actually facilitated butchering as a profession. "There is no longer any necessity of a butcher providing a slaughter-house for himself. . . . This charter, therefore, is not a monopoly in the sense that it prevents any one from being a butcher; instead of that, it makes it easier to be a butcher than before."

Although the claim of bribery remains unresolved, surely it is reasonable to ask why the legislature granted one company an exclusive right to build and maintain a slaughterhouse. As will be seen, such an approach to slaughterhouse regulation was not new to Louisiana in 1869. There is no doubt, however, that, as was true of other Southern Reconstruction legislatures at the time, what Michael Ross calls "ambitious modernization plans" had been proposed. To bring them to fruition, however, either tax or bond revenues were essential. But by 1869, tax revenues were very scarce, in part because of economic hardship, as well as white taxpayer recalcitrance. State bonds also remained unappealing to investors. This resulting shortage of state revenues may well have pointed legislators toward a policy of granting exclusive privileges to companies that, in return for the "favor," had to meet various public health requirements and conditions of open access. The context in which the 1869 statute was adopted needs to be carefully reexamined.

Speaking for the Court in *Slaughterhouse*, Miller emphasized the limited scope of his decision. "We now propose," he wrote, "to announce the judgments we have formed in the construction of those articles [the Reconstruction amendments], so far as we have found them necessary to the decision of the cases before us, and beyond that we have neither the inclination nor the right to go." This point is important, because Miller may not have intended his opinion to be taken as an "all embracing construction" of the Fourteenth Amendment. Rather, it was a response to the uncomplicated question of whether the Louisiana legislature's exercise of the police power concerning slaughterhouses had been affected by the new amendment. Echoing Chief Justices Marshall and Shaw, as well as Chancellor Kent, Miller had no doubt of the answer.

In referring to recent incidents, including the Civil War, Reconstruction, and enactment of the Southern black codes, events "almost too recent to be called history," Miller noted that "on the most casual examination of the language of these amendments, no one can fail to be impressed with the one pervading purpose found in them all, lying at the foundation of each, and without which none of them would ever have been suggested; we mean the freedom of the slave race, the security and firm establishment of that freedom, and the protection of the newly-made freeman and citizen." Yet the Fourteenth Amendment's language was broad, and Miller acknowledged that "if other rights are assailed by the States which properly and necessarily fall within the protection of these articles [the three Reconstruction amendments], that protection will apply, even though the party interested may not be of African descent." Miller emphasized, however, that "what we do say, and what we wish to be understood is, that in any fair and just construction of any section or phrase of these amendments, it is necessary to look to the purpose which we have said was the pervading spirit of them all, the evil which they were designed to remedy."

Nine years after his decision, during oral argument in another case involving the Fourteenth Amendment, Miller emphasized that "I do not know that anybody in this Court — I never heard it said in this Court or by any judge of it — that these articles were supposed to be limited to the Negro race." To which the lawyer replied, "there is a notion out among the people . . . that it was the intention of this Court to give this provision . . . as restricted and limited application as possible." Miller responded that "the purpose of the general discussion in the *Slaughterhouse Cases* on the subject was nothing more than the common declaration that when you come to construe any act of Congress, any statute, any Constitution, any legislative decree you must consider the thing, the evil which was to be remedied in order to understand fully what the purpose of the remedial act was."

It can be argued that Miller's goal, as evidenced by the language he used, was to prevent the Fourteenth Amendment from being diluted and diminished by its application to the issue of localized infighting among white butchers over which group would control the lucrative meat trade in New Orleans. Even if one accepted the contention of broad language, as Miller had from the outset, his majority may well have considered this dispute so far beyond the amendment's purview as to warrant rejection. A similar point can be raised concerning Miller's treatment of the privileges and immunities clause, which apparently remains a viable and sometimes visible part of our living Constitution. It might be noted that since Miller based his decision on police power precedents, there was no need to specify in any great detail exactly what the privileges and immunities clause might be interpreted to mean in future litigation. This could be explored later. Whatever "the privileges and immunities of citizens of the United States" were, however, they did not extend to the rights claimed by the bickering butchers.

The major criticism levied against Miller is that through his opinion, he sought to hinder — if not to derail entirely — the course of congressional Reconstruction. Once again, not only is there no evidence for such a claim, but its best rebuttal is the opinion itself. Miller did more than accept the well-established presumption of constitutionality doctrine. He upheld as legitimate the action of a biracial reconstructed legislature committed to a program of change, reform, and modernization that — had the legislature persevered — augured well, he believed, for the future. Far from gutting Reconstruction legislation, his opinion endorsed it.

The traditional view of *Slaughterhouse* ignores these facts, somehow assuming that what happened after 1877 was inevitable in 1873 — and this is not so. Miller's Court had no inkling at the time that Reconstruction would wither in the climate of the 1877 compromise, that Congress would lose its sense of commitment, or that an older racial and economic order fundamentally unsympathetic to Louisiana's postwar legislation would regain power. Moreover, Miller never denied the inherent potential in the due process and equal protection clauses. But their very legitimate purpose "was not to prevent states from passing health regulations that had nothing to do with race." Miller's opinion should be seen in the context of his previous training and career as a physician, his firsthand observations and experiences concerning the spread of cholera, and the terrible results of improper sanitation and inadequate safeguards related to the location and operation of slaughterhouses.

Finally, this overview should mention subsequent judicial commentary on *Slaughterhouse*, beginning most appropriately with Miller himself. Miller served on the high court until his death seventeen years after *Slaughterhouse*, and he remained proud of that decision. Very soon after the case was decided, in April 1873, he wrote to his brother-in-law that his two Fourteenth Amendment decisions (*Slaughterhouse* and *Bradwell*) were "undoubtedly the most important opinions delivered in this Court in many years. I believe they were decided rightly, though no questions have ever given me more trouble in making up my own mind than those therein discussed." (Decided immediately after *Slaughterhouse*, the *Bradwell* case reiterated Miller's conception of the Fourteenth Amendment within a narrow context. Bradwell, a female attorney, had sought to use the amendment as a basis to compel Illinois to admit her to the practice of law.)

Eleven years after his decision, Miller spoke for a unanimous Court upholding the right of a new (and all white) Louisiana legislature to repeal the 1869 statute dealing with slaughterhouses. State authority to enact such a law "was the exercise of the police power which remained with the States in the formation of the original Constitution . . . and had not been taken away by the amendments adopted since." A law resulting from such authority, "so long as it remains on the statute book as the latest expression of the legislative will, is a valid law, and must be obeyed, *which is all that was decided by this Court* in the *Slaughterhouse Cases*" (emphasis added to illustrate, once again, Miller's belief in the very limited scope of his earlier decision).

Later legal history appears to have rejected Miller's perception of the Fourteenth Amendment. Both congressional and public support for Reconstruction waned, and with it, any hope of multiracial legislatures working to bring reform and economic modernization to the South also faded. Miller's legal positivism had given great deference to legislative discretion. But with the enshrinement of "liberty of contract" came the accompanying view that the Fourteenth Amendment protected, but did not in itself create, such liberty. Any legislation that limited it was suspect, on its face. Thus judicial deference to state legislation became unwarranted and unnecessary.

The great distance the Court had traveled since *Slaughterhouse* can be seen through a brief comparison with *Lochner v. New York* and *United States v. Carolene Products Co.* The ghost of the earlier decision hangs over these cases, and it is most prevalent in the *Lochner* dissents. In noting, for example, that "the word liberty in the Fourteenth Amendment is perverted when it is held to prevent the natural outcome of a dominant opinion," Justice Holmes echoed Miller. So did Justice Harlan when he insisted that "neither the [Fourteenth] Amendment — broad and comprehensive as it is — nor any other amendment was designed to interfere with the power of the State, sometimes termed its police power." Actually, Harlan was quoting Justice Stephen Field in *Barbier v. Connolly* (113 U.S. 27 [1885]). Writing for a unanimous Court that still included Miller, and without any citation whatsoever, Field had sustained a San Francisco municipal ordinance regulating the hours during which public laundries could operate. Moreover, "legislation which, in carrying out a public purpose is limited in its application, if within the sphere of its operation it affects alike all persons similarly situated, is not within the [Fourteenth] Amendment." Miller had said much the same thing about the statute at issue in *Slaughterhouse*, whereas Field probably had it in mind when he added that "class legislation, discriminating against some and favoring others, is prohibited."

Between 1873 and 1938, when the *Carolene Products* case was decided, liberty of contract reached its apogee. The concept of strict judicial scrutiny concerning legislation had come a long way since 1873. But in *Carolene Products*, once again Miller's descendants — so to speak — argued successfully that it was now acceptable and reasonable to defer to the legislature. Justice Stone held that the existence of facts supporting the legislative judgment is to be presumed, "for regulatory legislation affecting ordinary commercial transactions is not to be pronounced unconstitutional unless in the light of the facts made known or generally assumed, it is of such a character as to preclude the assumption that it rests upon some rational basis."

"For all sad words of tongue or pen," according to John Greenleaf Whittier, "the saddest are these: 'It might have been!'" Do these words represent a fair and accurate summary of *Slaughterhouse*? There is no doubt that things did not turn out as Miller assumed they would in 1873, and it may be that somehow he and his majority looked back to what had been, while the dissenters anticipated what was yet to come. Yet Miller endorsed legislative deference and a healthy respect for federalism — values that, for better or worse, have continued to influence contemporary constitutional interpretation.

One source of significance for *Slaughterhouse* may be what it offered for the future, even though public policy as it evolved after 1877 declined to follow its direction. Certainly such a course led to tragic results, but that they followed inexorably from *Slaughterhouse* is neither an accurate nor, we believe, an acceptable conclusion. What Loren Beth wrote of this landmark decision in 1963 remains perceptive and persuasive. "Such a case," he observed, "never dies; there is always interest and importance in its reevaluation, and the final word about it is never said." We agree and offer the following chapters as our contribution to its further understanding — one based on context, controversy, contents, and consequences.

CHAPTER 2

Private Gain, Public Health, and Public Policy in Antebellum New Orleans

The Louisiana slaughterhouse statute of 1869 was not merely an example of misguided or corrupt Reconstruction-era policy. The act had roots in both the political and economic history of New Orleans. It was also the product of a long process by which sanitary reform was brought to a city that desperately needed it. The next several chapters place the act in its context and explain why it was so controversial, even as they offer ample justification for its passage.

At one point, as it meanders across the marshes and prairies of southern Louisiana, the Mississippi River makes a radical turn southward. It then circumscribes a curve some 5 miles wide before making another sharp turn to resume a southeastern course. Here at this second crescent-shaped bend about halfway between existing French outposts near Mobile and Natchez, Jean Le Moyne de Bienville established a new settlement in 1718 that he named New Orleans. From Bienville's perspective, the site had a number of advantages. It offered ample dockage along the river's muddy bank and a certain amount of high ground along its natural levee. It was only about 110 miles from the Gulf of Mexico and provided an ideal accommodation for vessels moving either up- or downstream. Further, the location was barely 6 miles from Lake Pontchartrain, a saltwater lake that provided access from the gulf without the problem of strong river currents. Finally, the narrow strip of land that divided the two bodies of water was already traversed by a bayou and could accommodate a future man-made connection.

Thomas Jefferson — whose actions as president had made New Orleans part of the United States — predicted that "New Orleans will forever be . . . the mighty mart of the merchandise brought from more than a thousand rivers. . . . With Boston, Baltimore, New York, and Philadelphia on the left, Mexico on the right, Havana in front, and the immense valley of the Mississippi in the rear, no such position for the accumulation and perpetuity of wealth and power ever existed." And for a time, it seemed as if Bienville's outpost would indeed become the key city in a great commercial empire.

After the Battle of New Orleans in 1815 (an engagement that ended the War of 1812, even though the peace treaty had already been signed in Paris), British blockades were removed from eastern ports, and wave after wave of immigrants landed on the eastern seaboard. As a result, settlement of the Mississippi River valley beyond the Appalachian Mountains expanded tremendously. Settlers moved first into the western states and territories along the valleys of the Ohio River and the upper Mississippi above Cairo, Illinois. Between 1840 and 1860, they migrated into the lower portion of the Mississippi valley. The movement was of such magnitude that between 1790 and 1860 the U.S. population center shifted westward from a spot near Baltimore, Maryland, to a point southeast of Chillicothe, Ohio. Between 1810 and 1820, the population of the western states and territories doubled, and by 1840, it had quadrupled to nearly 5 million people, or almost one-third of the entire population. Twenty years later it doubled again, embracing 37.8 percent of the American populace.

The West generated vast surpluses of agricultural products in search of a market. The Appalachian Mountains prevented most of this trade from directly reaching the eastern ports of New York, Philadelphia, and Baltimore. Rather, the route to market followed a southward direction, along the Ohio and Mississippi Rivers. New Orleans, situated at the base of the great river system, was a natural recipient for this produce. After 1816, the steamboat arrived. New Orleans–born writer George Washington Cable observed that this innovation "held out to the merchants of New Orleans, and the newcomers that daily poured into the town, not only present wealth, but the delusion of absolute and unlimited commercial empire inalienably bestowed by the laws of gravitation." Indeed, the Crescent City entered a "golden period of its commerce." In 1840, more than half a million tons came to New Orleans, valued at almost $50 million. At least 80 percent of these goods were products of the West.

The city had become a world-class trading center from and through which goods were shipped upriver to ports on the East Coast, to Latin America, or to Europe. Within a decade after the arrival of the steamboat, the New Orleans population increased by 70 percent, from 27,176 to 46,082. By 1840, it had expanded by another 121 percent to 102,193. On the eve of the Civil War, the New Orleans population had increased more than 500 percent since 1820. Only New York, Philadelphia, and Baltimore were more populous. *DeBow's Review*, a leading Southern periodical based in New Orleans, stated categorically that "no city of the world has ever advanced as a mart of commerce with such rapid and gigantic strides as New Orleans." It appeared to be the richest city in America, a growing metropolis that seemed "invulnerable to competition."

But appearances were deceiving. If Yankee ingenuity could design a steamboat, it could also provide more direct and less costly ways of transporting goods to market. Beginning in the 1830s, a system of newly constructed canals and railroads in the North brought about a revolution in transportation that proved very detrimental to New Orleans as a trade center. Now, trade from the West tended to bypass the Crescent City, and by 1858, the proportion of total receipts coming from the West had declined from a high of almost 80 percent to barely 18 percent. In fact, the flow of western trade reversed itself. *DeBow's Review* captured the significance of these events: the economic unit known as the Mississippi Valley had been turned on its head, so that the Mississippi River was flowing north.

> Where is New Orleans now? Where are her dreams of greatness and of glory? Where her untold wealth in embryo? Whilst she slept, an enemy has sowed tares in her most prolific fields. Armed with energy, enterprise, and an indomitable spirit, that enemy, by a system of bold, vigorous and sustained efforts, has succeeded in reversing the very laws of nature and of nature's God — rolled back the mighty tide of the Mississippi and its ten thousand tributary streams, until their mouth, practically and commercially is more at New York and Boston than at New Orleans. Thus have the fates mocked and deceived us in promising rank and greatness.

The forces of economic growth and industrial development turned with even greater vigor against New Orleans as a consequence of the Civil War. But the mighty Mississippi, the city's great natural endowment, continued to flow across its doorstep. It served as a constant reminder of past grandeur as well as future potential, and there were always those in the Crescent City who could not shake the notion that somehow they could recapture the dizzying prosperity of the past. As will be seen in the next chapter, the possibility of capitalizing on trade in Texas beef seemed particularly promising in the postwar period.

In spite of all the advantages Bienville may have perceived in the site he chose for New Orleans, the city's location presented a number of disadvantages as well. There was, for example, a problem with topography. George Washington Cable described the city's location as "a fragment of half-made country, comprising something over 1,700 square miles of river shore, swamp and marshland." New Orleans was founded on a site, noted another observer in 1853, "which only the madness of commercial lust could have tempted men to occupy."

The city is located in a subtropical zone, where in the nineteenth century the average temperature was 54.4 degrees in the winter months and 79.3 degrees in the summer. The annual rainfall averaged fifty-two inches, and it could be much more in some years. The highest point in the city was only fifteen feet above sea level, with much of New Orleans below it. To make matters worse, the earthen levees intended to keep the river at bay sometimes gave way in periods of unusually high water, and large portions of the city would be inundated. Throughout the nineteenth century, there were complaints about pools of stagnant water standing in low-lying areas, in vacant lots, and under houses.

In such an environment, drainage was a constant problem. Underground drainage did not exist, and the city depended on irregularly graded ditches and canals to carry water away from inhabited areas. Three mosquito-infested cypress swamps, situated like so many saucers between the occupied areas of the city and Lake Pontchartrain, exacerbated the drainage problem. These physical conditions, combined with a plethora of deplorable sanitary practices and a stubborn refusal by New Orleans officials to recognize and effectively resolve them, are important elements in the background of the *Slaughterhouse Cases.*

There was, for instance, neither an operable sewage system nor an effective method of garbage collection. It was common practice to dispose of refuse by throwing it into one of the swamps or by dumping it onto a vacant lot. In 1813, Governor W. C. C. Claiborne complained that "the pollution constantly striking a person walking on the levee, and which arises from the filth of the city thrown into the water's edge, is too offensive for a civilized person to submit to." Indeed, throughout much of the nineteenth century, the New Orleans citizenry routinely used the *batture*, the land between the river's edge and the levee, as a dumping ground for the contents of their privies, garbage, dead animals, and many other kinds of filth. Although the city required that dead animals and garbage be promptly removed from the streets, in reality, days passed without any action. The contractors employed by the city to collect garbage were subject to little supervision. There were complaints that they retired for the day after collecting only a few pints of material and that during rainy weather they filled potholes in the unpaved streets with the contents of the garbage carts. One butcher defended his practice of throwing the offal from his slaughterhouse into the street by insisting that it was an effective way to keep the thoroughfare in good repair. Given their circumstances, many nineteenth-century New Orleanians became apathetic about environmental cleanliness. In the 1820s, a visiting French physician reported that "with the exception of the homes of the elite, the condition of the yards is such that you would think that savages lived there."

Fortunately, mid-nineteenth-century New Orleans was gifted with a very active medical community, and leading physicians frequently remonstrated against the city's wretched sanitary conditions. In 1853, for instance, Dr. Edward H. Barton produced a "sanitary map" showing that tanneries, bone-boiling factories, cattle yards, slaughterhouses, cemeteries, and areas of standing and stagnant water were scattered throughout the urban incorporated area. The next year Dr. Barton wrote, "New Orleans is one of the dirtiest . . . and consequently the sickliest city in the Union." An inveterate spokesman for sanitary reform, Barton knew whereof he spoke. A host of diseases continually plagued this bustling city, in particular, epidemics of cholera and yellow fever. Time and again they struck and exacted terrible tolls. Between 1796 and 1869, New Orleans endured thirty-six epidemics of yellow fever. Eleven epidemics of cholera descended on the Crescent City between 1832 and 1869. In 1851, Dr. Barton had aptly characterized his city as "a great Golgotha."

It was not until the 1880s that the *Aedes aegypti* species of mosquito was identified as the vector of yellow fever. Prior to this discovery, the medical community had to make do with explanations of disease grounded in both conjecture and common sense. Some held, for example, that disease was transmitted from person to person. New Orleans physicians of this persuasion were apt to favor a naval quarantine to protect the city from imported sickness. Another group emphasized the importance of sanitation over quarantine. Doctors in this group typically argued that disease was caused by breathing the gases (which they called "miasma") given off by decaying animal and vegetable matter.

Whatever its scientific shortcomings, the miasma theory had the effect of focusing attention on the relationship between good health and environmental cleanliness. As early as 1834, for example, Barton had written that the warm and humid New Orleans climate could at times produce "an epidemic atmosphere," which, in combination with animal and vegetable decay, created a uniquely noxious mix. He repeatedly called for sound sanitary practices as a way of avoiding pestilence in the Crescent City. "Filth," he claimed, "is the electric spark which fires the other elements." Dr. Erasmus D. Fenner, coeditor of two New Orleans medical journals and publisher of a short-lived but well-respected journal of his own, agreed. He insisted that proper sanitary measures, properly enforced, could remove yellow fever from the city.

Various boards of health organized in New Orleans offered similar remonstrations against the deplorable sanitary practices that were an everyday occurrence in the city. Their annual reports often provided a forum for some of the best-respected advocates of reform. But these boards were political bodies, existing in an atmosphere of conflicting interests. All they had to offer were politically unpopular suggestions about quarantine, regulation, and costly drainage and sewage projects. The boards were inevitably established in response to a crisis, such as an epidemic, and when it subsided, support for the board waned, making it easy prey for detractors. New Orleans saw three separate boards of health come and go between 1800 and 1825.

Several factors help explain why effective reform came so slowly. To begin with, local observers repeatedly insisted that their city was a veritable health spa. As the editor of the New Orleans city directory put it in 1838, "no country in the world has suffered more unmerited obloquy than New Orleans, in relation to health." Indeed, he added, "probably there is no portion of America where the mortality is less than with our native and acclimated population." Whatever their political differences, Creole and American residents were united in their insistence that the Crescent City "was far more salubrious than the great cities to the north."

Many New Orleanians departed the city during the sickly summer months, leaving a population in which newcomers and the poor were overrepresented. This made it possible to argue that, for the most part, the only people affected were the poor, who, in their ignorance, led dissolute lives, or newcomers to the city who had not had sufficient time to become accustomed to the climate, or "creolized." Many agreed with an 1850 assessment by the board of health that yellow fever was a "stranger's disease." Although the disease might claim a few "deeply lamented citizens, it has principally affected the newly arrived immigrants, or those ghastly specimens of humanity that occasionally arrive from California."

Then, too, city officials were loath to concede the presence of disease because of the effect it might have on the city's commerce. As medical historian John Duffy wrote, even "the rumored presence" of an epidemic "was enough to start thousands of panic stricken residents pouring out of the city." It would certainly discourage businessmen from coming to the Crescent City if they could do business elsewhere. The main "business of a commercial port was business, and this could not be carried on when the public was alarmed and frightened."

Finally, there was a resistance generated in part by inertia. Epidemics came and went, and sentiment for reform inevitably seemed to wane, as did the virulence of the disease. Also, given the prevalence of a laissez-faire attitude toward governmental authority, it was not clear who was responsible for municipal health. When he stepped down as chair of the Louisiana State Medical Association in 1852, Dr. Barton commented that his group was "compelled to meet opposition of a character peculiar to a republican government, where every man claims the right to follow any occupation or profession most congenial to his own feelings." Moreover, if care for the sick was a moral obligation, and many held that it was, such a burden was considered an obligation of an individual, not a municipality.

In short, the path to reform, though seemingly clear, was not easy. First, the public had to be convinced that there existed a serious *public* health problem. Second, political decision makers, in spite of conflicting opinions and viewpoints, somehow had to be persuaded to use their power to overcome the problem. And indeed, signs began appearing in New Orleans that the status quo was no longer acceptable.

Sixteen years elapsed between the collapse of the last board of health in 1826 and the city's appointment of another. In that period, New Orleans was visited by epidemics of cholera or yellow fever almost every year, and pressure for sanitary reform accumulated from the medical profession, the newspapers, and even the general public. When a particularly severe epidemic struck in 1841, the city council finally created a new board of health, headed by veteran sanitarian Dr. Edward Barton. It collapsed the next year.

But by this time, reform had developed a more lasting impetus. In 1844 the city council asked the local medical society to serve as a board of health, and in 1846 it created a new and stronger board — the city's seventh since 1804. The new agency consisted of twelve physicians, headed by Dr. William P. Hort. Dr. Hort's contribution to the course of reform was a hard-hitting frankness and a single-minded insistence that the major impediment to reform was the refusal of city officials to enforce existing rules. In his first report for the board he insisted that the problem required not additional regulation but enforcement of what had already been enacted years before. Despite Hort's efforts, general health conditions in the Crescent City remained deplorable. When, in 1847, a new yellow fever epidemic struck the city, the state legislature itself created yet another board of health for New Orleans, the eighth in less than half a century.

There was at least a hint of Dr. Hort's insistence on more effective enforcement in the power of this new state-mandated board. It was given more power over sanitation in New Orleans than all previous boards had possessed. It had the authority to select health wardens for every ward, with the power to remove nuisances, file suits against stubborn property owners, and enforce the city's contracts with street cleaners. When little was accomplished, Hort used his 1848 report for the board of health to forcefully place the blame for the poor state of public health on the shoulders of public officials.

Hort assumed that there already existed sufficient authority to compel sanitary reforms. The 1848 report from the board of health — probably authored by him — emphasized that "wise police regulations have been adopted from time to time by our Councils, and commissaries have been appointed to carry them into effect." Yet the situation had not improved. "Of what avail are solutions and ordinances, if they are not rigidly enforced, and if the officers appointed . . . actually do, or permit to be done, the very things prohibited by the Board, and which have over and over again been spoken of as the most fruitful cause of our malignant epidemics." There appeared to be a simple solution. "We say, let *this* nuisance be at once abated; let the commissaries be compelled to do their duty and their whole duty, subject to fine or reform [removal] from office in default thereof."

Dr. Hort's arguments soon received compelling support from the publication of a new body of evidence. In 1848, Dr. J. C. Simonds, another New Orleans physician, attended a meeting in Boston, where he heard many negative comments concerning public health in his home city. Simonds returned to Louisiana determined to gather the evidence necessary to prove that the Crescent City was on a par with every other major urban center. But what he found proved just the opposite. His research led to the publication of reliable mortality statistics in New Orleans for the first time, and his remarkable findings received wide publicity.

In his study, Simonds compared the average annual mortality rates for the major urban centers of Philadelphia, New York, Boston, Baltimore, and Charleston from 1811 to 1849. All, he found, were between 2.4 and 2.9 percent. In New Orleans, based on only a four-and-a-half-year sample, the mortality rate was 8.1 percent, "or 1 in every 12, nearly." Dr. Simonds's comparison of New Orleans and Boston proved particularly shocking. Looking at an approximately nine-week period between February and April 1851, he found that there were more than twice as many deaths in New Orleans than in Boston, despite the fact that there were more than 8,000 more persons in the latter city. By insisting on a degree of public health in New Orleans that did not exist, the people were deceiving no one but themselves. Simonds emphasized that "an honest statement of the truth with regard to the health of the city, would ultimately promote its true interest and permanent prosperity."

Simonds's efforts reflected the emergence of still another factor in the reform process: an *organized*, reform-minded medical community. This trend paralleled similar developments on a national scale. When, for example, the American Medical Association was organized in 1848, doctors from New Orleans had been in attendance. New Orleans had had its own medical school since 1835. The city was also home to the *New Orleans Medical Journal*. With the publication of Simonds's mortality tables in 1851, the editors of the journal were among the first to admit that New Orleans was in fact one of the most unhealthy of American cities. Henceforth, with few exceptions, the periodical stoutly supported the cause of sanitation and public health. So did *DeBow's Review*. Its editor confessed that "we have been the last to yield to the proposition that New Orleans is an *unhealthy city*, very unhealthy, and have done as much, perhaps, as anyone circulating the contrary opinion. . . . The facts are, however, against us."

Hort and Simonds were joined by Barton, who in an 1851 article criticized not only the poor public health in New Orleans but also the apparent lack of official interest in making lasting improvements. Like Simonds, he conceded the poor quality of public health in his city. Indeed, it had "a mortality exceeding any city" in America. Moreover, "the present system of police is a mere mockery, leaving the public here, and those interested in our city abroad, with the impression that its salubrity is unimprovable."

Simonds, too, had had the police power in mind when he warned his readers not to attribute the high mortality rate to "the want or imprudence of strangers and the unacclimated." Rather, "commence immediately . . . an examination of the causes of the prevalence of disease, and proceed vigorously to remove them." Most important, "revise your sanatory [*sic*] regulations; compel your Board of Health to do its duty, and . . . institute such new police regulations as may be found necessary, and consider the protection of human life against disease and crime, as paramount in importance to every other question. Until this be done New Orleans will always remain unhealthy." The confluence of Hort, Simonds, and Barton in the 1850s is important. As John Duffy put it many years later, "although the struggle between the public health reformers and the conservatives was to continue for many years, never again was New Orleans to feel the sense of complacency which had characterized the townspeople in the period prior to 1850."

Unimpeachable evidence was now available; valid explanations for the city's health problems had been published. Yet in themselves, these facts still were not sufficient to bring about needed changes. Between 1853 and 1858, however, New Orleans endured the worst yellow fever epidemics in its history. The 1853 outbreak killed one-tenth of the population in a single summer. The city came to a virtual standstill during this time while residents cared for the sick and disposed of the dead. This was followed by yellow fever epidemics almost as severe in both 1854 and 1855; still another onslaught of yellow fever in 1858 was second in severity only to the epidemic of 1853. Another medical reformer, Dr. Stanford Chaillé, later declared the six years between 1853 and 1858, and especially the three years between 1853 and 1855, "a culminating epoch in the yellow fever and mortality history of this city, from its foundation to the present day; . . . in the entire history of New Orleans, no three successive years can be found at all comparable in fatality with those mentioned."

The city council convoked a sanitary commission to study the 1853 tragedy and named Barton as chairman. He had repeatedly contended that the city's health problems were entirely removable by an effective use of the police power. Now, in the commission's final report, he declared, "The 'let alone' system has been tried long enough. . . . The trial has been full and unsatisfactory. All unite in saying there must be sanitary reform." Between the medical community's repeated calls for an effective exercise of the police power and public officials' occasionally being forced into action by dire circumstances, an assumption had been created that public officials had some responsibility for public health. Persuading these officials to fulfill their responsibility remained another matter, however. In 1854, for the first time in its history, Louisiana established a statewide board of health. Yet despite the continued yellow fever epidemics, New Orleans failed to implement changes.

In 1859, for example, Dr. A. F. Axson, president of the board of health, denounced the city's condition and lamented the incredible tolerance for "scandalous nuisances" shown by its officials. "Populous hotels poured their ordure from brimming sinks through the chief avenues of the city; gutters sweltered with the blood and drainings of slaughter-pens; sugar refineries opened their sluices and whole streets reeked of their rank odors; and every highway that chanced to be unpaved was broadcast with the rakings of gutters and the refuse filth of private yards and stables." The board remonstrated against these outrages and the city council's habitual inaction without success. Two years into the Civil War, however, the reformers received aid from a most unlikely source. It came not from the city fathers but from the general commanding the Union forces that occupied New Orleans: Benjamin Butler.

———

New Orleans surrendered to Union naval forces late in April 1862. Admiral Farragut promptly turned control of the city over to General Butler, and on May 1, Butler assumed responsibility. He was shocked by the unsanitary condition of his surroundings "The streets," he later recalled, "were reeking with putrefying filth." He later learned that prayers were being offered in local churches for the arrival of a robust epidemic of the "saffron scourge." If the South was unable to defeat the military might of the Union, perhaps the disease could decimate the occupying forces from the North. Butler ordered city officials to enforce all existing public health regulations. A few days later, however, on a carriage ride with his wife, he encountered a basin near Lake Pontchartrain. The general later recalled that "the air seemed filled with the most noxious and offensive stenches possible, so noxious as almost to take away the power of breathing. The whole surface of the canal and the pond was covered with a thick growth of green vegetable scum, variegated with dead cats and dogs or the remains of dead mules on the banking." His response was to hire a force of up to 2,000 men to restore the streets, squares, and unoccupied areas to suitable conditions.

Butler's approach to enhancing public health involved both quarantine and sanitation. A member of his staff, Colonel T. B. Thorpe, assumed responsibility for the cleanup, and Butler's biographer described his efforts: "He waged incessant and most successful war upon nuisances. He tore away shanties, filled up holes, purged the canals, cleaned the streets, repaired the levee, and kept the city in such perfect cleanliness" that even die-hard secessionists admitted that "the federals could clean the streets, if they couldn't do anything else."

Dr. Elisha Harris, a member of the U.S. Sanitary Commission during the Civil War and the superintendent of the New York Metropolitan Board of Health, documented the New Orleans experience. He lauded Butler's efforts. Private premises were "kept in a state of unusual cleanliness by an absolute authority. . . . Privies and garbage, stables and butcheries . . . were all brought under police control." Livestock was impounded, and cattle boats were scrubbed before receiving permission to enter the city. According to Harris, "so clean a city had never before been seen upon the continent."

General Butler moved on to another assignment in December, declaring as he went, "I have demonstrated that the pestilence can be kept from your borders." His successor, Major General Nathaniel Banks, maintained the policy of civic cleanliness, and New Orleans was spared from epidemics throughout Federal occupation. Native son George Washington Cable would one day accuse New Orleans of "an invincible provincialism" for its failure to recognize and remedy important problems in the first half of the nineteenth century. Change had finally come about at the insistence of outsiders. Once the military returned the city to civilian control on March 19, 1866, however, the question arose whether the new sanitary conditions would be maintained. It did not remain an open question for long.

CHAPTER 3

Law, Politics, and
Slaughterhouse Reform

The idea that slaughterhouses ought to be centralized was not new to New Orleans or — as will be seen — to other nineteenth-century American cities. Early in the century, slaughtering in the Crescent City had been confined to a small area located directly across the Mississippi from the city and known as "Slaughterhouse Point." From there, slaughterhouse waste could be dumped into the river, and the powerful current would sweep it downstream toward the Gulf of Mexico. Butchers accomplished their slaughtering at night and transported their daily supply of meat across the river to the city markets.

By the mid-nineteenth century, however, the New Orleans population had increased by about tenfold. Wharves, landings, and warehouses were established farther and farther upstream to deal with the commerce flowing downriver. The expanding population followed, leading to the establishment of suburbs such as Lafayette and Jefferson City. For the sake of convenience, the butchers moved their operations from Slaughterhouse Point into the city and its suburbs, and they steadily migrated upstream with the population. The demand for dressed meat increased, as did the number of stock dealers and butchers. They became prosperous and politically influential.

New Orleans soon found itself plagued with all the nuisances that accompany the business of providing meat to the markets of a growing metropolis through a system of private slaughterhouses. The slaughterhouses required stockyards to be maintained nearby, and they gave rise to related enterprises such as bone-boiling (tallow) factories and fertilizer plants. Moreover, private slaughterhouses made it virtually impossible to enforce either the rules of cleanliness or an effective system of meat inspection. In New Orleans, animals were routinely herded through the streets. Slaughtering sometimes took place out in the open within sight of the public. Carts loaded with slaughterhouse waste were driven, leaking and reeking, through the streets to "nuisances wharves," where the waste was supposed to be dumped into the river. But much of it was simply discarded into the streets and gutters or left to rot and fester in butchers' backyards. By 1868 there were perhaps as many as 150 slaughterhouses in the New Orleans area. In 1869 the board of health reported 40 such establishments in the Fourth District alone.

By the 1850s, leading New Orleans physicians began insisting in various published reports that the slaughterhouses be removed from the city limits. However, both legal and political realities made reform a very slow process. In the eighteenth and nineteenth centuries, slaughterhouses were not generally considered to be *legal* nuisances. Most courts presumed that a slaughterhouse could be operated in a way that would not give offense. And the New Orleans butchers were a politically strong, cohesive group that always seemed to have effective representation on the city council.

Loopholes impeding effective municipal slaughterhouse regulation were numerous. An ordinance might be enacted calling for slaughterhouses to be kept clean, but it provided no penalties for violators. A statute might be passed requiring council approval before a new slaughterhouse could be established within the city, but such approval could be easily obtained. Still another enactment might forbid the operation of any slaughterhouse on the river upstream from the intake pipes of the city's water supply, but it would be so qualified as to make it ineffectual. In truth, more often than not, the city ordinances were not enforced, and they had little effect on limiting the number of slaughterhouses. Yet, in spite of all the obstacles thrown in their path, would-be reformers were able to point to a well-established body of regulatory law — the "police power" of the state — and municipal practices elsewhere that supported effective slaughterhouse regulation.

The practice of requiring butchers to accomplish their slaughtering in a single facility can be traced back to public slaughterhouses in Germany in the mid-thirteenth century and in Paris in the twelfth century. In 1807, Napoleon ordered the establishment of five public slaughterhouses to serve Paris; by 1818, private slaughterhouses had been forbidden in the city. In 1867, the year in which the Louisiana legislature first considered compulsory consolidation of the New Orleans slaughterhouses, the five separate Paris abattoirs were consolidated into one "grand" establishment at La Villette. In 1869, when the controversial Louisiana statute was enacted, there were compulsory public slaughterhouses in Germany, Scotland, Spain, Switzerland, Belgium, Austria, and Poland.

But spokesmen for slaughterhouse reform in New Orleans did not have to rely on Europe for support. Similar developments were occurring in the United States. By the 1850s, public health had become a national issue. Between 1857 and 1860, four national sanitary conventions were held, attended by leading exponents of public health, including a number from New Orleans. At the 1859 convention, Dr. John Bell presented a report in which he stressed the importance of removing slaughterhouses from cites and urged widespread adoption of the French concept of a centralized abattoir.

In his outstanding study *The People's Welfare*, Professor William Novak cites *Commonwealth v. Alger* (1851), a decision by Chief Justice Lemuel Shaw of the Massachusetts Supreme Judicial Court, as the prototype for police power decisions. It was one that occupied a "central place in nineteenth century jurisprudence," a holding that accurately articulated a vigorous and expansive police power doctrine. Shaw stated that "every holder of property, however absolute and unqualified may be his title, holds it under the implied liability that his use of it may be so regulated, that it shall not be injurious to the equal enjoyment of others . . . nor injurious to the rights of the community." Novak emphasizes that this decision, which came as New Orleans was poised at the brink of major demands for sanitation reform, was "firmly entrenched in the intellectual, political, and legal traditions of nineteenth-century America."

Indeed, the reasoning of the *Alger* decision can be detected in many nineteenth-century state cases. In 1849, in *Green v. The Mayor and Aldermen of Savannah*, the Georgia Supreme Court ruled that "every right, from an absolute ownership in property, down to a mere easement, is purchased and holden [*sic*], subject to the restriction that it shall be so exercised as not to injure others." In *Commonwealth v. Upton* in 1856, the Massachusetts Supreme Court insisted that "the public health, the welfare and safety of the community, are matters of paramount importance, to which all the pursuits, occupations and employments of individuals, inconsistent with their preservation, must yield." And in 1867, in *Ex Parte Shrader*, the California Supreme Court upheld the authority of San Francisco to prohibit slaughtering outside of a certain area, notwithstanding the argument that slaughterhouses were not nuisances per se. "Now there are many things," the court held, "not coming up to the full measure of a common law or statutory nuisance, that might . . . pave the way for the introduction of contagion and its uncontrollable spread thereafter. Slaughterhouses, as ordinarily and perhaps invariably conducted in this country, might, within the limits of reasonable probability, be attended with these consequences."

Yet not all courts were sympathetic toward municipal efforts to regulate slaughterhouses. Most notably, in *City of Chicago v. Rumpff*, decided in 1867, the Illinois Supreme Court rejected an effort by the city of Chicago to establish a single public slaughterhouse. By the mid-nineteenth century, Chicago was well on its way to becoming the nation's leading livestock market and meatpacking center. The city's slaughterhouses, its meatpacking and fertilizer plants, and its tanneries and glue factories created a pollution problem of staggering proportions that defied solution both logistically and politically.

Toward the end of 1865, the Chicago city council, impelled by the threat of cholera, undertook to establish the nation's first compulsory municipal slaughterhouse. In an ordinance that was later emulated in New York, Milwaukee, Boston, and New Orleans, it awarded a franchise to maintain a slaughterhouse in Chicago to a single company in return for the company's agreement to erect and maintain a sufficiently large and well-equipped slaughterhouse to accommodate all the city's butchers. In return, the city banned slaughtering anywhere in the city except at the new facility. The company agreed to allow its facilities to be used without charge, except that it could retain the usual slaughterhouse waste for its own profit. The statute was promptly denounced by the butchers as a monopoly and an unreasonable restriction of their right to slaughter wherever they wished.

In a unanimous decision, the Illinois Supreme Court agreed. In his opinion for the court, Justice Pinkney H. Walker readily recognized the city's power "to adopt and enforce all needful sanitary regulations." But he claimed that the ordinance was not an exercise of the city's regulatory power at all but simply an offer by the city to contract with the favored company. The resulting contract, he said, was invalid because in his view it created a monopoly, which was beyond any power the legislature had intended the city to have. The council did indeed have the right "to so regulate the business of slaughtering animals, as to prohibit its exercise, except in a particular portion of the city, leaving all persons free to erect slaughtering houses, and to exercise the calling at the place designated." But "an ordinance confining such a business to a small lot, or even a particular block of ground, is unreasonable, and tends to create a monopoly." Walker insisted that "when privileges are granted by an ordinance, they should be open to the enjoyment of all, upon the same terms and conditions." It would seem that there was ample precedent to justify this statute as a simple police measure. But possibly because of political factors, the judges, all of whom had to face the exigencies of an electorate, declined to emphasize the police power and opted instead to denounce the alleged nonregulatory features of the ordinance. The *Rumpff* opinion is notable for its total lack of case citation, and indeed it would have been difficult to find much support for it in the case law of the day. Nonetheless, it would prove very useful to those opposing slaughterhouse reform in New Orleans only two years later.

The distinction of having the first centralized abattoir in North America, some 200 years before *Slaughterhouse*, appears to belong to New York City. Established in 1676 and privately owned but franchised by the city, it had the effect of both confining slaughtering to a single place and facilitating some sort of municipal inspection. It lasted well into the next century but eventually fell victim to the city's expansion and the great increase in the number of butchers.

Like so many other municipalities, by the mid-nineteenth century, New York City had a critical public health problem. According to medical historian John Duffy in his *History of Public Health in New York City*, "Municipal regulations, slowed down by Jacksonian democracy and the principle of laissez faire, had simply not kept pace with the city's expansion." And when ordinances were adopted, they often were not enforced. When local politics prevented the city council from adopting effective reform, would-be reformers took their complaints to the state legislatures. In 1866 the New York legislature adopted the Metropolitan Health Act. According to Duffy, it marked a new era for New York and American public health.

Almost immediately, the newly established Metropolitan Board of Health clashed with local butchers. There were more than 200 slaughterhouses in New York in the mid-1860s, and it would take years of pressure before the last slaughterhouse was finally relocated. The arguments and tactics used by the butchers to thwart reform would become all too familiar in other cities. A slaughterhouse, they insisted, was not a nuisance per se; it could be operated in an inoffensive manner. In addition, efforts to centralize slaughtering would lead to a vast monopoly. Further, the butchers claimed that the cost of relocating their businesses beyond the city limits would cause many of them to fail and seriously impair the city's meat supply. Finally, they claimed that schemes to force them into consolidated facilities interfered with their property rights. And time and again, the butchers went to court and obtained injunctions from sympathetic judges that nullified the board's orders.

Inevitably, the need for slaughterhouse reform in New York attracted the attention of private parties who saw it as an opportunity for profit. In August 1866, the magazine *Scientific American* reported that "a new abattoir, somewhat on the French plan, is now in the course of construction at the foot of 106th Street." Similarly, a group of railroad stockholders from Chicago obtained a charter from the New Jersey legislature for a slaughterhouse near a railroad on the Bay of New York. They hoped that it would serve the New York market. In still another private effort that closely paralleled the forthcoming New Orleans dispute, a New York coal dealer with no experience in the livestock industry threw up a set of cheap buildings and attempted, unsuccessfully, to foist them on the city council as "the New York Abattoir."

After making little progress in discussions with the butchers, in 1867, the board of health prohibited all cattle from being driven or slaughtered anywhere in New York City below Fortieth Street. Butcher Jacob Heister violated the order by driving cattle and slaughtering them at a slaughterhouse he owned in the restricted area. When the board went to court to enforce a fine against him, Heister argued that the board's order violated a provision of the New York State Constitution holding that "no person shall be deprived of life, liberty or property without due process of law." The case of *Metropolitan Board of Health v. Heister* reached the New York Court of Appeals in 1868, just one year before adoption of the Louisiana slaughterhouse statute. It is of special interest because it was authored by Chief Justice Ward Hunt. In 1873, Hunt would be appointed to the U.S. Supreme Court by President Grant, and the first major case he participated in would be *Slaughterhouse.*

Speaking for a divided court, Chief Justice Hunt upheld the statute and observed that "no one has been deprived of his property or of his liberty by the proceedings in question." Contrary to Heister's claim, the board's "regulations take away no man's property." If "Mr. Heister owns cattle," Hunt explained, "his ownership is not interfered with. He may sell, exchange and traffic in the same manner as any other person owning cattle may do. If he owns a slaughterhouse, his property remains intact. He may sell it, mortgage it . . . and may use it just as any other man or all other men in the State combined may do." Simply put, "the health regulations of the district operate upon his cattle and his slaughterhouse in the same manner that they do upon live [like] property owned by all others, and the use of the streets for dangerous purposes of the prosecution of a business dangerous to the public health is regulated by the ordinances in question. This practice is not forbidden by the Constitution, and has been recognized from the organization of the State government, and is to be found in nearly every city or village charter which has been granted by the legislature."

Heister had also insisted that the regulation unlawfully conferred on the board of health quasi-judicial power, in violation of the New York Constitution. Again, Hunt rejected the contention and in so doing clarified an important dimension of the police power. "The power to be exercised by this Board upon the subjects in question is not judicial in its character. It falls more properly under the head [*sic*] of an administrative duty. . . . It is no more judicial than is the action . . . of the metropolitan police board, who . . . discuss the question of whether a license shall be granted to an individual to keep an inn or to sell spirituous liquors. . . . But such powers have never been held to be of a judicial character."

In short, the famous Louisiana case with which this study is concerned must be seen in the context of these earlier state holdings. By the time slaughterhouse reform was brought to the Louisiana legislature in 1869, the script for the drama had already been presented in many different theaters. Every scene — recognition of the sanitary problems, initial unsuccessful efforts for reform at the local level, resistance by butchers, resort to the state legislature, and eventual vindication of the state's use of the police power — would be faithfully replayed in New Orleans. However heated, the New Orleans drama was a rerun, not a new production.

The police power of the states was recognized and well defined in leading nineteenth-century legal treatises. The twelfth edition of James Kent's *Commentaries on American Law* was published in 1873, only eight months after the *Slaughterhouse Cases*. In his discussion of property rights, Kent notes that while these rights are important, they "must be made subservient to the public welfare." Certain trades, like the operation of slaughterhouses and the keeping of combustible materials, are subject to regulation on the "general and rational principle, that every person ought so to use his property as not to injure his neighbors, and that private interest must be made subservient to the general interest of the community." Two years after *Slaughterhouse*, another contemporary treatise by Howard G. Wood, specifically on the law of nuisances, insisted that "no man is at liberty to use his own without any reference to the health, comfort or reasonable enjoyment . . . by others." As will be seen, the *Slaughterhouse* litigation stands as a watershed among police power cases. In the future, the focus would be less on the limitations and sacrifices that private property owners had to accept in the name of the police power, and more on the right to pursue one's chosen calling free of any police power limitations except those that fell equally on all who pursued it.

By 1862, the New Orleans livestock and slaughtering industry was centered in Jefferson City, a separately incorporated municipality that fronted on the river adjacent to and just upstream from the Fourth District. On April 7 of that year, the city council there took a significant step toward both slaughterhouse reform and the great constitutional litigation with which this study is concerned. By a unanimous vote the council awarded a franchise to three businessmen, William Hepp, Albin Rochereau, and Raymond Pochelu, authorizing them to erect "at their expense" a "general slaughterhouse" and giving them "during twenty-five years from the completion thereof the exclusive privileges of slaughtering animals within the limits of [Jefferson City]." The ordinance provided that once the new facility was completed, "all private slaughterhouses within the incorporated limits of the City of Jefferson shall be closed and . . . it will no longer be permitted to slaughter cattle or swine there; under a $100 penalty for each violation, all animals must be slaughtered in the general slaughterhouse." The ordinance set tariffs to be charged by the company for use of its facilities, and it authorized the mayor to appoint inspectors of beef.

Jefferson City's 1862 ordinance was a sign that the complaints about unsanitary conditions in New Orleans, the city's doleful experience with epidemics, and the medical community's insistent call for reform were at last having some effect. The ordinance seems to have been adopted with little debate and no recorded opposition. Yet it was identical in all essentials to the measure that would be adopted seven years later during Reconstruction and that would cause bitter opposition and prolonged litigation. For reasons that are not entirely clear, the Jefferson City slaughterhouse was never constructed.

Perhaps Hepp, Rochereau, and Pochelu were unsuccessful in persuading other investors to join the venture. Quite possibly, there were fears of the enormous resentment that would almost certainly arise when the butchers learned that they would no longer be permitted to operate private slaughterhouses. The most important reason, however, may be that about three weeks after passage of the ordinance, General Benjamin Butler occupied New Orleans. As Randell Hunt, one of the attorneys in the forthcoming *Slaughterhouse* litigation later explained, the city "was cut off from trade and commerce, and from intercourse and communication with other parts of the Union. General Butler was here; a large number of citizens were expelled; the city was walled in by military rule. Is it a wonder, then, that Hepp and Rochereau could not use the powers and privileges conferred upon them by the ordinance?"

General Butler came and went. By March 1866, New Orleans had reverted to civilian control. Immediately, fears arose that, without the military present to enforce strict sanitary practices, the city would revert to its former dirty and unhealthy self. Only days before the return of civilian control, the mayor issued a lengthy proclamation warning against a possible epidemic and urging strict adherence to all sanitary requirements, including the ordinances regarding the condition of slaughterhouses. Less than two weeks later, the *Daily Picayune* noted that nobody was doing anything to comply with the mayor's request.

The street commissioner urged the city council to take over the job of cleaning the streets because the contractor was not performing that duty, and "our country is threatened by a direful epidemic." In

August 1866, the editors of a local medical journal complained, "This city is now filthy in the extreme." The specter of disease in major proportions quickly returned. Cholera struck the Crescent City twice in 1866 — first in March, and again even more virulently during the summer. A year later, yellow fever revisited New Orleans.

Shortly after the end of occupation, on April 16, 1866, the Louisiana State Board of Public Health was reorganized. It had been created by the legislature in 1855 but had not functioned since the imposition of martial law in 1862. The newly resurrected board created a committee to recommend measures that it deemed "necessary to enforce a thorough sanitary police for the city during the present season," and it urged the city to form a similar committee of its own. The problem of the slaughterhouses was a prominent item on its agenda.

The reconstituted board of health was not a Reconstruction body. That would occur, but not until November 1868, when newly elected Governor Henry C. Warmoth appointed a board consisting entirely of fellow Republicans. Nevertheless, the interests and constituencies represented by the board of health, on the one hand, and the city council, on the other, had always been quite different. Even before Reconstruction, ordinances proposed by the board did not sail through the council to easy adoption. Shortly after its reorganization, the board submitted a comprehensive sanitary ordinance. Predictably, the city authorities dragged their feet, and the proposed ordinance did not clear the lower chamber of the council until late July.

Impetus for the ordinance had come from a petition presented to the city council on May 29, 1866, signed by about 500 citizens and later supported by spokesmen for the waterworks. It denounced the large number of slaughterhouses located near the municipal waterworks. In turn, the Committee on Police and Health recommended that the council take action "to move or cause to be moved all slaughterhouses now established . . . in the First and Fourth Districts of the city, the same being injurious to the health of the city." According to the *Picayune*, this led to "considerable discussion," but no ordinance.

In the same period, however, the council entertained a plan to establish a single municipal slaughterhouse. Two butchers, Henry Bezou and V. Gaschet Delisle, offered competing bids of $40,000 and $50,000, respectively, for the privilege of building and operating an exclusive slaughterhouse of "great dimensions" (and fireproof as well) in the city's sparsely settled Third District, *below the city.* The plan called for the closure of the slaughterhouses located above the city (the great majority of such establishments). This was the second such proposal for a centralized slaughterhouse that New Orleans had seen, and it met with determined opposition, much of it from John Kaiser, the member of the council from the Fourth Municipal District.

Kaiser was a faithful and energetic representative of the butchers' interests. Although not involved in the livestock industry himself, he had resided in the Fourth Municipal District for nearly thirty years. He could always be counted on to oppose any effort at regulation or to testify in favor of a particular butcher whose slaughterhouse had been singled out as a public health nuisance. In his view, there was nothing particularly unhealthy or deleterious about slaughterhouses, and probably more important, "there is a very large amount of capital invested in the slaughterhouses in the 4th district, and in the Parish of Jefferson, and if they were to move them, it would be the ruination of those people."

A good example of Kaiser's watchfulness and political agility occurred during Bezou's and Delisle's efforts to establish a centralized slaughterhouse in the Third District. For reasons that are not clear, the Delisle proposal went no further, but on May 29, 1866, the board of assistant aldermen granted Bezou permission to establish a single stock landing in the Third District. Kaiser, however, succeeded in gaining reconsideration, and in the end, both Delisle's and Bezou's proposals were rejected. Instead, ordinances were adopted to award contracts for a term of fifteen years to the highest bidders for the construction of two separate slaughterhouses — one in the Third District and the other in the Fourth. Thus, Kaiser ensured rejection of the reformers' primary goal: centralization of the slaughterhouses in one district. His "solution," in fact, was a self-defeating ploy, because no one would go to the expense of constructing (nor would many butchers utilize) a grand slaughterhouse below the city as long as there was at least one to serve the many butchers whose businesses were located in and around the Fourth District.

Kaiser also took on the 1866 health ordinance. Hopes had been high for this proposal. While it was making its way through the city council, the *Times* had hailed it as being on a par with similar ordinances enacted in New York, Philadelphia, and Baltimore. Kaiser disagreed, denouncing the proposed legislation as "more tyrannical than the military law," and when it reached the board of assistant aldermen, he saw to it that the draft was referred to a special committee of four, with himself as chair. What ultimately became law on August 2, 1866, was far from what its petitioners had sought. It required all slaughterhouses and similar facilities to be kept clean and forbade the throwing of "dead animals . . . or other . . . injurious matter into the river above the waterworks." It also imposed a fine for the establishment of a slaughterhouse on the river above the waterworks, "the offal . . . from which, may, by being discharged [into the river], . . . spoil the water supplied by said waterworks to the city."

It had been widely expected that this ordinance would prohibit slaughterhouses from operating above the waterworks, thus compelling their removal from the Fourth District once and for all. But it did no such thing. A close reading of the new ordinance indicates that it remained perfectly legal to keep a slaughterhouse on the river above the waterworks, as long as its offal was not discharged into the river in such a way as to contaminate the water supplied to the city. Left open were a variety of modes of discharging offal into the river that, arguably, would not do this. Moreover, the ordinance did not provide for the closure of any offending slaughterhouse, but only a fine of between $50 and $100 in the unlikely event that anyone was successfully prosecuted under the new law.

This ordinance of August 2, 1866, might have been considered a failure, just another abortive attempt at reform, except for one provision that proved to be of unexpected significance. It provided for the appointment of physicians "of standing and reputation" to serve as health officers for each of four sanitary districts, corresponding with the existing municipal districts. More effectively than the board of health itself, these officers institutionalized a revived concern for sanitation and public health throughout New Orleans. They made complaint books available to the public; conducted regular inspections; reported problems to the board of health, the police, and the city council; and ordered the abatement of minor nuisances. The inspector for the Fourth District decried "the multitude of slaughterhouses," but this problem was beyond his power to rectify. Although it is not clear whether the publicity resulting from the inspectors' efforts contributed to the growing pressure for change, at a minimum, their activities were helpful from the outset in proving both the ineffectiveness of present regulation and the need for further legislation.

Besides the perennial lack of commitment to real health reform in New Orleans, the problems of the Crescent City were compounded because their causes extended beyond its geographical boundaries. Although many of the slaughterhouses were located in the city's Fourth District, the center of the industry was in adjacent Jefferson City. Even if strong regulatory measures had been taken in New Orleans, they would have had no application in Jefferson City, where they were most needed. The stock landing that served the entire metropolitan area was situated there. It was the axis around which all the stockyards and slaughterhouses revolved.

Obviously, Jefferson City would have to be included in any plan for sanitary reform. Not surprisingly, proponents of reform turned from the city council and urged — at last — that relief be provided by the Louisiana state legislature. On August 10, 1866, a grand jury sitting in the First District Court formally recommended that the slaughterhouse problem be referred to the legislature and that it be urged to remove "the greatest of all nuisances." Four days later, the superintendent of the municipal waterworks addressed a supporting letter to the grand jury. In response, the grand jury issued a special report on August 21, released the superintendent's letter, reminded the public of its earlier submission, and once again called for remedial action by the state legislature. "We recommend that the city authorities should take this matter into immediate consideration, and besides passing the requisite ordinances they should petition the legislature asking that if it be in their power, they pass an act that there should not be allowed to exist, any slaughterhouses or similar places above the city within a specified number of miles."

———

The legislature that convened in New Orleans in January 1867 should not be confused with the one that would later be elected under congressional Reconstruction. Indeed, the First Reconstruction Act had not yet been passed. To be sure, the new state constitution had been drafted in 1864 during military occupation and by a convention that represented only a portion of the state. But the first elections held under its auspices in November 1865 had resulted in a legislature that would, according to the *Picayune*, "represent and express the will of the real citizens of the state, the *bona fide* people of the state." As such, it gave serious consideration to the issue of slaughterhouse relocation. Introduced in the house by G. F. Thieneman of Orleans Parish, the measure would have prohibited slaughterhouses on either bank of the river at any point above the waterworks and as far as the upper line of Jefferson Parish. The bill received prompt and favorable endorsement from the appropriate committee, but once it reached the floor, a lengthy and heated debate ensued, mainly among representatives from New Orleans. Their arguments would become familiar rhetoric in the *Slaughterhouse Cases*. Why should the legislature substitute its judgment for that of the city council, which had always rejected such proposals? In particular, critics predicted that the proposal would be the "entering wedge of a vast monopoly," one "to benefit speculators" while at the same time depriving "constituents of the benefits of investments of hundreds of thousands of dollars."

In reply, Thieneman argued that the welfare of the city should not be sacrificed to the interests of a few wealthy butchers, "only about 100, no more," who wanted to keep the slaughterhouses where they were. Another house member noted that the only men "interested in opposing the measure were a few cattle dealers, a few cow buyers, a few lasso throwers, and a few grog shops."

After more debate, the house referred the removal bill to a special committee composed of ten members — two from each of the four New Orleans municipal districts, plus one from Jefferson Parish and one from St. Bernard. The committee met four times over a three-week period. It collected evidence from private physicians, all four of the city's health officers, the superintendent of the waterworks, a representative of the board of health, several wharf managers, and a number of other knowledgeable individuals. The result was a comprehensive and authoritative record in support of the argument that the New Orleans slaughterhouses and stockyards represented a serious sanitary problem, requiring their removal from their present location above the city. In other words, almost two years before enactment of the famous (or infamous) slaughterhouse statute, the Louisiana legislature had for its consideration all available evidence, options, alternatives, proposals, justifications, and rebuttals concerning relocation of the slaughterhouses. Much of the testimony echoed points raised earlier. But what ultimately became law in 1869 was not new, original, or unexpected.

Most of the evidence focused on the relationship of the slaughterhouses to the key essentials of public health — pure air and clean water. The great majority of the slaughterhouses were located in well-populated areas of the city, only about one and a half miles upstream from the two large intake pipes for the city's water supply. The result was described by the health officer for the Third District: "The amount of filth thrown into the river above the source from which the city is supplied water, and coming from the slaughterhouses, is incredible. Barrels filled with entrails, livers, blood, urine, dung, and other refuse portions in an advanced stage of decomposition, are being constantly thrown into the River, but a short distance from the banks, poisoning the air with offensive smells and necessarily contaminating the water near the banks for miles."

Additional witnesses focused on the way other nations, such as France and England, had resolved the slaughterhouse problem. Dr. James Burns, the health officer for the First District, reminded the committee that "throughout the civilized world the danger of slaughterhouses have been recognized and earnest efforts have been made to remove them."

It was not only medical men who took note of the problem. The presiding judge of the grand jury that had urged removal of the slaughterhouses testified to having seen carts of "bloody fetid matter" dumped into the river above the waterworks. Others verified that the carcasses of animals that had died en route to New Orleans were routinely thrown overboard at the stock landing. These were sometimes retrieved by individuals who skinned them for the hides and tossed what remained back into the river. "Some people," noted one witness, "drank water directly from the river and when in port, vessels filled their water casks" from the same source.

Testimony received by the special committee made it clear that any attempt either to relocate the slaughterhouses to the other side of the river or to dispose of refuse in midstream would do little good. This would have been unfair to the people who lived across from New Orleans in Gretna or Algiers. In addition, the prevailing winds and river currents made it impossible to prevent slaughterhouse debris from the east side of the river from being disbursed among the shipping lanes and wharves located on the other side. Similarly, Dr. James Burns dismissed the suggestion that offal should be transported to some point below the city as "a clumsy, thriftless, ineffectual substitute for the proper remedy."

One might have thought that the board of health, the agency whose revival had rekindled the move toward slaughterhouse reform, would have enthusiastically supported their removal. But the board remained ambivalent concerning a final solution. It was, in fact, a political body, limited in what it could accomplish and doubtful about what it could or should propose when property rights in homes and businesses might be adversely affected. Ultimately, the board concluded that it was unnecessary to relocate the slaughterhouses, provided that their offal was transported and discarded below the waterworks.

Armed with the committee's thoroughgoing study, a majority of its members (eight to four) urged passage of the bill to remove the slaughterhouses. Undaunted, the four dissenting members offered a substitute bill that allowed the slaughterhouses to remain where they were and merely imposed a duty on New Orleans and Jefferson City to prohibit dumping in the river. In mid-March 1867, the house turned its back on all the evidence amassed by the special committee and passed the substitute bill by a vote of fifty-three to thirty. After futile efforts to construct its own version of a removal bill, the senate simply acquiesced in the house version, and the governor signed the bill into law on March 23, 1867.

A well-coordinated and well-supported effort to bring about reform had resulted in a statute that neither forbade existing slaughterhouses to operate above the waterworks nor barred the building of new establishments nor required the consolidation of existing facilities. It simply returned the cause of reform to the city councils of New Orleans and Jefferson City, where it had always been defeated in the past. Even so, private investors continued to be intrigued by the possibility of profiting from needful reform, as can be seen in developments that were soon to take place in Jefferson City.

In 1868, an effort was made to revive the franchise that Jefferson City had granted to Hepp, Rochereau, and Pochelu in 1862. On March 15, a new corporation, the Slaughterhouse and Chemical Manufacturing and Warehouse Company, announced that it had acquired the old franchise and was now seeking the capital needed to begin operations. It offered stock worth $100,000 to the public at $50 per share. Once the new company was in operation, all slaughtering in Jefferson City would have to take place in its facilities, in accordance with the 1862 ordinance. It was a butcher-friendly effort. The company gave assurances that its fees would amount to only about half the present costs for slaughtering, and it promised to continue the common practice of allowing butchers to keep the hides and other parts of their slaughtered cattle.

Authors of this prospectus pointed out that they were offering the stock first to the "butchers and property holders of Jefferson City. If they do not take the stock, they must not complain if they lose control of it." They cautioned that "unless this establishment does away with the nuisances complained of, all the slaughterhouses will be driven out of the cities in a very short time, to the great injury and detriment of property holders in Jefferson City." The *Picayune* had high praise for the plan. It would substitute the nuisance of 150 private slaughterhouses with a central facility, and it would not require the butchers to relocate their homes or shops.

For whatever reason, the stock of the new company was undersubscribed, and it never went into operation. Yet it is clear that by the time New Orleans and Louisiana prepared to function under congressional Reconstruction, there existed a body of evidence and an inventory of ideas concerning the slaughtering industry and its reform that had been accepted by different groups and from which an ultimate solution might be crafted. A system of virtually unregulated private slaughterhouses scattered all over New Orleans constituted a sanitary nightmare and no longer seemed feasible. A district court judge who had testified before the 1867 legislative committee explained his support for relocating the main stock landing with this comment: "I think it would be politic to remove it if it can be done justly and without personal injury. . . . I am satisfied it will ultimately be done, and another reason is that the people seem dissatisfied for it to be where it now is." Significantly, by 1868, the concept of a centralized abattoir — praised by some and denounced by others — had come to be widely regarded in the local livestock industry as a fit subject for a profitable franchise.

Time and again, New Orleans had had an opportunity to reform, either by local action or by legislative initiative, and it had managed to squander every chance. All that was needed as events in 1868–1869 unfolded was an aggressive group of entrepreneurs willing both to take risks and seek profits. Those who had ensured a seemingly permanent continuance of the status quo were not in a position to complain if the old problems were now resolved in a new manner, within the context of a new political environment. As Boss Plunkitt once remarked of his activities as a loyal member of Tammany Hall in New York City, "he [had] seen his opportunities, and he took 'em." The same might well be said of a new association of individuals that would soon surface, eager to profit from long-overdue reform.

CHAPTER 4

A Centralized Abattoir for New Orleans

In the period of Reconstruction that followed the Civil War, President Lincoln and later his fellow Republicans in Congress sought to reconstitute the Southern states and persuade them to accede to the principles of the Union and to the rights of the newly freed slaves. It was a particularly turbulent time in Louisiana. It was one of only three Confederate states in which blacks formed a majority of the population. Moreover, according to Reconstruction historian Eric Foner, New Orleans was the South's "largest and most distinctive city." Although whites (many of whom were foreign born or from the Northeast) had always controlled the city government, New Orleans was home to the "largest free black community in the deep South." Often light skinned in complexion, many of the so-called free men of color identified more with French or foreign culture than with American. They had much in common with the New Orleans Creoles, who were whites of French and Spanish ancestry and were apt to consider themselves the aristocrats of the population. A number of free blacks were wealthy, and although as a group they could not vote, they could travel freely, testify in court against whites, and work in various skilled crafts, some of which they came to dominate. Inevitably, a tension existed between the growing numbers of newly freed blacks and the well-established free black community, yet they were united in their interest in the right to vote.

But both Lincoln and Congress were unable to move toward black suffrage, although Lincoln had tentatively suggested to Louisiana governor Michael Hahn that "some of the colored people . . . be let in — as for instance the very intelligent." However, the all-white constitutional convention that met in 1864 ignored Lincoln's proposal, and the legislature that convened under the new enactment demonstrated no interest whatever in either black suffrage or education. Further progress toward the reconstruction of Louisiana would have to await the establishment of a viable state Republican party.

The Louisiana Republican party was formed by a combination of local antislavery whites, the large African American community, and a large number of recent arrivals from the North, commonly known as carpetbaggers. One member of this last group, Henry Clay Warmoth, deserves special mention. At the age of twenty-six, he would become the youngest governor in the history of Louisiana, if not the nation. He would also sign into law the slaughterhouse bill so important to this study. Ultimately, he would become a victim of the intense factionalism that helped destroy the Republican party in Louisiana.

A native of Illinois, a lawyer, and a competent but undistinguished Union army officer, Warmoth was attracted to New Orleans by the city's lifestyle. In 1864 he was befriended by its current military commander, General Nathaniel Banks, and for a few months served as a judge of the local provost court. Upon leaving the military in 1865, Warmoth determined to enter politics and soon became a leader in the attempt to establish and maintain the Louisiana Republican party.

From 1865 to 1867, both the Louisiana legislature and the state government were dominated by former Confederates whose idea of Reconstruction was to return Louisiana to its prewar status in as many ways as possible. Eventually their determination to limit the rights of the freedmen alarmed both radical and moderate Republicans and even the unionist governor James M. Wells. He supported a plan to reconvene the 1864 constitutional convention for the purpose of enfranchising blacks and prohibiting former "rebels" from voting. The first meeting of the convention on July 30, 1866, resulted in a bloody clash between white New Orleans policemen and a group of 300 to 400 blacks. It left at least 37 dead and more than 100 injured, mostly black. General Philip Sheridan wired Washington that it was "an absolute massacre by the police." Louisiana had done its share to transfer the responsibility for Reconstruction from the state legislatures to Congress.

Congressional Reconstruction took the form of a number of acts that divided the South into five military districts, one of which included Louisiana and Texas. They provided, in part, that former Confederate states could seek readmission to the Union only after fulfilling a number of requirements — one of which was to prepare and ratify a new constitution "drawn up by a convention of delegates elected by all adult male citizens except those disenfranchised for rebellion or other." When registration, conducted under military supervision, was complete, the vast majority of Louisiana Republicans were black. For a number of reasons, including apathy, economic hardship, and racial antagonism, many more blacks registered to vote than did whites. For the moment, at least, Republicanism triumphed in the state. The vote to convene the convention was 75,083 in favor, with barely 4,000 votes in opposition. Furthermore, of the ninety-eight delegates, half were black, and only two called themselves Democrats.

Most of the black delegates were literate, former freemen of color, and at least half of them were natives of Louisiana. Many of them had served in the Union army, and most were property owners. The constitution produced by this convention included the state's first bill of rights. It also provided for a racially integrated public school system (public schools were virtually nonexistent outside of New Orleans) and for state institutions for people with disabilities. There was little in it that was radical, except, perhaps, that blacks now had the vote, and this portended that there would never be a return to the old Louisiana.

The constitution of 1868 was ratified by a vote of 66,152 in favor and 48,739 against. It owed its approval to the black vote. Louisiana historian Joe Gray Taylor has pointed out that there were perhaps only 2,500 white supporters of radical Reconstruction in the entire state. In the same vote, Warmoth won election as governor, and a decisive majority of Republicans were chosen for both chambers of the state legislature. In the Louisiana house, the party division was sixty-five Republicans, which included thirty-five blacks, and thirty-six Democrats. The division in the state senate was twenty-three Republicans, seven of whom were black, and thirteen Democrats. For the first time in Louisiana's history, there were black legislators. They were never in a position to control the legislature, however, and any measures they favored required support from their white colleagues.

Members of the legislature were not required to take a loyalty oath either to run for office or to serve in the legislature; General Grant had decided that members needed to take only the oath of their office. As a result, both houses contained many former Confederates. But that did little to dispel the impression of most Louisianians that this was a legislature that could do no good: blacks were involved, and their presence was seen as an effort toward black equality.

When Warmoth became governor, both Louisiana and New Orleans were practically bankrupt, and corruption was rife. Indeed, Foner notes that "throughout the country, public honor was among the casualties of the Civil War." Years later in his memoirs, Warmoth recalled that at the time, "New Orleans was a dirty, impoverished, and hopeless city with a mixed, ignorant, corrupt and bloodthirsty gang in control. . . . Many of the city officials, as well as the police force, were thugs and murderers." Democrats and even some members of Warmoth's own party harbored doubts concerning his own trustworthiness. To their criticisms he once replied, "I don't pretend to be honest. I only pretend to be as honest as anybody in politics. . . . I tell you [that] these much abused members of the Louisiana legislature are at all events as good as the people they represent. Why damn it, everybody is demoralizing [*sic*] down here. Corruption is the fashion."

But accusations of corruption were not the only problems of Warmoth's administration. As Taylor observed, the "vast majority of the white people of Louisiana never accepted [his government] as legitimate." Indeed, "the background presence of federal military power was essential to the survival of the Republican state administration." In the antebellum period, New Orleans businessmen and rural planters had dominated the government. Yet Warmoth's government contained no one from this class. From the perspective of these people, the state government in 1868 was dominated by men who had served on the enemy's side in the late war. As the *Daily Picayune* saw it, this was a time when the "real people" of the state had been deprived of power and "a set of new men, greedy for the rapid acquisition of wealth and utterly unscrupulous as to the means of getting it, have come among us, and joining with the lately emancipated slaves and the meanest portion of the resident white population, have concocted plans for public plunder which they have not found it difficult to put through."

Louisiana's defeat had indeed come home. The most galling reminder to white New Orleans Democrats that they were now being governed by the victors was the fact that the Louisiana legislature of 1869–1871 included blacks. They constituted about 37 percent of the members of the house and 25 percent of the senate, and for legislation to pass, their support was essential. Historian Michael A. Ross has observed that "this alliance of blacks and carpetbaggers enraged many New Orleans whites." They described the new legislature as a horde of "ignorant negroes cooperating with a gang of white adventurers." Any and all enactments by such a body were suspect. During the first three months of 1869, comments to this effect became more frequent. One newspaper editor insisted that laws passed by this legislature "are of no more binding force than if they bore the stamp and seal of a Haytian [*sic*] Congress of human apes instead of the once honored seal of the state." Within this time frame, Ross notes, the legislators passed a statute enforcing open accommodation in public places, including hotels, railroad cars, and barrooms. Another ordinance required integrated public schools in the state. Sandwiched in between these two laws was the slaughterhouse bill.

Undoubtedly, opposition to the Slaughterhouse Act would have been vigorous regardless of the racial makeup of the legislature. Unlike other exclusive franchises awarded by the legislature at this time, the Slaughterhouse Act posed a direct threat to the interests of a large and coherent group of tradesmen who knew how to complain. Nonetheless, race was an inseparable element in the opposition. As the *New Orleans Republican* pointed out, the legislature's critics "failed to see any good in the work of those who have been called upon to take part in the state government under the new constitution. . . . [E]verybody has been proclaimed infamous, vile, ignorant and corrupt, that has had anything to do with a state government that recognized the civil and political equality of the colored man." Thus did the issue of slaughterhouse relocation become one with Reconstruction measures in general, and all were unacceptable.

———

The act that provided the butchers and stock dealers of New Orleans with an opportunity to litigate the provisions of the Fourteenth Amendment for the first time was entitled "An Act to Protect the Health of the City of New Orleans, and to Locate the Stock Landings and Slaughter Houses." It incorporated seventeen persons into the Crescent City Live Stock Landing and Slaughter House Company and granted the company "the sole and exclusive privilege" for twenty-five years of conducting the business of landing, keeping, or slaughtering animals for food in the contiguous parishes of Orleans, Jefferson, and St. Bernard. The company was required to erect, by June 1, 1869, "a grand slaughterhouse of sufficient capacity to accommodate all butchers," together with stockyards for all animals received at the port. Thereafter, no stock was to be landed, confined, or slaughtered for the New Orleans market except at the company's facilities. However, the act also provided that if the company refused to allow healthy animals to be slaughtered in its facility, it was to be fined $250 "in each case." In short, all who sought to slaughter beef had to do it in the new facility, and the company had to permit access to the slaughterhouse to anyone who wished it. The benefits to the company were both a detailed schedule of fees that it was authorized to charge for the use of its facilities and provisions allowing it to retain portions of each slaughtered animal for their value as raw material for agricultural fertilizer. An inspector of beef was to be appointed by the governor, and the inspector's certification was required, at set fees, before any animal could be slaughtered.

Although adoption of the New Orleans Slaughterhouse Act of 1869 was part of a national movement aimed at bringing long-overdue regulation to slaughterhouses, the statute also reflected a more general transformation of the livestock industry that occurred in the years following the Civil War. Even as it passed, and as the judicial drama it provoked was being played out in the courts, several factors were coming together that would modernize the nation's meat industry. As described by economic historian Rudolf A. Clemen, these were, "first, the opening and developing of a new source of supply of livestock; second, the extension of railroad transportation to the source of supply; third, refrigeration; fourth, men to organize the distribution of livestock and meat in the most efficient way."

Prior to the Civil War, the center of stock raising in the United States had steadily migrated westward with the frontier, in responses to the spread of industrialization in the East and a general rise in population. By 1860, it had shifted from Illinois to Texas, and the relatively unknown Texas longhorn overtook short-horned English stock as the country's most plentiful source of beef. In the years immediately following the Civil War, Texas boasted an enormous supply of beef. It was a commodity in great demand everywhere else, and it begged for transportation. It had always been difficult to find a market for Texas cattle. The state was relatively isolated from the rest of the country, and the skinny-legged, fierce-looking longhorns were considered uneatable in some places. Their meat had a reputation for being "coarse and stringy," with a taste "almost as wild as the buffalo." Joseph McCoy, a pioneer of the Texas cattle industry, wrote that until postwar shortages sharpened eastern appetites for red meat, longhorns were "as unsaleable in eastern markets as would have been a shipment of prairie wolves."

The Civil War proved disastrous for the Texas cattle industry, as the Lone Star State was cut off from all its major markets. According to McCoy, "then dawned a time in Texas that a man's poverty was estimated by the number of cattle he possessed." By 1865, there were between 6 million and 8 million head of cattle in Texas. But beef was in short supply everywhere else. Whereas there were between five and eight head of beef per capita in Texas in 1865, as late as 1870, the ratio in New York was still less than half a head (0.46) per capita, and only slightly higher (0.53) in Ohio. These discrepancies between supply and demand were reflected in prices. In 1865, high-grade steers could be had for $3 to $6 a head in Texas; when bought by the herd on the range, they cost as little as $1 a head. The same animals brought ten times as much in northern markets. The price in New Orleans in early 1869 was $50 a head. It had been over $60 a head for a brief period in 1867.

New Orleans was a legendary center of trade to which ambitious men had always been attracted. Inevitably, some of them recognized the economic potential of the tremendous supply of beef available not far to the west. Even as the Slaughterhouse Act was debated and assaulted, New Orleans newspapers were replete with allusions to the importance of the Texas cattle trade. The *Daily Picayune* predicted that "the time is coming when the products of the West will constitute the chief feature of our commerce" and that New Orleans would become "the depot of the trade of the west."

Indeed, New Orleans had been the chief market for Texas cattle before the war. But prewar drives had typically been small, and none of the existing routes could reliably deliver cattle to New Orleans in sufficient numbers to satisfy postwar demands. The most promising route to New Orleans was by way of the Gulf of Mexico from Galveston and Indianola aboard steamships owned by Charles Morgan.

In 1857, the New Orleans, Opelousas and Great Western Railroad was completed from New Orleans to Berwick Bay at Brashear City (later Morgan City), a distance of eighty miles. It made a railhead available to which Morgan's steamers could deliver cattle for a quick overland run to New Orleans. But the Morgan line had a reputation for high rates and monopolistic practices. Besides, when cattle were shipped by water, they often arrived in a bruised and sickly condition.

There was no rail connection between New Orleans and Texas, and the importance of remedying this problem was repeatedly and vociferously recognized. Cautioned the *Daily Picayune*, "Texas can do without the railroad to New Orleans, but New Orleans cannot do without the railroad to Texas." The press reiterated time and again that a delay in completing a rail connection could cause the Texas trade to find another path to market, and New Orleans would "be forever competing with the Northern states for the Texas trade." In the end, this is precisely what happened.

By late 1865, Texas farmers and men from as far away as Iowa and Illinois were gathering herds and making preparations to drive them north to market. The first of the great cattle drives took place in 1866 when a group of northern drovers and local cattle farmers attempted to drive herds of about 260,000 head northward to Sedalia, Missouri, a stop on the Missouri Pacific Railroad. Bad weather, rough terrain, thieves, and irate Kansas and Missouri farmers fearful of Texas cattle fever all combined to turn this first effort into an unprofitable disaster. In Texas, the ranching industry was thrown into a momentary depression, and in New Orleans, cattle fever of another kind soared. But the New Orleans window of opportunity to preempt the cattle trade did not remain open for long. In 1867, only 35,000 head were driven north from Texas. In the same year, arrangements were concluded with the Union Pacific Railroad to establish a cattle depot in Abilene. In 1869, 350,000 head were delivered to railheads in Kansas, and the potential of the Texas cattle trade became manifest from New Orleans to Chicago. It was the beginning of the fabled Texas cattle-trailing industry, which, by 1885, would deliver almost 6 million head to railheads in places such as Abilene, Wichita, and Dodge City.

Yet at the time the Slaughterhouse Act was enacted, there was enough speculation about railroads to justify a feverish interest in the Texas trade. Two enterprises actively competed for the state aid and franchises necessary to push westward. One of them, the New Orleans, Opelousas and Great Western, with its eighty-mile leg to Brashear City, was purchased by Charles Morgan in May 1869 with a boast that he would "now show the people of New Orleans how to build a road." The other line was the New Orleans, Mobile and Chattanooga Railroad. By the spring of 1869, it had secured from the Louisiana legislature both a charter giving it permission to construct a line westward and a pledge of state bonds amounting to $12,500 for every westward mile it constructed. Predictions in the press of the "glorious day" when Texas and New Orleans would be linked by rail ranged from two years to eighteen months. Actually, the connection with Texas would not come about until 1880, but as late as 1871, when 600,000 longhorns were driven to market along the northern trails, New Orleans had not lost hope. "In our railway connection with Texas, which is to mark one of the events of the near future," the *Times* predicted, " New Orleans will become the cattle and beef mart of the continent."

Advances in the science of refrigeration made it possible to reap the full benefits of the vast postwar improvements in the railroad industry. The first American patent for the manufacture of ice was issued in 1851. By 1866, it had become easy enough to manufacture ice that the *Daily Picayune* urged the formation of a company to slaughter beef on the Texas coast and transport it under refrigeration to New Orleans and other markets beyond. In fact, the first shipment of refrigerated beef to New Orleans from Texas arrived by water in the summer of 1869 in the midst of the slaughterhouse dispute. The first American patent for a refrigerated car was issued in 1867, and by 1875, a trade in dressed beef had been established between Kansas City and the East. Only one more element was needed to transform the meatpacking industry from a seasonal, local enterprise to an industry of truly national proportions. This was the energy and ambition of the men who made it all happen.

The livestock industry had always been marked by a tendency toward consolidation. This was reflected in the development of cities such as Boston, New York, Philadelphia, and Chicago as central markets. By the mid-nineteenth century, further developments were occurring within existing markets that suggested a way for individuals in New Orleans to profit from the Texas cattle trade. This was the replacement of the chaotic system of private stockyards in central markets with the more businesslike and profitable consolidated stockyards. The prototype of this improvement was the Union Stockyard and Transit Company, incorporated by the Illinois legislature in 1865 at the behest of a group of railroad men and stock dealers. It opened for business in Chicago on Christmas Day 1865 amid great fanfare. The company consolidated the city's stockyards in a "great bovine city" served by nine railroads just south of the city. In terms of convenience, efficiency, and improved sanitation, it was a major advance over the former system of having private stockyards distributed throughout the city. The concept spread rapidly to other markets.

Among its most important effects, the consolidated stockyard ensured a crucial role in the cash livestock market for the livestock commission merchant. The first firm of livestock commission merchants had been established in Chicago only in 1857. These men acted as intermediaries between the cattle drovers and the buyers. They made the market their business, and the drovers could consign their herds to them and rely on the commission merchants' expertise and self-interest to find the best price for their stock. According to Clemen, they became the "most important factor in a cash livestock market" and "contributed more to the prosperity and progress of the market than any other single cause."

Nineteenth-century New Orleans was a city of middlemen. An enormous amount of money was earned by brokers and commission merchants. Both these agents tended to specialize in a single commodity such as groceries, liquor, cotton, hogs, and, eventually, beef cattle. The business section of Gardner's city directory for 1869 listed 398 firms of commission merchants (not including cotton brokers), making them easily the most numerous group of businessmen in New Orleans. Not all commission merchants grew rich, but it was a game that almost anyone could play, and it was *the* game, or some imagined and possibly grandiose variation of it, that attracted the ambitious men who organized the Crescent City Company.

For all the controversy the slaughterhouse franchise would provoke, even as late as the middle of the nineteenth century, municipalities were still uncertain what functions were proper for them to perform, and it was not uncommon to farm out certain services to private companies. The New Orleans waterworks, for example, had been organized in 1833 as a private company with an exclusive franchise to furnish drinking water to the city. In the postwar years, New Orleans became a bustling city again, and many new men arrived. They were quick to see opportunities for personal profit in badly needed internal improvements, particularly if they could be undertaken in partnership with the state in terms of either authority or funding. As the power of the state passed from traditional elites into the hands of the interests that had won the war, a great many sinecures and exclusive franchises for such things as a state lottery, state printing, hay inspection, and state aid for the construction of navigation and drainage canals were adopted. Similar measures had been enacted before the war, but now there were many more of them, and they were accompanied by a greater amount of state aid. They met with intense resentment because of the widespread perception that they had been obtained dishonestly.

The Slaughterhouse Act is a prime example of these controversial postwar acts. Indeed, the view of the act as a product of bribery was endorsed by the courts. About the same time as the *Slaughterhouse Cases* were filed in the New Orleans district courts, a spate of stockholder suits broke out over claims that some of the company's organizers were being denied their rightful number of shares. One of these suits was filed by William Durbridge in Judge William H. Cooley's Sixth District Court in May 1871. Cooley rendered a judgment in Durbridge's favor, but he refused to grant him any relief. The evidence disclosed, he said, that the court was being asked to distribute an illicit fund. In Judge Cooley's view, the stock over which the litigants were fighting had been allocated to the organizers of the company "in order to bribe the members of the General Assembly and other men who stood in their way in order to obtain the final passage of the bill and its signature by the Governor." It was evident, he wrote, "that members of the House of Representatives were bribed for their votes and members of the Senate were also bribed for their votes. . . . It further shows that other parties occupying official positions in the City of New Orleans were also bribed, and I think the evidence is irresistable [*sic*] that the Governor's signature to that bill was obtained by the same soft sawder [solder]." In 1875, on appeal, the Louisiana Supreme Court reached the same conclusion and affirmed Cooley's dismissal of the action. "We will have nothing to do with it."

In spite of the courts' emphatic rhetoric, as will be seen in the next chapter, the New Orleans butchers were never given an opportunity to prove their hard-pressed claims of bribery. Historians have been left to debate this charge among themselves. Michael A. Ross, for example, cautions against a reliance on Cooley's conclusions on the grounds that the judge was a disaffected Republican who had left the party over the radical wing's civil rights agenda. Herbert Hovenkamp found that, at best, the evidence proves only that the organizers were guilty of aggressive lobbying. And it is entirely plausible that both Cooley and the state supreme court resorted to a finding of bribery as an excuse for dismissing a case mired in circumstances so unfathomably complex and conflicted that it could not be resolved, but only terminated, by a court.

However, even though the claims of bribery and corruption remain uncertain, a review of the records in the Durbridge suit and related stockholder actions enables us to see why it was feasible for Judge Cooley and the state supreme court to conclude that the act had been obtained by bribery. These records, along with the legislative debates and other sources, also make it possible to glimpse the Crescent City Live Stock Landing and Slaughter House Company in its formative stages and gain some insight into the identity, motives, and methods of the incorporators.

First, who were the entrepreneurs behind the Crescent City Company? How did they occupy themselves, and how did they relate to one another? The man who claimed to be the originator of the slaughterhouse project was William Durbridge, a native of London and longtime resident of New Orleans. His primary occupation was proprietor of a popular hat store. "The idea originated in my brain," he claimed. He knew that efforts had been made for years to relocate the slaughterhouses to some point below the city, and he had just bought property in that vicinity. He shared his idea with two business acquaintances, Oliver Mudgett, an employee at the U.S. Custom House, and businessman A. J. Oliver, who in turn discussed it with others. Oliver and Mudgett "took hold and the thing started from that." Before long, Oliver came to Durbridge "and proposed advances of money" and a contract for shares in a slaughterhouse company. In all, Durbridge claimed to have sunk between $13,000 and $14,000 in the enterprise, "which I never got back yet."

The entrepreneurs who were eventually favored by the legislature with an exclusive slaughterhouse franchise, and their associates, were the kind of motley group that could always be gathered up in New Orleans. Some of them conformed to the popular image of the carpetbagger as an unscrupulous northern adventurer, but others challenged this stereotypical view. They included natives of both the North and the South, longtime residents of New Orleans as well as newcomers, and veterans of both the Union and Confederate armies. Several of the nineteen organizers spent only a short time in New Orleans, but at least six died there.

In terms of occupation, nine of the nineteen were commission merchants or brokers in 1869 or would soon be occupied in that way. They were all keen to take advantage of the opportunities of postwar New Orleans. For a number of them, the Slaughterhouse Act was not their only venture into the domain of semipublic enterprise. Their names can be found on state contracts to remove debris from the Red River and among the incorporators of a controversial company formed by the legislature to construct a canal linking the Mississippi with the Gulf of Mexico. In 1869 the legislature awarded still another of the incorporators, John Lockwood, and others an exclusive contract to furnish illuminating gas to Jefferson City. By 1872, Lockwood had become the president of the Jefferson City Gas Light Company. In earlier years, he had won a similar contract from the city of Milwaukee, which he quickly assigned to an illuminating company. This practice of obtaining a valuable franchise and then selling it to a more appropriate proprietor at a profit was to be repeated in the slaughterhouse affair.

The organizers appear to have been a devious lot, given to counterletters and side agreements among themselves. Five of the original organizers divested themselves of their interests as soon as the bill was signed into law. One of these was N. W. Travis, an editor of the *New Orleans Republican;* his paper opposed the act on the grounds that it created a monopoly. The company's first president, Franklin J. Pratt, once denied having any occupation at all. He was a speculator who seemed constantly on the move, traveling to New Orleans, New York, and his home in Greenfield, Massachusetts. In 1871, when the U.S. Supreme Court was poised to rule on a motion that might have had an adverse effect on Crescent City Company stock, Pratt made arrangements with one of the state's attorneys to be sent a coded telegram in case the decision went against him. Evidently, he had no intention of keeping his stock if the price was about to decline.

Even the carpetbaggers among them, however, did not look so terrible on close inspection. Captain Samuel P. Griffin, a cotton broker, was a New York native and a graduate of the U.S. Naval Academy at Annapolis. He had once commanded a vessel in a polar expedition. The Crescent City Company employed him as its first superintendent. In 1869, Edward B. Benton was a thirty-seven-year-old native of Vermont who had practiced law and participated in a number of businesses in other states before arriving in New Orleans in 1867. In New Orleans, he became the director of several companies and the president of the Accommodation Bank. James G. Clark, a member of the original board of directors, was a native of Virginia and a Confederate veteran. A cotton broker and dealer in building materials, he was active in public affairs and eventually served as president of New Orleans's prestigious Pickwick Club.

Nor was it entirely true, as the ultraconservative newspaper the *Bee* claimed, that all the organizers were "newcomers here. . . . Not a name among the seventeen is familiar to any old citizen." Joachim Viosca Jr., for example, was the forty-one-year-old son of a prominent local wholesale merchant. Testimony in the Durbridge litigation showed that members of the 1869 legislature regarded him as "the only honest man" among the company's organizers. "Viosca's checks were better than anybody's."

Only one of the organizers seems to have had any experience as a butcher. He was Jonas Pickles, who owned one of the many slaughterhouses in Jefferson City, as well as a liquor business and other property. In city directories for 1872 and 1873, his occupation is given simply as "capitalist." He also served for a time as superintendent of the streets. Pickles was recruited into the enterprise in a chance encounter on Canal Street with one of the company's organizers. Apparently, the capitalist in Pickles could not resist the opportunity to acquire for only $10,000 an interest in a new company that he was told was worth between $40,000 and $60,000. He subscribed for $10,000 worth of stock, paying $3,000 in cash and signing promissory notes for the balance. A night or two later, the incorporators elected him to the board of directors.

Six men assumed a leading role in the organization of the Crescent City Company and in the passage of its enabling act, but from the start, it appears that Franklin Pratt was primus inter pares among them. The Six admitted three other individuals into their privileged subgroup: W. H. Henning, Charles A. Weed, and Robert Bloomer. Henning was a partner in a prominent firm of commission merchants that included two of the organizers. Bloomer, a longtime resident of New Orleans, was employed to manage the bill in the legislature. He was a partner in a firm of cotton brokers that included other organizers. Several years later, while working with the legislature again, he was implicated in a bribery scheme related to the purchase of land for Audubon Park in New Orleans. Though no stranger to bankruptcy, he seems to have been a resourceful lobbyist.

Charles A. Weed deserves special mention as an individual who may well have had a clear idea of the value of a monopoly over the Texas cattle trade. A prominent Republican from Stamford, Connecticut, Weed had come to New Orleans in 1862 on the heels of General Butler and worked as a commission merchant for a time. It was rumored that in partnership with Butler's brother, Colonel A. O. Butler, Weed had brought Texas cattle into New Orleans at a time when such trade was forbidden by General Butler himself. Perhaps it was Weed's experience with the Texas cattle trade that explains the unusual interest he showed in the Crescent City Company. At the height of the slaughterhouse furor, he served as a sort of mediator, trying to convince individual butchers to acquiesce in the new franchise.

Weed shared a residence with Franklin Pratt, the company's president. Eventually, he became a stockholder in the Crescent City Company to the extent of 800 shares and a member of its board of directors. His name appears among a list of board members in 1872, when all the original incorporators had divested themselves of their interest in the company. In 1869, Weed became proprietor of the *New Orleans Times*. With him at the helm, the *Times* served unflinchingly as the company's staunchest apologist.

One of the incorporators' chief advantages was the ready access they enjoyed to Governor Warmoth. Pratt and Weed had frequent discussions about the slaughterhouse venture with Warmoth both in the street and at his home and office. In testimony offered later in federal court, the governor readily admitted to being acquainted with these men and with other leading slaughterhouse figures and acknowledged that he had taken action to aid the company at several crucial junctures. But he insisted that he had acted "not in the interest of the Slaughter House Company nor to the detriment of the butchers, but simply to enforce the law." Warmoth steadfastly maintained that he had no personal interest in the slaughterhouse venture, and no evidence has surfaced to contradict him.

However grand the idea for the new abattoir, the company was never well capitalized. Witnesses in the Durbridge actions readily testified that advances had to be paid in order to have the bill passed. To establish the company, property needed to be purchased, a slaughterhouse outfitted, and a legislature persuaded to sanction its enterprise and no one else's. Some of this initial capital was in the form of cash, but a good deal of it was in promissory notes elicited from various parties for no consideration or for promises to transfer stock — all of which seems to have been used either to attract investors or possibly to buy votes in the legislature. It was a series of these none-too-clear transactions that underlay Durbridge's claim to stock in the Crescent City Company and that explained his resort to legal action.

———

The legislative history of the measure that was to become the Slaughterhouse Act of 1869 began on January 22, 1869, when House Bill 88 was introduced by John McVean. Representative McVean had already guided another controversial monopolistic enterprise, the Ship Island Canal bill, through the house, and since his home in Caddo Parish was located far from New Orleans, his sponsorship emphasized the point that the slaughterhouses were a proper subject for state action and not exclusively a New Orleans affair.

McVean almost lost control of the bill at the start when opponents succeeded in having it sent to a special committee consisting of ten representatives from the parishes directly affected, namely, Orleans, Jefferson, and St. Bernard. This tactic had been used to defeat slaughterhouse reform in the 1867 legislature. He soon managed, however, to bring the bill back before the whole house, where he would always be present and, apparently, could command a majority vote.

Even so, the bill had its detractors. When it was first introduced, Representative Mitchell Raymond, a radical and freeman of color from Jefferson Parish, where opposition by the butchers and stock dealers was strongest, promptly suggested that it be referred to the Committee on Immigration. Another opponent ridiculed it by proposing an amendment ensuring that the new facility would "admit all cattle, without distinction on account of sex, color or previous condition." Some of the opponents readily admitted the need to relocate the slaughterhouses, but they all objected to the bill on grounds that it created a monopoly. Said one, "No objection can be made to the removal of the slaughterhouses below the city; but it does not follow that there should be a monopoly of the slaughterhouse business."

In the Committee of the Whole, opponents resorted to frequent roll calls, petty bickering, challenges to the chair, and other dilatory tactics. Complained McVean, "There is too much frivolous discussion in committee for purpose of killing bills." Another of the bill's proponents commented that the house was in "too good humor to discuss a bill relating to the health of the city." Indeed, this was not an orderly house. Besides being largely a legislature of first-time officeholders, slaughterhouse reform had long been ignored and even derided both by past legislatures and by much of the political leadership of New Orleans. It is little wonder that the sanitary value of this private effort was not taken seriously by most members of the legislature, or that opponents used every stratagem at their disposal to oppose it.

The task of articulating the case against House Bill 88 fell to two conservative members in particular: John Page of Jefferson Parish, home of the stock landing and most slaughterhouses, and William Pope Noble of Orleans Parish. Denying the nuisance aspects of the livestock industry, Page argued that the bill proposed to take from his constituents property they had accumulated by "years of industry. . . . All they have for their old age is there." And "who are the men composing this company? Who are they? They are not butchers. They are not cattle dealers. . . . We do object that these men should come along to rob our people, to steal away their property, to disturb our firesides."

Noble was a Democrat who had come to New Orleans around 1860. He had served as a high school principal and in the Confederate army. He struggled mightily over a two-day period to persuade the house to adopt an amendment striking out the words "sole and exclusive" in the bill, thus depriving the company of any monopolistic claims. His amendment was defeated by a vote of thirty-one to twenty on the afternoon the bill was adopted. It was an indication of the reservations engendered by the monopolistic aspects of the bill that this amendment elicited the highest vote against the measure recorded in the legislature.

The house passed the slaughterhouse bill on Saturday, February 6, 1869, by a vote of fifty-one for and eighteen against. One-third of the house members either were absent or abstained from voting. It was clearly a victory for the radicals; they had furnished forty-four of the fifty-one favorable votes. Only nine radicals voted against it. Five conservatives voted for the bill and nine against it. It is possible that the rate of nonvoting reflected a reluctance on the part of some representatives to oppose a measure, however controversial, that promised to remedy a serious and long-standing municipal problem.

That House Bill 88 was a favored measure whose passage was assured was evident in the way it was handled in the senate. When the measure passed in the lower chamber, the senate was considering a rival bill that would have awarded the slaughterhouse franchise to another company. But when H.B. 88 reached the senate, the rival measure was quickly tabled. In short order, H.B. 88 was reported favorably by the Committee on Health, and on February 18, 1869, after mustering a four-fifths vote to set aside the constitutional rule requiring bills to undergo three readings on separate days, the bill was read for a third time and adopted as a whole by a vote of twenty-one to five, without ever having been printed. The opposition consisted of two conservatives and three radicals who had consistently argued against the bill. Radicals had provided sixteen of the favorable votes and three against, with five not voting. Among the conservatives, the vote was four in favor, two against, and seven not voting. The heat of the controversy in New Orleans is reflected in the fact that of eleven senators from that area, four (two radicals and two conservatives) voted in favor, two radicals voted against it, and three radicals and two conservatives abstained. All that remained was for the bill to be signed into law.

The *Picayune* deplored passage of the act as an "outrageous bartering away of birthrights" in a first-page article and urged the governor to veto it. Meanwhile, the house returned the bill to the senate for repassage on the grounds that it had been rushed through so quickly that it had been improperly engrossed. According to the minutes of one of the organizational meetings of the Crescent City Company, the organizers hurriedly appointed Robert Bloomer as chairman of a committee to go to the senate "and employ their best efforts in getting the Bill through." They had good reason to be concerned. When the issue was taken up in the senate, the president, Lieutenant Governor Dunn, ruled that the body had already acted on the measure and could not take it up again. The organizers succeeded in having this ruling overturned, however, and the bill was immediately read and passed. The next day, the senate enacted it a second time. In due course, Governor Warmoth signed the bill into law, making it Act No. 118 of March 8, 1869.

Over the next three weeks, the incorporators met nearly a dozen times at the offices of commission merchant J. H. Henning and Company to perfect the organization of the company and to live up to its legislative mandate to have a grand slaughterhouse ready for the butchers by June 1. As the corporation got under way, it was important to know precisely who owned it. To this effect, they employed Randell Hunt and Christian Roselius, two prominent New Orleans attorneys, to advise them concerning the validity of the maze of transactions among the organizers that had preceded passage of the act and to advise them on the most important issue of all — the very constitutionality of their Slaughterhouse Act. The slaughterhouse men showed good judgment in choosing legal counsel. Hunt and Roselius were two of the most distinguished members of the New Orleans bar, and they had excellent credentials as scholars and statesmen. They would play a leading role in defending the Slaughterhouse Act in the state courts. At the time, Hunt was president of the University of Louisiana and taught law there, and Roselius served as dean of the law faculty. They had both opposed secession but remained in the state as constitutional unionists.

The organizers also employed Randell Hunt's younger brother, William J. Hunt, a Republican and associate of the governor, to write the articles of incorporation. This instrument was signed by the incorporators on March 20, 1869, after which, in true Louisiana fashion, they celebrated at the popular Moreau's Restaurant. On the same day, a committee was appointed to select a site for the new, centralized slaughterhouse and suitable quarters for the company's offices.

Finally, what evidence is there that the Slaughterhouse Act was a product of bribery? The *Picayune* had no doubt. Only a few days after the bill had passed in the senate, it charged that "no sensible man" could deny that bribery was being practiced for "the creation of monopolies designed to enrich a few." According to the paper, the act had cost the incorporators a million dollars, "though only one hundred thousand could be raked up in cash." The *Picayune* believed that even Governor Warmoth was implicated. When he failed to veto the bill after its legislative opponents had allegedly refrained from making amendments in order to present it to him "with its most repulsive features untouched," the conclusion seemed inescapable that "the Governor holds stock to a very large amount." Presciently, the *Picayune* predicted that "an immense amount of litigation" would follow.

The most fertile sources of information available today on this subject are the records in the suits by William Durbridge and other stockholders mentioned earlier in this chapter. As a whole, the testimony is inconclusive, and some of it is patently suspect. Nonetheless, elements of it ring true and clearly tend to incriminate. According to these records, the six principal organizers "took the lead in the passage of the bill and had charge of it. . . . They were in the room most of the time; took a great deal of interest night and day." It was also generally agreed that The Six "were outside the board. They formed a board themselves."

Soon after the act was passed, the incorporators agreed that the company would issue $2 million of stock and that only half of it would be offered to the public. The other half was considered to be preferred, fully paid up, and nonassessable, and it was to be divided among the seventeen incorporators as follows: each of the six principal organizers was to receive $100,000 worth of stock, or 1,000 shares each at a par value of $100; the remaining four-tenths of this privileged half was to be divided equally among all seventeen organizers, giving 235 shares to each. Judge Cooley referred to this arrangement as "a grand division of the spoils."

It was repeatedly acknowledged that this special allocation of stock was made to The Six to compensate them for their personal expeditures and to underwrite passage of the act. It was never expected that they would actually receive this stock. The secretary of the company, John H. McKee, said that Pratt kept a separate stock book. Pickles, a member of the board of directors, testified that Pratt "had the issuing of that stock and he just took charge of that six thousand shares and gave us our stock 230 [*sic*] shares and we never paid attention to the rest." Durbridge seems not to have understood that he was not to receive any of this stock, and when he sued for it, there was none left. Under Pratt's administration, the $600,000 in "trustee stock" was entirely depleted.

Just what this stock, or other funds expended in securing the act, was actually used for, however, remains unclear. Most witnesses would not admit to having personal knowledge that money or stock actually found its way into the hands of members of the legislature. They referred instead to "expenses, champagne, sandwiches and such like stuff." The questioning of Jesse R. Irwin is typical:

Q: Was it not to your knowledge that it was necessary to make expenditures either of stock or funds or something of the kind, for the purpose of facilitating or securing the passage of the law creating the Slaughterhouse Company?

A: Yes, Sir. It was.

Q: Is it not to your knowledge . . . that a portion of that stock went into the hands of parties connected with the Legislature?

A: No. I never seen any.

By the Court:

Q: Have you not a rather strong suspicion that some did?

A: [Witness laughs.] I have heard a great deal—heard a great deal on the street for two or three years but I never seen it.

Pickles testified that he never saw any member of the legislature with shares of stock or checks in their hands. But, he said, it was customary for members of the legislature to go to the Henning office and "loaf around there."

Durbridge himself testified only that money was furnished for "fires, committee rooms, sandwiches, whisky, brandy." But it should be noted that Durbridge was in no position to admit to anything more. The company's defense to his claim was that the stock in question had been allocated by the company for the illicit purpose of bribing the legislature and that the court should not enforce such an arrangement. Had

Durbridge admitted to anything more than ordinary lobbying activities, he would have admitted himself right out of court, which is indeed where he ended up on the testimony of others.

It should also be noted that, ultimately, Durbridge's adversaries in the litigation were not Pratt and his fellow original incorporators but a new group of stockholders. During the pendency of the stockholder suits, the Crescent City Company had been sold to a group of New Orleans livestock dealers and butchers. Earlier, these new owners had been among the company's most fierce opponents. They had no interest in defending the misdeeds of their predecessors. Indeed, victory in the Durbridge litigation lay in *proving* them.

E. B. Benton, who served as an unofficial vice president of the company whenever Pratt was out of town, seemed to invite questioning about the machinations of The Six. Their affairs, he said, "were always a secret and a matter to be kept confidential. I should hate to state the whole facts unless absolutely necessary."

When assured by counsel that it was indeed necessary, he readily acknowledged that The Six had given Robert Bloomer authority to make good on promises to legislators and said that he had actually seen members of the legislature with the stock. "I think there was some considerable money advanced, and in fact I have seen members of the Legislature have the money and saw them get it. So I am positive there was money paid."

McKee, the company's secretary, testified that Pratt had devised a method that allowed stock to be delivered to members of the legislature without their names appearing in the stock book. He was aware that "a great many hundred shares" of stock were owned by members of the legislature, mentioning, as examples, J. D. Beares, C. C. Antoine, William McMillen, A. L. Lee, and Michael Hahn.

Benton even admitted that stock had been given to men close to Governor Warmoth as a means of ensuring that the governor would sign the bill into law, but he was careful not to implicate Warmoth in bribery. Anyone familiar with the frequent criticism leveled against the bill in the house by the governor's close associate and friend, Representative William L. McMillen of Carroll Parish, had reason to doubt the governor's support. McMillen was a former general in the Union army, a leading radical, and one of the owners of the *New Orleans*

Republican. Both he and his newspaper condemned the monopolistic aspects of the Slaughterhouse Act. Though not a member of the team that had opposed the act, as an individual, he seldom missed an opportunity to criticize it. He had urged the house to inquire whether members had been bribed to vote for the bill. He once suggested that the house waive a reading of the bill "in order that gentlemen not be troubled with qualms of conscience." And he had underscored his opposition by changing his vote from "abstain" to "nay," even after the bill had passed by a substantial majority.

According to Benton, after the bill had passed in both houses, the incorporators "met and it was deemed advisable — good policy for the Company to give Lee, McMillen and Deane some stock — not as a bribe so far as that went." (Lee was another member of the legislature. Deane was the clerk of the Louisiana Supreme Court.) All three were known to be close to Governor Warmoth.

As Benton explained under oath, McMillen, Lee, and Dean "had been bitterly opposed to the bill all through its passage through the legislature and it was thought that it might induce them to use their influence to the final success of the enterprise. It was no bribe. It was entirely unknown to them they were going to get it."

Q: It was a mere gratuity?

A: It was. And entirely unknown to them to my positive knowledge.

Benton said that he and his colleagues had had trouble from an unknown source with "our Ship Island Canal Bill" and wanted to make sure it did not happen again. They later discovered, Benton added, that Governor Warmoth had "nothing whatever" to do with the act after he signed it, "and we felt we had been great asses to make the donation."

With the adoption of the Slaughterhouse Act, an interest in financial speculation accomplished what a sense of civic duty had failed to do. However controversial, the act represented an effective means of addressing a persistent public problem in a manner consistent with the mid-nineteenth-century emphasis on minimal government. The contemporary understanding of the act may have been captured best in the words of a Republican district judge in 1871. "For years," wrote Judge Henry Dibble, the butchers of New Orleans had defied public opinion and the express provisions of laws and ordinances in relation to the locality of the slaughter houses. . . .

The legislature therefore did a wise and practical thing; the corporate defendant was created. . . . Such a corporation with such large interests involved became powerful and strong enough to throttle the butchers. The Company did what the officials of the law had failed to do; they forced all butchering and stock landing below the city and instituted a thorough system of inspection in obedience to other provisions of the law aforesaid.

This is a view of the act that accepts the profit motive as a legitimate incentive to reform precisely because it is likely to be effective. Indeed, the widely perceived linkage between the slaughterhouses and ill health provided the energy to reform, the development of the centralized abattoir elsewhere provided the form, and the public franchise to a private company offered a readily available means of implementation. The accomplishment of public tasks by this means was consistent with the early-nineteenth-century ideological penchant for minimal government and had frequently been used in New Orleans and elsewhere for a variety of purposes, including early sanitary reform. To a great extent, the slaughterhouse bill was indeed a reform measure. And if the organizers of the Crescent City Company obtained their franchise by means that left a good deal to be desired, it was also true that these methods were not new to Louisiana; nor did they disappear with the end of Reconstruction. As historian Joe Gray Taylor wrote many years later, "Louisiana state government was corrupt before Warmoth's administration and was corrupt afterward. It was corrupt when the Republicans were in power and was corrupt when Democrats held the reins."

CHAPTER 5

The Order of Battle in the Lower Courts

The Slaughterhouse Act became a topic of heated conversation everywhere in New Orleans, from its markets to its houses of worship. News articles, editorials, letters, and formal reports of judicial proceedings in the city's several newspapers kept the public informed about every turn of events. With the exception of the *Times*, all the New Orleans newspapers were critical of the Slaughterhouse Act. The *Daily Picayune* condemned it as just the sort of act that could be expected from a legislature organized "under the oppressive usurpations of the federal Congress." It charged that in this instance the legislative power of the state had been used to create a uniquely odious monopoly covering a staple item of food. In effect, the act placed "the whole community under embargo to a few rich men."

When the *Times* attempted to defend the act as a bona fide health measure, the *Picayune* dismissed its arguments as "sophomoric scribbling." The men behind this act "have none but a pecuniary interest in Louisiana and . . . are only desirous of keeping off sickness" to the extent that it results in "the transfer of money from the pockets of our people, into their capacious iron safes, located in colder climes." The measure had been "conceived in iniquity and carried through by the boldest and most unscrupulous of means," and the *Times*'s support for it could only be explained by the fact that its publisher, Charles Weed, was financially interested in the company.

Even the *Republican* (whose owners at one time or another included both Governor Warmoth and his fellow partisan in the house, William L. McMillen) and the *Tribune*, the city's black newspaper, editorialized against the monopolistic aspects of the act. The *Republican* admittedly eschewed a discussion of "the manner in which the charter was obtained." But it noted that the public was sympathetic with the "plea of sanitary reform." And it reiterated the old claim that up to now, the butchers had exercised a sort of monopoly of their own.

But the *Republican* considered the monopoly charge to be "a most formidable position." "The new company sought to monopolize the whole business and deny to all persons the right to pursue the avocation of butchers without the proper consent of the Slaughter House Company. . . . The monopoly charge is well founded." It advised the new company to "lay aside its pretensions to a monopoly of the business and enter the lists boldly as a competitor. . . . The public health will not suffer from three or four small slaughterhouses at proper points."

Most of the New Orleans butchers were French-speaking immigrants from the Gascony region of France or had ethnic roots there. Taking the level of discourse down a step, the *Times* complained that there was not "an American in the business." These men are "not allied to our people either by nativity or community of interests." The act threatened the Gascon butchers' ability to keep prices artificially high by means of their own informal monopoly, and *that*, charged the *Times*, is what explained their "garlic-scented" cries of "monopoly."

From the earliest stages of the dispute, the butchers were advantaged by the existence of the Butchers Benevolent Association of New Orleans. The association had been formed in 1866 and incorporated in 1867 by a group of French and German butchers to combat the informal monopolies of the large stock dealers and to provide some organizational strength against the frequent municipal efforts to regulate slaughterhouse practices. It pooled small capital and made livestock available to individual butchers at low prices. The very existence of the association was evidence of an occupational, economic, and social divide that existed between most of the butchers on the one hand and the stock dealers on the other. In the spring of 1869, the association could boast about 50 members, but that number grew to perhaps 250 in a year. On June 4, only days after the effective date of the act, the association held a protest meeting at one of the city's markets. A throng of butchers, stock dealers, judges, politicians, and other sympathizers turned out. The gathering authorized the association's president, Paul Esteben, to appoint a "Committee of Five" to employ attorneys, solicit funds, and institute necessary actions. Before long it was reported that the butchers had raised $40,000 for their lawyers. On June 18 at another such gathering, a committee of thirteen leaders was appointed to steer the opposition.

Opponents of the act insisted that the dispute was not merely a matter of money but that ultimately it involved the inherent rights of the citizens. This transcendent theme became part of the popular outcry. One *Picayune* reader wrote that the dispute had a "higher significance" because it involved "the personal rights of the masses." Opponents at the June 18 meeting angrily resolved that they held "these truths to be self evident," that "every man in this community has a property in his person and his faculties. That no less sacred than this is his right to the product of those faculties which implies a right to the possession of property, to accumulate property by his labor, and to employ those faculties in any lawful avocation without the control, domination, or direction of any other person or persons in the community for their own emolument."

In short, all the makings of a great legal argument were there. As Walton Hamilton described the plaintiffs' position: "American institutions were being flaunted; a monopoly, odious at law and to the people, had been given a legislative blessing; the laborer had been denied his biblical doom and God-given right to work. The enemy was an octopus of a corporation; the cause was the cause of the workingman; the rights at stake were the rights of man." All that was needed was suitable legal representation. That role was filled by no fewer than three firms of attorneys, but the most prominent legal spokesman was John A. Campbell.

A native of Georgia, Campbell had first been admitted to practice law by a territorial court in Florida at the age of nineteen. In 1830 he was admitted to practice in Alabama, and in 1853 President Pierce appointed him to the U.S. Supreme Court. Opposed to secession but loyal to the South, he left the Court in 1861 to serve as assistant secretary of war for the Confederacy. At the close of the war, he resumed the practice of law in New Orleans as an advocate of legendary reputation. Reportedly, a former slave to whom Campbell had given the money to purchase her family's freedom said of him on her deathbed, "Put your trust in God and Mr. Campbell." In the postwar period, not a few clients, mostly corporate, availed themselves of his services.

When Campbell died in 1889, Justice Joseph P. Bradley wrote to the *Picayune:* "The esteem in which he was held by the members of the

Supreme Court amounted to reverence. For myself, from the time I first heard him in New Orleans in the *Slaughter House Case* until his death, he was the *beau* idea of forensic perfectness." Bradley's colleague on the Supreme Court, Justice Samuel F. Miller, did not share his admiration of Campbell. In 1870 he described Campbell "as a man of honor and an unfortunate one," but he had harsh words for the former justice seven years later. "I have neither seen nor heard of any action of Judge Campbell's since the rebellion," Miller wrote, "which was aimed at healing the breach he contributed so much to make. He has made himself an active leader of the worst branch of the New Orleans democracy. Writing their pronunciamentos, arguing their cases in our Court, and showing all the evidences of an unsuccessful partizan [*sic*] politician."

In the weeks following adoption of the act, the Crescent City Company set out to fulfill its statutory obligation to have "a grand slaughterhouse of sufficient capacity" to accommodate all butchers ready for business by June 1. The company purchased riverfront property for $48,000, making a down payment of a quarter of the price and agreeing to pay the balance over the next three years. The property was located opposite the city on the west bank of the river, at Slaughterhouse Point in Algiers, the very site where the New Orleans slaughterhouses had been confined during the city's colonial period. This location could be defended both on sanitary grounds and by the presence of a railhead belonging to the New Orleans, Opelousas and Great Western Railroad, a line that ran westward for eighty miles and was expected to be part of a line that would eventually connect New Orleans and the beef-rich Texas plains. Two river ferries were located nearby. But the site meant that the butchers would have to relocate their operations, commute to their slaughter pens across the river, and either pay fees to transport their meat to market or move it themselves.

An architect was employed to help plan the facilities. A stock landing was constructed, and holding pens and sheds were thrown up in unpainted pine. A building formerly used as a sheet iron warehouse located on the property at the water's edge was hastily outfitted to serve as a slaughterhouse. Capital was in short supply, and once the facilities were completed, they were criticized for being makeshift and a poor imitation of the European abattoir. "This ridiculous specimen of an abattoir," wrote a veterinarian from France, was unsuited to serve as the *backyard* of any respectable French abattoir. The company's architect was never fully compensated for his services and eventually had to sue for his fee. Several years later, when it served the company's purposes to abandon the Algiers slaughterhouse, the facility was dismantled in a matter of hours.

While work on the slaughterhouse progressed, the Crescent City Company served notice through the newspapers that it would be ready to comply with the conditions of its charter by June 1. The notice included a schedule of charges authorized by the act. At the same time, the company made an effort to quell the rising tide of opposition. It disavowed any interest in interfering with the smooth operation of business or retaining any parts of the slaughtered animals that were customarily sold in the markets. It even gave 1,500 shares of paid-up preferred stock to one of the principal firms of stock dealers associated with the Jefferson City stock landing in return for the firm's agreement to relocate its operations to the new facility and to try to persuade other firms to follow suit. None of this was sufficient to quell the mushrooming opposition, however, and before long, the New Orleans courts were embroiled in a confusing tangle of litigation involving more than 300 suits and many more individual injunctions. As complicated as the controversy was, however, it is possible to reconstruct the contours of the battle by focusing mainly on the half dozen actions that were eventually appealed, initially to the state supreme court and ultimately to the U.S. Supreme Court, where they were consolidated for decision as the *Slaughterhouse Cases.*

When the judicial collision came, it could not have been more head-on. The judicial system of Orleans Parish in 1869 was made up of seven district courts. Three of these exercised specialized jurisdiction, but the remaining four had identical general civil jurisdiction, which they exercised without regard to the area of the parish in which an action arose or where the parties resided. The first suit was filed on the morning of May 26 when the Butchers Benevolent Association, represented by its president, Paul Esteben, brought a petition to Judge William H. Cooley in the Sixth District Court seeking an injunction to prevent the Crescent City Company from asserting any of its rights under the act. Judge Cooley was a Republican, but he was also a native of Louisiana and a veteran of the Confederate army, and the *Picayune* had given him high marks for taking conservative positions. His handling of the association's suit illustrates how things were done in the New Orleans courts during this chaotic period.

In a long and wordy petition, the association asserted that its members were engaged in a "lawful and necessary" trade that had been conducted for more than thirty years in the area covered by the act. A thousand people, allegedly including 400 members of the association, had invested "capital and labor" in establishing their businesses, and the members of the association alone now owned property in the affected area valued at more than half a million dollars. In seeking to enforce its exclusive privileges, the company proposed to force the petitioners to abandon the purposes of their organization and destroy important property rights.

The petition charged that the Slaughterhouse Act was an absolute nullity. It established "an odious and burdensome monopoly . . . against common right and the common interest," and it had been obtained "by the use of corrupt, fraudulent and illegal applications of bribes"; in fact, both the governor and members of the legislature were stockholders. The provisions of the act indicating that it was a health measure were "mere disguises" designed to conceal its real purpose, which was to create a profitable monopoly at the butchers' and the public's expense "for the benefit of a body of adventurers." More specifically, the petition charged that the Slaughterhouse Act violated the privileges and immunities clause of the newly adopted Fourteenth Amendment, which "secures to all protection from state legislation that involves the right of property the most valuable of which is to labor freely in an honest avocation." And it alleged that the act violated the power of Congress to regulate interstate commerce, as well as several unnamed provisions of the state constitution that the petitioners contended emancipated labor and guaranteed "equality of right." The ultimate aim of this action was to have the Slaughterhouse Act declared unconstitutional , but until that issue could be decided, Judge Cooley imposed a preliminary injunction to prevent the company from asserting any of its rights under the act or from interfering with the business conducted by the association.

One of the striking features of the controversy as it played out in the lower courts was the sheer number of efforts made by counsel on both sides — and the energy invested in them — to stymie or defeat the opposition short of arguing the merits of the cases. The lawyers filed exceptions (demurrers, in common law) to one another's petitions rather than answering them directly, and they argued these motions heatedly and at length in open court. They challenged the soundness of the sureties offered in support of injunctions. They moved to replace injunctions with monetary bonds. And if their losses in these interlocutory efforts could be appealed, appealed they were. Like prizefighters, counsel returned blow for blow as though the contest would ultimately be decided by the sheer expenditure of energy.

An example of the earnestness of these preliminary encounters is provided by an exception filed by the company against the association's suit in Judge Cooley's Sixth District Court. The company moved to dismiss the butchers' suit because the plaintiffs had failed to make a valid case against the act and the allegations concerning bribery were "impertinent, scandalous and criminous," too "loose and railing" to admit of proof. John Campbell's oral argument in rebuttal spanned nearly two days and took the *Picayune* almost ten columns of its finest print to report. He contended that every man has a natural right of "property in his person and a right to employ that in every lawful trade." He did not deny the regulatory power of the state, but he scorned the contention that this act could be justified as a health measure. "What do they say on their part?" he asked of the incorporators' motivations. "That this monopoly is just? That this monopoly is right? . . . No, sir. They say that the great object of the bill was to secure the health of the city; that the great purpose of this bill was to convey pure air and pure water, nutritive food, wholesome food, to the members of this community." Campbell dismissed this contention as pretense. Quite to the contrary, he contended that the act was a private financial scheme of unprecedented audacity, a "grinding and odious monopoly" obtained by fraud from a legislature all too willing to be corrupted.

Campbell made it quite clear that he was arguing for a greatly expanded role for the courts — for "all the judiciaries of the country" — in the defense of fundamental rights against unreasonable legislative intrusions. The legislative and executive branches had defaulted in their obligation to respect fundamental rights, he argued. "Woe! woe! woe! to this country if these tribunals falter in the performance of their duty." Campbell concluded his long argument by making his expectations of the judges even more explicit. "All modern civilization is derived from the ascendancy which the legal profession acquired.

All the constitutions of Europe emanated from the professional mind and I pray that the judges of the land may fulfill their high vocation, and defend, and protect and guard the liberties that are embodied in these constitutions."

Judge Cooley did not rule on the exception until December. Though similar arguments were held in other courts, the argument of this motion in Cooley's court before a capacity crowd in late June proved to be the most celebrated and most prolonged public hearing that any of these cases received in the lower courts.

The second of the six suits to be appealed was initiated only hours after the Butchers Benevolent Association filed its suit. William H. Hunt, an attorney for the Crescent City Company, filed a short petition with Judge Charles Leaumont in the Fifth District Court asserting the company's exclusive privileges and alleging that the Butchers Benevolent Association had publicly made known its intentions to thwart the company in the exercise of its rights. In response, Judge Leaumont issued an injunction against the association. The butchers replied to this action with an exception and answer in which they moved that the suit be dismissed on the grounds that the Slaughterhouse Act was unconstitutional and because it violated the first section of the Civil Rights Act of 1866, which they claimed protected citizens in all their civil rights.

In Louisiana, as elsewhere, the writ of injunction was an extraordinary remedy available only if a plaintiff could convince a judge that some action by the defendant was about to cause him or her irreparable harm and that the court should intervene immediately to prevent it. In such a case, a preliminary restraining order would be issued ex parte, without waiting to hear from the defendant. If the defendant believed, however, that the plaintiff did not stand to suffer irreparable harm, he or she could ask the court for permission to substitute a surety bond for the injunction. The bond would compensate the plaintiff for any damages he or she might suffer because of the lifting of the injunction, should the case ultimately be decided in the plaintiff's favor. As an extraordinary remedy, an injunction could not be maintained, even as a preliminary order, if the potential damage to the plaintiff was readily ascertainable in dollars and cents.

William Hunt lost no time in seeking permission from Judge Cooley to substitute bonds for the injunction imposed at the behest of the

Butchers Benevolent Association. On June 6, Cooley's courtroom "was crowded with representatives of both sides" for their first encounter in open court in an extraordinary Saturday hearing. John Campbell argued strenuously that his clients stood to suffer irreparable harm. The act "would break them up and disperse them." To require the butchers and stock dealers to relocate to the new facilities across the river was tantamount to having an ax "put to the root of a whole community." But Judge Cooley found that immediate compliance with the act by the butchers and stock dealers was merely a matter of dollars and cents. He ordered the dissolution of the injunction, provided that the company furnished a bond of $100,000.

This ruling left the Crescent City Company free to assert its rights under the statute, while the butchers remained enjoined from interfering with the company by Judge Leaumont's order. The company's victory seemed only to stiffen the resistance, and at a mass meeting held that night, the butchers adopted resolutions "with three cheers and a 'tiger'" denouncing the company as "an iniquitous and grinding monopoly," "a nefarious scheme of public plunder," "a willful violation of the Constitution." As if to show its own resolve, the company went back to Judge Leaumont's court on Monday morning and caused the president and three other members of the Butchers Benevolent Association to be fined and briefly jailed for slaughtering outside the company's facilities in violation of its injunction. Rumors of bribery remained rife in this climate. The *Picayune* reported, "We learn that the governor holds stock to a very large amount" and that several legislators are "heavily interested." Warmoth felt compelled to obtain a handwritten statement from the president and secretary of the Crescent City Company certifying that "to the best of our knowledge and belief Governor Henry Clay Warmoth neither is nor has been at any time, directly or indirectly, openly or disguisedly, immediately or prospectively, either a stockholder in the above company or interested in its affairs in any pecuniary sense whatsoever."

The attorneys for the Butchers Benevolent Association now undertook a series of moves aimed at restoring their injunctions against the company so that their clients could conduct their businesses undisturbed, pending the outcome of the litigation. First, they sought to suspend Judge Cooley's finding that the butchers did not stand to suffer irreparable injury and his decision allowing the injunctions to be bonded out until the issue of irreparable harm could be appealed to the state supreme court, as allowed under Article 566 of the Code of Practice. Under Article 575, if the appeal were taken within ten days, the effect of the decision would be suspended until the appeal had been decided. This motion afforded the opportunity for a second major confrontation in open court. Once again, John Campbell argued, "My clients tell you their businesses will be broken up, their calculations for business disturbed and irreparable injury will be caused." But Judge Cooley refused to allow the appeal. For the second time, he dumbfounded counsel for the butchers in his interpretation of the law, this time by holding that Article 566 could not have been intended to apply to a case like this, since it would have the effect of canceling out Article 304, which allowed the injunctions to be bonded out in the first place. In reaching this decision, Judge Cooley ignored an impressive line of state supreme court decisions that uniformly and explicitly supported the practice of allowing suspensive appeals in such cases. In fact, all the decisions cited by Judge Cooley to support his denial of a suspensive appeal actually *acknowledged* the availability of such an appeal.

The butchers now launched a second effort to restore their injunctions. They attacked the bonds given by the Crescent City Company in substitution for the injunction, arguing that the persons who had signed them were not qualified under the law because they neither resided in the parish nor owned property there. At a hearing they were unable to prove this charge, however, and Judge Cooley dismissed the motion. On June 19, in yet another attack, Campbell attempted to substitute a bond for the injunction the Crescent City Company had obtained in the Fifth District Court. The *Picayune* reported that Judge Leaumont's court was "crowded to suffocation" for the hearing, but the motion was a long shot at best. Only the day before, Campbell had failed in his effort to prevent Leaumont from convicting Paul Esteben and his colleagues of contempt of court. It came as no surprise when this judge refused to permit the company's injunction to be bonded out.

This decision was loudly denounced at the mass meeting held at a Tchoupitoulas Street saloon that night. The butchers were quickly running out of judicial means of keeping the Slaughterhouse Act in abeyance until the merits of the case could be decided—or so it seemed. The saloon crowd shouted its support for a resolution calling for a boycott of the markets. Days followed when fresh beef was a scarce commodity in New Orleans, making it impossible for the general public to escape involvement in the dispute. Not long afterward, the butchers denounced the *New Orleans Times* as "an enemy of the people and butchers — the organ of a monopoly," and its proprietor, Charles A. Weed, as a "Northern adventurer."

But before the June 19 meeting ended, Paul Esteben emerged from a long, secret session of the leadership to suggest another strategy that would allow practically all the butchers to go on selling meat. Fresh from his confinement in the parish prison, he chose his words carefully to avoid incurring Judge Leaumont's wrath again. But his message was clear: the company's injunction did not bind anyone who was *not* a member of the Butchers Benevolent Association. Therefore, individual butchers could extricate themselves from the injunction simply by resigning from the association. They would then be free to obtain individual injunctions against the company in another court. The New Orleans legal landscape would soon be covered with crisscrossing injunctions.

The first shot in the war of injunctions that followed was fired by Inbau, Aycock and Company, a prominent firm of stock dealers in Jefferson City. Represented by the same team of attorneys who had brought suit on behalf of the Butchers Benevolent Association, Inbau carefully avoided Judge Cooley's court and filed a similar action in the Seventh District Court — whose judge, T. Wharton Collens, had actually appeared at one of the mass meetings in support of the butchers' cause. This action would become the third of the *Slaughterhouse Cases* on appeal.

Inbau made a very strong case for an injunction against the company. As one of the principal lessors of the stock landing in Jefferson City, it had invested thousands of dollars in yards and related facilities and regularly received cattle for sale from customers both in and out of the state. Many butchers depended on the firm for their supply of beef. Judge Collens responded by ordering Franklin Pratt into court, and on June 21, he enjoined the Crescent City Company from interfering with the conduct of the plaintiff's business.

Predictably, the Crescent City Company moved immediately to dissolve the injunction upon its posting of a bond, and a short time later, it filed an exception to the action. The motion to dissolve was extensively argued in early July, but Judge Collens took the matter under advisement and did not rule on it until November, when the controversy was in a much different phase. Meanwhile, Inbau's injunction remained in effect, and the firm continued to do its business undisturbed for the time being.

Other stock dealers and a crowd of angry individual butchers followed Inbau into Judge Collens's friendly Seventh District Court. By the end of June, counsel for the butchers had filed at least 170 new suits to enjoin the company and its functionaries, making a total of approximately 500 injunctions to be issued against the company. These actions were lodged by means of printed forms in which each petitioner piously disavowed membership in the Butchers Benevolent Association and attacked the Slaughterhouse Act as a violation of both the state and national constitutions in general and "specially the Fourteenth Amendment."

Meanwhile, from Judge Leaumont's Fifth District Court, the company replied with a volley of its own, consisting of two dozen suits and approximately 200 new injunctions against individual butchers, stock dealers, and steamship operators to force compliance with the act. One of these actions was filed against the steamboat *B. L. Hodge No. 2* and its owners to collect wharfage fees for 226 head of cattle landed at a place other than the company's wharf. It would become the fourth of the *Slaughterhouse Cases* on appeal.

The most controversial action in this barrage was one filed by the man appointed by Governor Warmoth as the first inspector of stock under the act, George W. Carter. In April, the *Times*, realizing the need to bolster the legitimacy of the new abattoir, had urged the governor to appoint to this important position "an old and experienced butcher, one whose character is well known to the community." Carter was a native of Virginia and formerly a popular Methodist minister who had served the Confederacy as a colonel in a Texas regiment. At the time of the Slaughterhouse Act, he was traveling in Governor Warmoth's circles, trying, as he once publicly explained, "to bear defeat manfully." Later, Warmoth would have the legislature create Cameron Parish to make a seat in the house of representatives available to Carter. Shortly after being appointed inspector of beef, Carter had served public notice of his determination to use the police pow-

ers given him by the act "to secure the rigid execution of the law."
The fact that he was a far cry from the "experienced butcher" the
Times had recommended, coupled with the vigor with which he exercised his police power, made him an ideal target for popular resentment of the entire slaughterhouse enterprise.

It became apparent even before the end of June that the merits of
the cases would ultimately have to be decided by the state supreme
court. When that day arrived, it would be important to make the
strongest possible case against the monopoly. From the beginning of
the litigation, the butchers and stock dealers had been under enormous pressure to relocate their operations away from the residential
areas of the city. It was not long before they realized that any plan to
defeat the Crescent City Company would have to be grounded on a
willingness to relocate the slaughterhouses.

In mid-July the leadership of the butchers and stock dealers revealed their ultimate strategy to defeat the Slaughterhouse Act. A
group of thirteen stock dealers and prominent butchers announced
the incorporation of a new entity, the Live Stock Dealers and Butchers Association of New Orleans, naming William Fagan as its first
president. The new corporation had been formed for the express purpose of purchasing property in St. Bernard Parish, just below New
Orleans, from Charles Cavaroc, a prominent banker and merchant,
and erecting a huge slaughterhouse capable of accommodating the
needs of the whole city. By voluntarily relocating the slaughterhouses,
the livestock dealers hoped to make it impossible to rationalize the act
as a necessary health measure. The new corporation filed suit immediately in the Seventh District Court, challenging the constitutionality of the Slaughterhouse Act on both state and federal grounds, and
Judge Collens dutifully issued an injunction to prevent the Crescent
City Company or George Carter from interfering with its plans. This
would be the fifth of the cases on appeal.

It was now clear to all parties that the dispute was heading for the
state supreme court. But before it got there, it was important for the
Crescent City Company to mount one final assault. That attack came
a week later when Louisiana's attorney general, Simeon Belden,
entered the fray on behalf of the company and its legislative mandate
in an action that would become the sixth of the *Slaughterhouse Cases*.

The company was, after all, endeavoring to defend a state legislative act. Why should the state not assume some of the responsibility — and the cost — of the fight? In an action filed before Judge Leaumont in the Fifth District Court, the attorney general insisted that the act was a bona fide health measure and that the state had an interest in seeing it successfully implemented. He obtained an injunction to prevent the Live Stock Dealers and Butchers Association and Charles Cavaroc from attempting to consummate their plans. An effort by the livestock dealers before Judge Leaumont to substitute a bond for this injunction came to nothing, but no matter: Cavaroc promptly obtained an injunction of his own against the attorney general from the Third District Court. At that point, Belden informally agreed to take no action to prevent the construction of the new slaughterhouse, although he predicted — correctly — that the butchers would eventually lose the case in the state supreme court. By mid-September, thus shielded, construction of the new slaughterhouse and wharves began.

Far from makeshift, the new facility would take nearly a year to complete and, including the price of the land, would cost the Live Stock Dealers and Butchers Association around $200,000. On a Sunday in January 1870, only a day or two before the cases were argued in the state supreme court, the livestock dealers staged a grand opening of their new, almost finished slaughterhouse. Through the streets of New Orleans went a brass band and a cavalcade of cattle and butchers dressed in the colorful European costumes of their trade. It was a bit of nineteenth-century public relations: the owners of the rival slaughterhouse were taking no chances that the availability of their new, state-of-the-art facility, safely located below the city, would go unnoticed, especially by members of the judiciary.

Any hope that the Crescent City Company's organizers may have had of easily and swiftly implementing their franchise had been shattered. Its judicial efforts had resulted in a stalemate that allowed the butchers to keep the markets supplied with beef slaughtered in Jefferson City, Algiers, or the new establishment below the city. The company had made several extrajudicial efforts to induce compliance with the act — by offering reduced slaughterhouse rates to any butcher who would patronize the new facility, for example — but these efforts had little result. By the end of June, there were rumors that holders of assessable stock were not willing to meet their installments, that dissension had broken out among the leaders, and that some of the original incorporators were selling out. The company had seen the price of its stock decline from about $40 a share when it was first offered in early June to less than $30 by the end of the month. In mid-August, it sold for about $18 a share and was about $15 in October. Suits over ownership of stock had broken out among stockholders. In late August, the *Picayune* reported that everything around the company's slaughterhouse had "a sleepy look."

As soon as the supreme court reconvened for its regular term on November 1, 1869, the litigants returned to the fray, determined to bring the proceedings in the lower courts to an end. Unresolved exceptions were quickly disposed of, clearing the way for the defendants to file answers and plead the merits of the cases if they had not already done so. In a formal agreement executed by the attorneys for both sides, the parties selected the six principal actions described earlier — three filed by butchers or stock dealers against the company, and three filed on behalf of the company — and agreed to submit them to the district courts for summary decisions on the basis of the documents already on file and a limited amount of additional evidence. The agreement provided that these decisions would then be appealed as a single consolidated action to the state supreme court and that the parties would abide by the high court's decision.

All six cases came up for trial and were submitted for decision in their respective courts on December 9 on the evidence stipulated by the parties in their written agreement. For the butchers, John Campbell introduced a transcript of out-of-court testimony taken from witnesses on both sides concerning the extent to which the slaughterhouse had been ready for business by June 1. Campbell also offered to prove that the incorporators of the company had never had any responsibility for the health of the city or any previous experience in the livestock industry and that the Slaughterhouse Act was a product of bribery. His offer of testimony on these points was refused by the court, and objection to this refusal was noted for purposes of appeal.

The first decisions were rendered by Judge Collens in the Seventh District Court in the actions filed by the Inbau firm and the newly organized Live Stock Dealers and Butchers Association. Collens had never concealed his sympathy for the butchers' cause and had hinted at how he would decide the cases as early as November 2, when he denied the company's motion made in July to dissolve the Inbau injunction. At that time, he had declared the act unconstitutional, holding that it created a monopoly in violation of the Fourteenth Amendment and Articles 1 and 2 of the Louisiana Constitution, which recognized basic human equality and an equality of civil rights. Now, a month later, and on the same day the cases were submitted to him, he rendered judgments in favor of both Inbau and the Live Stock Dealers and Butchers Association, perpetuating their injunctions against the company.

The lengthiest opinion was rendered by Judge Cooley in the suit filed by the Butchers Benevolent Association in the Sixth District Court. Cooley had never ruled on the exception taken by the company in that suit, which Campbell and others had resisted so passionately. But Cooley had also disappointed the butchers earlier by allowing the company to bond out the injunction he had ordered in favor of the butchers and by refusing to suspend this decision until the issue of irreparable injury could be adjudicated on appeal. Now, in an elaborately reasoned opinion that the *Picayune* called "long and able," citing out-of-state legal authorities, the Federalist Papers, and even the writings of Benjamin Franklin, he held that the Slaughterhouse Act was invalid because it had been signed by the governor four days after the legislature had adjourned.

According to Judge Cooley, the governor had violated two articles of the Louisiana Constitution of 1868. Article 39 limited legislative sessions to sixty days and nullified "any legislative action" beyond that period. Thus, in signing the bill when he did, the governor had engaged in prohibited "legislative action." Moreover, Article 66 provided that if the governor were prevented from vetoing an act by the adjournment of the legislature, he had until the first day of the next legislative session to reject the measure, or it would become law. The effect of this provision, Cooley held, was to prevent the governor from signing a measure into law after adjournment of the legislature. In his view, a bill could become law without the governor's signature on the first day of the next legislative session, but it could not become law *with* his signature sooner. It was a patently incorrect interpretation that would not pass muster in the state supreme court, but it enabled Judge Cooley to express his disapproval of the radical slaughterhouse measure without embracing that grander radical project, the Fourteenth Amendment. Cooley's interpretation must have offered the butchers' attorneys some vindication for initiating their action in his court, even though, at this point, it made little difference how he decided the cases.

The remaining three actions — the company's suits against the Butchers Benevolent Association and the steamboat *B. L. Hodge* and Attorney General Belden's action against the Live Stock Dealers and Butchers Association — were pending in Judge Leaumont's Fifth District Court, which had been the company's court of choice from the beginning. Like Judge Collens in the Seventh District Court, Judge Leaumont had never made a single decision that was adverse to the interests of the slaughterhouse litigants who had initiated action in his court. On the day after the cases were submitted to him for decision, Leaumont dutifully perpetuated the injunctions against the butchers and stock dealers in all three cases without written reasons.

Suspensive appeals to the state supreme court were ordered in all cases on December 14, and the court heard oral arguments on January 27 and 28. Both sides were represented in these proceedings by some of the best legal talent available in New Orleans. J. B. Cotton and J. Q. A. Fellows joined with John Campbell to represent the butchers and stock dealers. William Hunt's brother, Randell Hunt, and Christian Roselius, eminent advocates associated with the local law school at the University of Louisiana, spoke for the company. Before turning to the Louisiana Supreme Court decision, however, a summary of the key points presented to the justices is appropriate.

In a printed brief of more than seventy pages, Campbell emphasized and embellished a number of points, of which three may be considered essential. In the first place, the statute establishing the Crescent City Company had been enacted through "the bribery of the members of the Legislature, and the purchase of their votes." Any statute, Campbell insisted, "can be set aside for fraud, and the bribery and corruption of the members of the Legislature which passed it." Moreover, the statute violated the Louisiana Constitution (1) because it had been signed by Governor Warmoth after the legislature had adjourned, and (2) because the statute had not been signed within the five-day period mandated by the constitution. Finally, the statute was unconstitutional because in enacting it, the legislature had granted a monopoly, "in every sense of that term." Here, Campbell, an ex-Confederate official who had glorified states' rights only five years earlier, now argued that "it is a mistaken idea . . . that the Legislatures of the States have powers of legislation limited only by the express prohibitions of the constitutions of the State or the Union, or by necessary implication." The exercise of legislative power to pass the slaughterhouse statute "is contrary to the fundamental principles and theory of our form of government." Though counsel had resorted to the Fourteenth Amendment in the initial pleadings, it was not until the next-to-last page of his brief that Campbell mentioned the amendment. He insisted that it represented "a new declaration of rights" and "that monopolies cannot be granted by a State Legislature without violating that article."

Extending to barely fourteen pages, Attorney General Belden's brief stands in marked contrast to Campbell's, if only in size. Whereas Campbell had sought to expand constitutional interpretation to new heights, Belden insisted that the Fourteenth Amendment as well as the Louisiana Bill of Rights "have not the remotest application to the solution of the question, presented by the record." The slaughterhouse statute was based on "police regulations, promotive of the health and cleanliness of the city. This is a subject of ordinary legislation, and it seems to us difficult to imagine on what legal ground the Constitutionality of such a law can be assailed." Belden dismissed Campbell's claim of monopoly with similar ease. "That the State itself, might constitutionally, in the exercise of its police power, erect an *abattoir*, where all animals intended for the markets of the city should be killed, . . . and that a reasonable retribution might be levied on those who use it, we suppose will hardly be denied by anyone." But because the state had delegated a corporation to construct at its own cost a central slaughterhouse, "with the right of charging a reasonable toll as a *quid pro quo*, fixed by law for the enjoyment of the facilities thus provided, it constitutes a monstrous monopoly!"

"Is there a single line in the act," asked Belden, "which hinders any one from following the occupation of a butcher?" The right of all who sought to run a meat shop was undisturbed. Only the *locality* where slaughtering of the animals could occur was restricted. All who sought to butcher their own meat *had* to be afforded the right to do so, albeit at the central slaughterhouse facilities. Moreover, Belden reminded the court that "our statute books are full of similar delegations of power." Nor did Belden see any validity in the claim that the slaughterhouse statute had been approved after adjournment. Describing Judge Cooley's "elaborate disquisition" on this point as "rather fanciful than sound," the attorney general insisted that the Louisiana Constitution spoke only to "a fatal delay" that limited the time in which the governor could veto a statute. "Not one word is said in any part of the Constitution that he shall approve a law within a given time, or return it to the Legislature after he has approved it."

It fell to Randell Hunt to comment on Campbell's frequent claims of corruption and bribery. First, he described Campbell's argument as "a grave, serious, vituperative, and lengthy address . . . abusive of the character and standing of seventeen citizens against whom there is no evidence in the record, and illegally and acrimoniously denunciatory of a coordinate branch of the government." Hunt summarized at some length the history of the efforts in New Orleans at sanitary reform. If Campbell had invoked constitutional limitations, Hunt invoked an expansive view of governmental power. Referring to the rhetoric of Hamilton and Marshall, he noted that "when a large and consolidated capital is necessary to accomplish works important to the public good, it is quite customary for the States to grant charters of incorporation to private individuals, with special and often exclusive privileges, to effect that end." Further, as had Belden, Hunt emphasized that the slaughterhouse statute "conferred no exclusive privilege on the company to slaughter . . . , but compelled it to furnish whatever is essential to the convenience and accommodation of the butchers for killing their cattle."

Hunt saved his most vigorous denunciations for Campbell's oft-repeated statement that the seventeen original incorporators belonged in a penitentiary. "I deny it. There has never been any legal charge made in a form susceptible of legal proof. . . . They pretend that my clients shrank in fear from the investigation. You shrink and you skulk. You skulk behind a generous railing and informal accusation. You say members of the legislature were bribed. Tell us who they are. Name them. Name any one. You say you have witnesses to prove it. Who are the witnesses?"

The state constitution of 1868, like the constitution of 1864, called for a supreme court composed of five justices appointed by the governor. Governor Warmoth had chosen five active fellow Republicans for these seats. James K. Taliaferro had run against Governor Warmoth in the gubernatorial election of 1868, nominated by a group of Republicans who feared that Warmoth was more interested in his own agenda than in advancing the ideals of the party. A firm unionist who had been briefly imprisoned by Confederate authorities, Taliaferro later served as president of the 1869 constitutional convention. "He represented," wrote Joe Gray Taylor, "the best of the native white element at the convention." Chief Justice John Ludeling had also opposed secession, and while his two brothers fought for the Confederacy, he refused to aid the Southern cause. A consistent supporter of congressional Reconstruction after the war, Ludeling, along with one John Ray, bought a bankrupt railroad for $50,000, according to Taylor, "by means of legal skullduggery and, probably, bribing the agent of purchasers willing to pay a much higher price." In addition, Ray got the Louisiana legislature to pass a bond issue for railroad repair, a piece of legislation that Ludeling, as chief justice, later ruled to be valid. In due time, the U.S. Supreme Court voided sale of the railroad to Ludeling and Ray, but not before they had profited considerably from the transaction. Ludeling's extrajudicial business activities should be kept in mind when his opinion for the court in the *Slaughterhouse Cases* is discussed.

Taliaferro and Rufus K. Howell were carryovers from the court under the previous constitution. Howell was a pro-slavery unionist who, with Warmoth's strong support, would later be selected as a federal judge. The remaining justices were William W. Howe and William G. Wyly. The *Picayune* had questioned whether the justices had the "forensic and judicial experience" of some of the justices of the past, but it had applauded some of their decisions and trusted that the justices would not sacrifice state law in their pursuit of Republican goals.

The Crescent City Company's stock traded for about $15 or $16 throughout January, until Randell Hunt concluded his argument and submitted the case for decision; then the price quickly climbed to $25 or more, apparently in anticipation of a quick decision in the company's favor. When this did not come about, the price began to slip. Throughout March and into April, Crescent City Company stock sold at around $21 or lower. Finally, on Saturday, April 9, word leaked out that the court was about to hand down its decision, and in a single day, several thousand shares were traded at prices ranging from $23 to more than $31. On Monday, the court formally handed down its decision, and an additional 2,000 shares changed hands at prices that rose to $34.

In a three-to-one decision, the Louisiana Supreme Court upheld

　　　　　{ *The Slaughterhouse Cases* }

the validity of the Slaughterhouse Act. The court's decision was announced in an opinion by Chief Justice Ludeling in which Justice William W. Howe silently concurred; Taliaferro concurred in a brief separate opinion. Justice William G. Wyly registered a single dissent, and Howell did not participate in deciding the case. The chief justice brushed aside the objections made by the butchers to Attorney General Belden's right to bring suit. The attorney general, he wrote, had ample authority to enter the dispute because the state had a right to enjoin anyone from interfering with the exercise of its laws. Further, added the chief justice, an 1868 statute specifically authorized the attorney general to take action to prevent the usurpation of public offices or *franchises*, referring here to the nullifying effect of the Live Stock Dealers and Butchers Association's charter on the Crescent City Company's exclusive statutory privileges. The butchers had contended that the act was merely a private measure aimed at enriching its sponsors and hence should be overthrown on grounds of fraud and bribery. Well aware that an argument concerning bribery of legislators might apply to instances besides the slaughterhouse statute, Ludeling, as had the lower courts, rejected this evidence because of the vagueness and indefinite nature of the accusations. Citing none other than John Marshall, Ludeling held that "courts are without warrant . . . to inquire into the motives which may have influenced or actuated the members of the General Assembly in enacting laws." Moreover, the act had all the makings of a public act, since it was addressed to the public at large and aimed at protecting important public interests. Ludeling considered it a well-settled rule that the courts were not entitled to look beyond the face of public acts at the legislature's motives in passing them.

Nor did the chief justice have any difficulty overruling Judge Cooley's decision that the act was invalid because the governor had signed it after the legislature's adjournment and more than sixty days after the commencement of the legislative session. Accepting the point made by Belden, he noted that Article 66 allowed the governor five days in which to veto an act by returning it to the legislature for reconsideration. If the legislature prevented its return by adjourning before the lapse of five days, the governor could return the bill to the legislature at the beginning of the next legislative session, or it would "be a law." That measure had obviously been designed to secure the legislature's right to override the governor's veto and not to restrict his right to approve legislation. Moreover, in limiting legislative sessions to sixty days and prohibiting legislative action beyond that period, Article 39 of the constitution could not possibly have meant to characterize the signing of a bill by the governor as "legislative action." This would have prevented the governor from vetoing legislation after adjournment of the legislature, which he was clearly authorized to do on the first day of the next legislative session.

The attorneys for the butchers had spent a good third of their brief attempting to demonstrate that by creating a monopoly in the Slaughterhouse Act, the legislature had exceeded fundamental boundaries on its power imposed both by the inherently limited nature of state legislative power — limitations recently confirmed and augmented by adoption of the Fourteenth Amendment — and by specific provisions in the state constitution. For its part, the court preferred to accept the arguments made by Hunt and to abide by well-settled state precedent, which acknowledged "that the legislature, in its sphere, is supreme in all respects, save when restricted by the constitution of the State or of the United States."

But for the first time in the history of the state, its constitution contained a bill of rights, and among its provisions was one guaranteeing to all citizens "the same civil, political, and public rights and privileges." How could an act that robs "one class of citizens of certain rights of property and freedom of action, not for the good of the community, but for the private gain of other individuals in the community," be consistent with such a provision?

Had this been the actual result of the statute, such an enactment might well have violated the Louisiana Bill of Rights. But, reasoned Ludeling, it was simply not true that rights were being limited solely for private gain. The Slaughterhouse Act was defensible as a genuine sanitary measure and was rooted in a long history of sanitary reform, which Randell Hunt had outlined in detail in his oral argument and from which Ludeling now quoted freely. In short, the act was a legitimate exercise of the police power of the state. There was sound precedent, based on the state's power (previously upheld) to restrict the sale of oysters in New Orleans to municipally established markets. The court reacted with incredulity to the suggestion that the Slaughterhouse Act infringed on constitutionally protected liberties.

"We think this is a fallacy," Lubeling wrote. "Liberty is the right to do what the law permits." It "presupposes the existence of some legislative provision, the observance of which insures freedom to one, by securing the like observance from the other." Placing his holding squarely within well-established police power case law, Ludeling cited Cooley's already famous *Constitutional Limitations.* "There are, unquestionably, cases in which the State may grant to specified individuals, privileges, without violating any constitutional principle, because, from the very nature of the case, it is impossible that they be possessed and enjoyed by all." Accepting the premise that it was reasonable to restrict slaughtering to one specific area of the city, it was within legislative discretion to conclude that in exchange for the expenses involved in purchasing the site and building and maintaining such a facility, the grant of exclusive privileges was not an unreasonable step.

Both Justice Taliaferro's concurring opinion and Justice Wyly's lone dissent turned on the equality of right guaranteed by the state constitution, but with opposite results. Taliaferro found that the constitution's equality of right had to yield to an effort to protect the general welfare. And, he added, it is not for the courts to gainsay the means selected by the state to pursue its legitimate goals.

In his dissent, Wyley found that the Slaughterhouse Act was a valid police measure to the extent that it required a change in the site of livestock operations. But in creating the Crescent City Company, with its exclusive privileges, the act went beyond what it was necessary to do to protect the public health. In this aspect the act could not be squared with the provisions of the Louisiana Bill of Rights guaranteeing freedom and equality. There is no mention in his opinion of the Fourteenth Amendment. The police power was not unlimited, Justice Wyly added, and it would not do for the legislature to be left alone to exercise it free from interference by the courts. He did, however, pay indirect tribute to Campbell. "I think the vast array of authorities . . . presented with such consummate ability by the counsel on behalf of the Butchers Benevolent Association, fully maintains the view I have taken."

The Louisiana Supreme Court had upheld the Slaughterhouse Act as a valid exercise of the state's police power. This decision was supposed to end the case, because the parties had agreed that the cases would be taken to the state supreme court for a final decision on the merits and that both parties "would abide [by] the result" in that court. The agreement had not specifically foreclosed an appeal to the U.S. Supreme Court, however, because, according to the company's attorney William H. Hunt, "no one believed it possible to get the question before that court." But once the state's high court handed down its decision, the attorneys for the butchers ignored their agreement and lost no time in initiating an appeal to the U.S. Supreme Court.

CHAPTER 6

Appeal, Repeal, and a Compromise

The attorneys for the butchers had made what they could of the various state issues, but none of them ever had much potential as a legal weapon against the Slaughterhouse Act, except in the hands of the most sympathetic state judges. Yet they had also raised federal questions, namely, the precise meaning of the limitations imposed on the states by the provisions of the Fourteenth Amendment. The state supreme court had summarily discarded these issues, but they provided the grounds for an appeal to the U.S. Supreme Court. It would take nearly three years of litigation and political maneuvering before the nation's high court would render its historic decision on the merits. The immediate aftermath of the state supreme court's decision was another summer of judicial confusion.

A few days after the Louisiana Supreme Court upheld the Slaughterhouse Act, the butchers' attorneys traveled to Galveston Texas, where Justice Joseph P. Bradley was attending to circuit duties, and obtained a writ of error to enable an appeal to the U.S. Supreme Court. Under Section 25 of the federal Judiciary Act, whenever a state supreme court upheld a state statute that had been challenged on grounds of the U.S. Constitution, the decision could be appealed to the U.S. Supreme Court by means of a writ of error. Moreover, if the writ were served on the state court within ten days of its decision, it would have the effect of a writ of supersedeas. This meant that the court's decision would be held in abeyance (superseded) until the Supreme Court disposed of the case.

At any rate, that would have been the effect of a writ of error in an ordinary action involving a monetary judgment. In such a case, the supersedeas effect of a writ of error postponed the losing party's obligation to satisfy the judgment until the dispute was finally resolved on appeal. But could the writ have such an effect in a case involving an injunction? An injunction is an equitable remedy granted only when it is necessary to prevent irreparable harm. To hold such an order in abeyance, even for a short time while the merits of the case were being decided, might allow the very harm it sought to prevent to occur. If, for example, an injunction given to prevent trees from being cut down were dissolved, would not the party seeking the injunction have a right to have it reinstated while the merits of the case were decided on appeal?

The Crescent City Company's first reaction to its victory in the state supreme court had been to file new suits against the Butchers Benevolent Association, the Inbau firm, and the Live Stock Dealers and Butchers Association, seeking damages allegedly suffered by the company as a result of the delay in the implementation of its franchise. The *New Orleans Republican* noted in its financial column that the company would soon boast a full treasury if these actions succeeded, but in fact, these suits were premature and were soon abandoned as the company's attorneys became occupied with the effects of the writ of error. The company had no intention of seeing its advantage put aside, even temporarily, without a fight. Indeed, it had never been in a better position to implement its franchise.

As soon as Justice Bradley arrived in New Orleans, the attorneys for the company met with him and their counterparts to discuss the legal effect of the writ of error. Bradley's decision was not quite satisfactory to either side. Although he had intended the writ to act as a supersedeas when he issued it, he had not specifically so ordered. Moreover, his research had convinced him that the effect of the writ of error was immediately to vest jurisdiction over the cases in the U.S. Supreme Court. As a result, all subsequent questions concerning the legal effect of the writ could be answered only by the high court and not by him. On this subject, he ruled, the "parties must take the law at their peril, as I cannot, sitting here, make any judicial determination which will bind them." The uncertainty of Justice Bradley's decision caused "wailing and rejoicing" on Carondelet Street, the center of New Orleans' financial district. Crescent City Company stock quickly slipped from $30 a share to around $25, and the question of the proper effect of a writ of error became a hotly debated topic among the city's financiers.

———

The New Orleans judicial system had undergone an important change during the time the *Slaughterhouse Cases* were pending in the state supreme court. Nothing could have demonstrated more clearly the impracticality of vesting concurrent jurisdiction over injunctions in the several district courts of Orleans Parish than the judicial stalemate and contradictions that resulted from the slaughterhouse melee. The *Daily Picayune* had denounced the "abuse of injunctions," and in a rare instance of consensus, both the *Times* and the *Republican* had joined it in calling for reform. To alleviate the problem, in March, Governor Warmoth persuaded the legislature to create a new court, the Eighth District Court, giving it *exclusive* jurisdiction in proceedings for injunctions and certain other writs and in all actions to settle election disputes. The latter was a significant power as Warmoth began to prepare for the election of 1870, and indeed, the *Picayune* saw it as a radical scheme to control elections. The act directed the other district courts to transfer all such cases to the new court.

The new statute departed from the constitutional practice of electing district court judges to the extent that it authorized the governor to appoint an interim judge to serve on the new court until one could be regularly elected in November 1872. For the position, Governor Warmoth chose Henry C. Dibble, a close associate, a sometime staff member of the Republican legislature, and the man who had drafted the bill creating the Eighth District Court. Dibble was an Indiana native in his mid-twenties. He had served as a colonel in the Union army and had briefly attended the University of Louisiana before being admitted to the bar in 1865. He confessed to feeling "painfully conscious" of his "inexperience" when he took office.

Although the legislature had acted well within its constitutional powers, this new tribunal was controversial nonetheless. From his seat in the Sixth District Court, Judge Cooley called it "no court at all," and Judges Collens and Leaumont joined him in protesting the statutory mandate to surrender jurisdiction in pending cases to Judge Dibble. It took a decision by the state supreme court in late May to settle the question of the Eighth District Court's legitimacy. By June, all the principal *Slaughterhouse Cases* (and many others) had been transferred to it.

Justice Bradley had declared himself unable to say whether the writ of error had a supersedeas effect when the question had been presented to him on June 3. But according to the *Republican*, "before the close of the day the slaughter house people, with invincible pluck, were on the war path again." Availing itself of the services of the new "octagon court" and its sympathetic judge, the Crescent City Company, represented solely by its president, Franklin Pratt, filed suit against the city of New Orleans, the administrators of both police and commerce, and the Board of Metropolitan Police to enforce its franchise without further delay. These defendants, the company alleged, were in charge of both the police and the markets of the city, and it was their duty to enforce the law. Instead, they were "countenancing and permitting" various infractions of the Slaughterhouse Act by the city's butchers and livestock dealers. In response, Judge Dibble ordered the issuance of an injunction, not to enjoin the defendants from taking any action but rather commanding them *to take positive measures* "to prevent" anyone from violating the various terms of the slaughterhouse franchise. The willingness of Charles A. Weed, the reviled publisher of the *New Orleans Times*, to serve as surety on the required bond added to the popular ire provoked by Dibble's action.

The Metropolitan Police was a force of nearly 700 men that had been created by the legislature in 1868 to serve the parishes of Orleans, Jefferson, and St. Bernard. In effect, it served as a military force on behalf of the Republican state government. The deployment of this force in the service of the Crescent City Company could be seen as another example of the cooperative relationship that existed between company leaders such as Franklin Pratt and Charles Weed and Governor Warmoth. Although the governor had not actually called out the Metropolitan Police himself, he admitted to having "instructed" the superintendent of police and, at the superintendent's request, to have "given him my views of what constituted his duties under the injunction."

Pursuant to Judge Dibble's injunction, in the predawn hours of Sunday, June 5, 1870, a posse of police converged on the rival livestock dealers' slaughterhouse and, without actually closing the establishment, refused to allow between 200 and 300 head of freshly slaughtered beef to leave. Carts laden with beef en route to market were seized and held until the meat spoiled. The police took up positions at the various city markets to prevent the sale of meat slaughtered at the livestock dealers' abattoir and lacking certificates from the inspector of beef. Butchers in large numbers were prevented from unloading carts at the French market. With only about 150 head being slaughtered daily at the Crescent City Company's abattoir, this new action caused an instant shortage of fresh meat and a sensation both in the press and among the public. When Louis Ruch, a butcher, confronted Weed and Pratt about the seizure, Weed told him that he could get justice from Justice Bradley — advice that Weed would later have good reason to regret. On Monday morning, June 6, Attorney General Belden dutifully intervened in this new action in support of the company's efforts at enforcement.

By midweek, disgruntled butchers had filed forty-two new suits against the Crescent City Company seeking a total of $18,000 in damages, but Judge Dibble's injunction remained in force. At yet another mass meeting, this one held at the Henry Clay statue on Canal Street, the butchers echoed the reasoning of the Declaration of Independence and accused the governor and the courts of having "abused the very reason why governments are established." Two leading butchers, Paul Esteben and James Stafford, swore out affidavits before Commissioner D. Urban in the Federal District Court seeking to have Pratt, Weed, and members of the Board of Metropolitan Police arrested for allegedly conspiring to violate rights protected under the Civil Rights Act of 1866.

This action led to personal appearances and testimony by Governor Warmoth, Lieutenant Governor Oscar Dunn, Judge Dibble, Franklin Pratt, Charles Weed, and other interested parties. It also resulted in a major argument between both Hunt brothers and Christian Roselius, representing Weed, and John Campbell and John Cotton, representing Stafford. Testimony focused on the extent of the monetary damages caused by the meat seizure, the "personal relationship" that apparently existed between the governor and principals in the Crescent City Company, and the lively and continuing interest that Weed took in this enterprise. Campbell sought once again to prove that Weed had conspired to deprive his clients of rights protected by the federal civil rights acts. Judge Edward Durell ultimately discharged Weed, however, and dismissed the matter on the grounds that Stafford could recover any damages from the state courts, if he was entitled to them.

Premature and crass though it may have been, Judge Dibble's enforcement injunction resulted in the opening of a new legal front, and it prompted a new line of argument from Campbell and his colleagues that had immeasurable — if also unknown — potential. On Monday, June 6, J. Q. A. Fellows and John Campbell presented Justice Joseph P. Bradley and Judge W. B. Woods in the U.S. Circuit Court with a lengthy petition in which they reviewed the history of the litigation and charged that the Slaughterhouse Act infringed on federal rights now protected by both the Civil Rights Act of April 9, 1866, and the new Fourteenth Amendment. They sought an injunction requiring the company to suspend all proceedings against them, thus enabling the butchers to construct the facilities they needed and generally to pursue their businesses "subject to no condition more severe than that of any other party." They also asked for an order removing the company's enforcement action from the Eighth District Court and transferring it to the Federal Circuit Court so that the validity of Judge Dibble's injunction could be tested. After a year of litigation, counsel for the butchers had found an unexpected opportunity to explore the potential of their federal arguments before a justice of the U.S. Supreme Court.

Interested spectators jammed the circuit courtroom for the argument two days later. John Campbell spoke for the butchers. He contended that the intent of both the Civil Rights Act of 1866 and the Fourteenth Amendment, which had been proposed by the same Congress in the same year, had been to secure for all citizens an equality of civil rights, which the act defined largely in terms of property rights. He pointed to the all-embracing language used in the documents, the object being "to place every citizen under the protection of the [federal] Government." "Is there," he inquired, "a law of Louisiana in which the rights of citizens are violated? There clearly is. One of the most abominable and outrageous acts that ever was passed." Campbell equated the 1869 slaughterhouse statute with "the vassalage of the Middle Ages." He insisted that the monopoly it granted was unconstitutional, and indeed, "the principles which vitalize our constitution grew out of the struggle against monopolies."

Opposing counsel William Hunt denounced the butchers for re-
neging on their agreement to abide by the state supreme court decision and insisted that Campbell was resorting to the civil rights law
"for a purpose for which it was never intended." Christian Roselius
denied that the 1869 statute established a monopoly. All who wished
to do so could become butchers, could slaughter their beef at the central slaughtering house, or could have others slaughter it for them.
The corporation, he reminded Bradley, "is compelled to prepare and
provide the necessary facilities for all butchers. Then where is the
monopoly?" Who was not free to pursue his business according to the
law of the land?

The irony of the situation was not lost on the *Daily Picayune*. Here
was John Campbell, a former justice of the U.S. Supreme Court and
a leading supporter of states' rights, now advocating that white butchers were to be protected by a Reconstruction measure. "Few of our
people would have dreamed," it observed, "that it would be found
necessary to appeal to the Civil Rights Bill to protect the rights of the
people in this or any other Southern city from invasion." In the opinion of the editors of the *Bee*, both the Slaughterhouse Act and the
Civil Rights Act were equally iniquitous. But there was no chance of
defeating the former act in the state courts. The only hope of success
lay in applying to the federal courts, and there employing "poison as
an antidote for poison."

In June 1870, Joseph Bradley had been on the high court for less
than six months. He had built a successful career as an attorney in New
Jersey, and until secession threatened the Union, he considered himself
"a conservative of conservatives." Shifting from a Whig to a Republican, he had denounced secession and slavery but insisted that "we were
always willing to concede to the South all their just rights — the entire
control and regulation of their own affairs." Although he had welcomed
the Reconstruction amendments, in common with many others who
had supported the Union, Bradley retained a strongly racist view of
society. To what extent it colored his perception of events in Louisiana
is uncertain. But it should be remembered that barely concealed in
Campbell's rhetoric was a denunciation of Reconstruction in general
and of the 1868 interracial Louisiana legislature in particular. Criticism
of Louisiana's reconstructed legislature and its policies was loudly touted
and widely shared. It is possible that Bradley was affected by it.

At the end of the week, Bradley announced a decision that landed like a bombshell in the litigation, although it did not alter the immediate positions of the parties. In an opinion that touched on all the major issues raised by the case, Bradley declared his belief that the Slaughterhouse Act was unconstitutional. He noted the very broad language found in the first section of the new amendment. It was possible, he conceded, "that those who framed the article were not themselves aware of the far reaching character of its terms. . . . Yet, if the amendment, as framed and expressed, does in fact bear a broader meaning, and does extend its protecting shield over those who were never thought of when it was conceived and put in form, and does reach social evils which were never before prohibited by constitutional enactment, it is to be presumed that the American people, in giving it their imprimatur, understood what they were doing, and meant to decree what has in fact been decreed." The prohibition in the Fourteenth Amendment that "no state shall make or enforce any law which shall abridge the privileges or immunities of citizens of the United States" was more than a guarantee of equality of rights among citizens. Rather, he wrote, it "demands that the privileges and immunities of all citizens shall be absolutely unabridged [and] unimpaired."

> Without venturing a complete list of all the privileges of citizenship, we may safely say it is one of the privileges of every American citizen to adopt and follow such lawful industrial pursuit — not injurious to the community — as he may see fit, without unreasonable regulation or molestation, and without being restricted by any of those unjust, oppressive, and odious monopolies or exclusive privileges which have been condemned by all free governments; it is also his privilege to be protected in the possession and enjoyment of his property so long as such possession and enjoyment are not injurious to the community; and not to be deprived thereof without due process of law. It is also his privilege to have with all other citizens, the equal protection of the laws.

Bradley then announced a key conclusion. "There is no more sacred right of citizenship than the right to pursue unmolested a lawful employment in a lawful manner. It is nothing more nor less than the sacred right of labor." Bradley recognized that this right was subject to various forms of legitimate regulation, as is implied by the issuance of occupational licenses, patents, or franchises by which a single concern is given the exclusive right to accomplish some task, such as the building of a toll road or bridge. These are things that in their nature cannot be allowed to all members of the public and ordinarily require public indulgence in some form. Admittedly, too, the right is subject to the exercise of a wide police power aimed at protecting the health, safety, or well-being of the community. He noted that certain pursuits or callings "should be regulated and supervised . . . in order to promote the public health, the public order and the general well being." But, Bradley insisted, "they are open to all proper applicants, and none are rejected except those who fail to exhibit the requisite qualifications . . . or who, after proper selections are made, would increase the number beyond what the interests and good order of society would bear."

A few questions arise concerning Bradley's position. In his eagerness to condemn the 1869 statute, he appears not to have considered the implications of permitting all butchers who wanted to maintain a slaughterhouse to do so, even if they maintained their establishments in a limited area. Would this not result in what Bradley had just called an increase of numbers "beyond what the interests and good order of society would bear"? The occupation of butchering, with all its aesthetic and sanitary hazards that are admittedly dangerous to the public health, was not a typical occupation. Was it therefore unreasonable for the legislature to decide that one slaughtering facility should be constructed, large enough for all who sought to use it, and that in return for the cost of building and maintaining such a public facility, those individuals willing to invest should have an exclusive franchise for a limited term of years?

Bradley denounced the effort to defend the Slaughterhouse Act as an appropriate exercise of the police power as "pretense . . . too bald for a moment's consideration." It conferred on a single corporation "a monopoly of a very odious character." Thus the question, admittedly "one of great delicacy and embarrassment," was whether such an arrangement could be permitted consistent with the Fourteenth Amendment's guarantee of fundamental privileges and immunities. Bradley had no difficulty whatsoever with this question. "It would be difficult to conceive of a more flagrant case of violation of the fundamental rights of labor than the one before us." The plaintiffs were prepared to conform to any and all police regulations governing their businesses. Yet they were required to land, keep, and slaughter their cattle at the defendant's facilities, and to pay tolls for the privilege of doing so, because "the ipse dixit of the legislature assigns a lawful and ordinary employment to one set of men, and denies and forbids it to another." Possibly with the Reconstruction experience in mind, Bradley added that "the injustice perpetrated under acts of irresponsible legislation has become a crying evil in our country."

Bradley's holding represented as strong a statement of the act's alleged invalidity as counsel for the plaintiffs could have sought. What followed next must have been a letdown for them. There was one insurmountable technical objection that the company had raised in its answer, and Bradley freely conceded that it would prevent him from affording injunctive relief, at least in the precise terms requested. An act of Congress passed in 1793 made it illegal for a federal court to grant an injunction to stay proceedings in a state court. He concluded that, under the circumstances, the parties would have to content themselves for the time being with their appeal of the state supreme court's judgment to the U.S. Supreme Court.

The following day, however, Justice Bradley amended his decision. Further consideration had convinced him that the Civil Rights Act of 1866 was intended to guarantee to all citizens the same rights protected by the Fourteenth Amendment *and to furnish remedies in the federal courts for their infraction*. The 1793 act prevented him from enjoining proceedings in any of the existing slaughterhouse actions. But under the Civil Rights Act he could, and he did, enjoin the Crescent City Company, the city of New Orleans, and the Board of Metropolitan Police from instituting any *new* suits to enforce the Slaughterhouse Act.

The *Bee* hailed the opinion as "luminous," and the *Picayune* called it "one of the ablest that has ever been delivered from the bench." The *Republican* gave first-page coverage to a letter extolling the decision as "sound Republican doctrine." It came as no surprise that Charles Weed's newspaper, the *Times*, bitterly criticized Bradley's holding. In its view, the Fourteenth Amendment had been written "with the sole purpose and intent of abolishing all distinctions of color," and Justice Bradley's interpretation of it would result in "a vast and indefinite extension of the power and authority of the judicial department of the Government." It would "convert our judges into constitution makers and amenders, with full power to lay down and proclaim what are the 'civil rights' of men." The week had begun with an aggressive use of state judicial power to enforce the company's alleged monopoly and had ended with an equally aggressive use of federal judicial power holding that the Slaughterhouse Act was unconstitutional. Crescent City Company stock had sold for as much as $30 the week before, but it closed at $18 the day Justice Bradley announced his modified decision. Within a few days, it had declined to as little as $15.

Meanwhile, in the Eighth District Court, Judge Henry Dibble regarded Bradley's opinion on the constitutionality of the act and the ban on any new injunctions as a direct challenge to his enforcement injunction. Moreover, the legality of Dibble's injunction was being challenged in separate motions filed by butcher attorneys J. Q. A. Fellows and J. B. Cotton and by the city of New Orleans. The city had even charged that Dibble's injunction violated the Fourteenth Amendment. To make matters worse, on June 14, the Board of Metropolitan Police entered the fray with a motion of its own protesting the legality of the injunction. The board complained that its efforts to enforce Judge Dibble's injunction had involved it in a "vast amount of litigation," and it was being sued for $50,000 in damages. Besides, it claimed, the Slaughterhouse Act provided for its enforcement by the company itself.

The Fellows and Cotton motion came up for trial before Judge Dibble only three days after Justice Bradley had declared the act unconstitutional and on the same day that the Metropolitan Police filed its motion against the injunction. Under the circumstances, Fellows and Cotton saw no reason to do battle and declined to argue their motion. This only enraged Judge Dibble. He complained angrily that state authority was being "blotted out and ignored by the simple dictum of a single Federal Judge." Dibble had hoped to use the motion as a means of upholding the validity of his injunction. Instead, he had to content himself with hearing the arguments of the city officials in opposition to the injunction. He then took their motion under advisement.

It is important to recall that Judge Dibble's enforcement injunction had not been addressed directly to the livestock dealers' slaughterhouse and did not have the effect of closing it. Therefore, a means had to be found of enforcing the original injunction against the rival slaughterhouse that had been granted by the Fifth District Court at the attorney general's behest and affirmed by the state supreme court. Belden had already seen to the transfer of his action against the butchers from the Fifth to the Eighth District Court. Now, taking advantage of Bradley's admitted inability to enjoin ongoing proceedings in a state court, Attorney General Belden moved in Dibble's court for the immediate enforcement of the state supreme court's decree upholding the Fifth District Court's original injunction against the construction of the livestock dealers' rival slaughterhouse. With that, Dibble announced that he would delay making a decision on the motions filed by the city officials and the Metropolitan Police until he had heard the attorney general's motion.

On the same day, inspector of beef George W. Carter was "persuaded" by Governor Warmoth to take parallel action to force the butchers to knuckle under to the 1869 statute. There was money to be made under the Slaughterhouse Act in the inspection of beef, and indeed, Carter had been inspecting on both sides of the river. "As soon as I saw in the newspapers that Mr. Carter was inspecting there," Governor Warmoth later testified, "I sent for him and gave him my views of the law." "These steps were taken," the governor explained, "not in the interest of the Slaughter House Company nor to the detriment of the butchers, but simply to enforce the law. . . . I came to this decision as to my duty after consultation with Messrs. Weed, Pratt, Beckwith, and others, but such consultation had nothing to do with my coming to that decision." Now, Carter took out newspaper notices and advised the public that in the future, stock would be inspected only at the Crescent City Company's facilities.

When the attorney general's motion to enforce the state supreme court's decree came up for trial before Judge Dibble on June 21, Fellows and Cotton replied with a motion to have the case removed to the U.S. Circuit Court under the Civil Rights Acts of 1866 and 1870, asserting that they could not get a fair trial in Dibble's court. Judge Dibble promptly fined them $150 each for contempt of court. Two days later, and again before Judge Dibble, counsel insisted anew on the supersedeas effect of their writ of error and, as an alternative, added a claim that the Slaughterhouse Act violated their clients' rights under both the Fourteenth Amendment and the civil rights acts. This time, Dibble agreed at least in part and dismissed the attorney general's motion, holding that Judge Bradley's writ of error did indeed operate as a writ of supersedeas, but *only to prevent the enforcement of the final decree rendered by the state supreme court.* This meant, however, that the writ did not suspend the enforceability of the *preliminary injunction* originally issued in the attorney general's favor by the Fifth District Court. "Under this ruling," the *Picayune* pointed out, "the butchers have no recourse until the United States Supreme Court acts."

With that, Attorney General Belden moved swiftly to enforce the *original injunction* rendered in the Fifth District Court against the livestock dealers' abattoir. His motion gave the two sides one final opportunity to argue the question of whether the butchers would be able to go about their business unhindered by the Slaughterhouse Act while the case was pending in the U.S. Supreme Court. Was there, in other words, any validity to the claim that this appeal had stalled or superseded all current attempts to enforce the original injunction obtained by Belden?

Again, Fellows and Cotton insisted that the answer to this question was affirmative, and they attacked the validity of the Slaughterhouse Act. Other arguments were raised — such as the written agreement to abide by the decision of the state supreme court, as well as allegations that the attorney general had informally agreed to take no further action pending a final resolution on appeal. In the course of the hearing, however, it became apparent that Dibble had no intention of ruling in favor of Fellows and Cotton. With that, the butchers' attorneys abandoned their effort and stormed out of the courtroom. The *Republican* called the event "the closing scene in the great Slaughterhouse controversy." It had been played out to yet another crowded courtroom. "This would seem to end the slaughterhouse controversy at least until it is revived in the Supreme Court of the United States."

At the end of the week, on July 2, Dibble formally upheld the attorney general's right to enforce the original injunction obtained in the Fifth District Court, at least until the U.S. Supreme Court decided the case. This meant that, for the time being, the stock dealers and butchers would have to land, keep, and slaughter their cattle at the Crescent City Company's facilities across the river. They had run out of state legal options. By mid-July, the butchers had relocated their operations to the Crescent City Company's slaughterhouse in Algiers. At the end of the month, sheriff's deputies took charge of the rival slaughterhouse and padlocked it. On October 17, 1870, however, as the U.S. Supreme Court prepared to resume its business after the summer recess, John Campbell was there with yet another motion for a writ of supersedeas. In mid-November, Campbell and an associate, Philip Phillips, argued the motion in the high court against Thomas J. Durant and Jeremiah S. Black.

Campbell's argument had a seemingly uncomplicated logic to it. In his view, the preliminary injunction that the attorney general now sought to enforce was the same injunction that had been made permanent by the Fifth District Court and ratified by the judgment of the state supreme court. But, he contended, the supreme court's judgment had been suspended by Justice Bradley when he issued the writ of error. Even Judge Dibble had admitted as much when he turned down Attorney General Belden's attempt to enforce the supreme court's decision. But now, Campbell insisted, at Belden's urging, Dibble was attempting to enforce the district court's original temporary injunction as though it had been "left flying" in the lower court.

Campbell added that by obtaining their enforcement injunction from the Eighth District Court, the company and the attorney general had acted to deprive the livestock dealers and butchers of everything they were contending for, even before their rights could be adjudicated on appeal. The Supreme Court should not permit its authority to be undermined in such a manner. Instead, it should step in and issue writs of supersedeas and injunctions suspending further proceedings and enjoining all parties — the state, its attorney general, the city of New Orleans, the Crescent City Company, the Metropolitan Police — from attempting to enforce the Slaughterhouse Act or from interfering with operations at the livestock dealers' slaughterhouse while the case was before the high court.

In reply to these arguments, Durant and Black (joined by Matthew H. Carpenter and Charles Allen) contended that a writ of error did not ordinarily have a supersedeas effect in a proceeding involving an injunction. "Supersedeas is a law term, and has no application to a chancery proceeding." It was a point supported by both logic and a number of authorities. A reluctance to stay proceedings could also be discerned in the decisions of the state courts, although the decisions were not uniform on the point.

The U.S. Supreme Court had little difficulty deciding the case, and by a vote of six to one, it denied Campbell's motion. There were no grounds for the issuance of a writ in this case because all the parties had conceded that nothing had been done by the Louisiana Supreme Court to modify, reverse, or execute its judgment. Moreover, the enforcement injunction obtained by the company in the Eighth District Court with the attorney general's concurrence had not been appealed, so the Court had never acquired jurisdiction in the matter. Speaking for the Court, Justice Clifford pointed out that it was precisely such circumstances that Congress had in mind when it passed the act of 1793 prohibiting state court proceedings from being enjoined. In a short dissenting opinion, Justice Bradley expressed concern that the Court was disclaiming too much jurisdiction, too quickly, over the state courts. With this decision, the possibility of delaying implementation of the Slaughterhouse Act through judicial intervention came to an end.

The slaughterhouse controversy now shifted from the judicial to the legislative arena, where political developments worked, at least briefly, in favor of the opponents of the Crescent City Company. Elections held in November 1870, midway through Governor Warmoth's four-year term, resulted in an enhancement of the Republican party's control of the state and of the legislature in particular. At the same time, however, there were signs that the governor's own power was on the wane. Black Republicans increasingly doubted his commitment to civil rights, and other members of the party had been disappointed by his failure to support their projects. Worse still, a serious rift had developed within the party between politically pragmatic elements represented by Warmoth and his allies and an antagonistic group based in the U.S. Custom House at New Orleans, who regarded themselves as more firmly committed to a radical agenda.

Evidence of this fissure surfaced early in the 1871 legislative session when Mortimer Carr, a Warmoth ally, was forced to resign from his position as speaker of the house. He was immediately replaced by the ambitious George W. Carter, whom Warmoth had earlier appointed inspector of beef under the Slaughterhouse Act. Carter owed his position in the legislature to Warmoth. But, as Louisiana historian Joe Gray Taylor noted, "loyalty was not one of Carter's virtues," and with his election as speaker, "the gentleman from Cameron promptly became the leader of the Custom House faction in the House of Representatives." It was an opportune time for a final assault against the Crescent City Company's exclusive privileges.

Opposition to the monopoly had never waned among some members of the legislature. As early as February 1870, for example, while the case was being argued in the state supreme court, W. Pope Noble, a representative from Orleans Parish who had passionately opposed the monopolistic aspects of the Slaughterhouse Act, had introduced a bill to deprive the company of its monopoly while at the same time restricting slaughtering to areas downstream from the city. The measure was promptly defeated in the house by a vote of twenty-four to thirty-five. This was a more narrow victory than the 1869 bill had won (fifty-one to eighteen), and it is yet another indication of anti-monopoly sentiment.

With Speaker Carter's cooperation, anti-monopolists were quick to take advantage of the new political dynamics of the 1871 legislature. In January, on the motion of Representative J. B. Matthews, a radical and Carter ally from Tensas Parish, the house had appointed a special three-person committee to investigate the Crescent City Company and specifically "to ascertain whether they have complied with the provisions of their charter." Carter followed suit not long afterward by announcing that he intended to file a bill amending the Slaughterhouse Act.

The committee heard witnesses and concluded that the company had failed in its statutory obligation to provide adequate facilities for the butchers and stock dealers. As a remedy, the committee proposed House Bill 209 to limit slaughtering to areas below certain defined points on each bank and to strike out the Crescent City Company's exclusive privileges. Speaker Carter took personal charge of the bill and saw to its passage by the house in a single day. The vote was ninety to six. Two days later, the senate's lobby was crowded with brokers and other interested parties as the upper chamber adopted the bill by a vote of thirty-one to one. A legislature dominated by radicals and led in the house by a former Confederate officer had approved a measure to deprive the company of its monopoly.

Warmoth promptly vetoed the act. He argued chiefly that the company had gone to great expense in reliance on the Slaughterhouse Act and that a contractual relationship now existed between the state and the company. A state act revoking the company's exclusive privileges amounted to an impairment of the obligation of contract, forbidden by Section 10 of Article I of the U.S. Constitution and Article 110 of the state constitution.

Though closely allied with the governor, the *Republican* had always had misgivings about monopolies, and it reported these repeal proceedings with equanimity. But once Warmoth vetoed the measure, the paper found that he had treated the bill with characteristic "perspicaciousness, ability and legal acumen" and predicted that the day would come when everyone would see the Slaughterhouse Act as "an important sanitary measure."

A vote on whether to pass the act notwithstanding the governor's veto was taken on the same day that the house received it. Speaker Carter surrendered the chair to a colleague and spoke for half an hour in favor of overriding the veto. He disputed the idea that the company had vested rights to protect in the slaughterhouse arrangement and contended that the issue was only a sanitary one. But the motion to override the veto failed by a vote of fifty-eight to thirty-seven. Under the circumstances, no vote had to be taken in the senate.

The *Daily Picayune* viewed this "whole affair" as being "rooted, steeped, saturated and drowned in chicanery from beginning to end." It accused the legislature of having undertaken the repeal project in order to profit twice more from the interests of the company, supposedly by taking money first to oppose the repeal act and then to support the veto. But, as the *Picayune* saw it, the company had outwitted the legislators. Rather than trying to buy votes in both houses to prevent passage of the repeal act, it had "preferred to trust to a veto." In this way, it needed to buy the votes of only a third of the house. The result was, the *Picayune* claimed, "the astounding vote of yesterday: thirty-five men who had voted for the repeal of the monopoly turned around and voted to retain it."

It is impossible to accurately discern the motivations of the members of the house who first voted to repeal the monopoly and then failed to vote to override the governor's veto. But several factors come to mind besides venality. One is the utter unpopularity of the monopolistic aspects of the Slaughterhouse Act. It must be remembered also that although the radicals held a majority in the legislature in both 1869 and 1871, the membership of the 1871 legislature was not identical to that of 1869. It is entirely possible that some new Republican members of the house harbored anti-monopoly sentiments. Moreover, a division had developed in Republican ranks, and Warmoth's ability to influence the vote of his party for favored projects was at a low ebb.

The tally of the vote to override the veto reveals this division. A total of ninety-five house members voted on the motion to override. Of these, twenty-four were Democrats, and all of them voted in favor of overriding the veto and repealing the monopoly. The remaining seventy-one votes were cast by Republicans. Thirty-seven of them voted to sustain the governor's veto and retain the monopoly, but thirty-four voted to override the governor's veto. The lobbying efforts of the butchers and stock dealers to bring about this result are not recorded but can safely be presumed. For all the record reveals, their methods may have been just as unseemly as those they attributed to the Crescent City Company's supporters.

———

In March 1871, a number of prominent butchers and stock dealers did something they had always insisted they would never do: they *compromised* with the Crescent City Company. This move may have been unexpected, but it was quite understandable. Since losing their appeal to the Louisiana SupremeCourt in April 1870, the butchers had tried twice to put aside the Crescent City Company's alleged monopoly, at least temporarily, only to see both efforts come to naught. In December 1870, the U.S. Supreme Court had turned away their motion for supersedeas, and in February 1871, they had won passage of an act repealing the company's exclusive privileges only to see it successfully vetoed by Governor Warmoth. The rival slaughterhouse built by the Live Stock Dealers and Butchers Association on the right bank of the river had been put out of operation by Judge Henry Dibble's injunction in the Eighth District Court. Most, if not all, of the butchers and stock dealers were now using the Crescent City Company facilities as required by law. And no matter how strong their feelings, the case for the validity of the Slaughterhouse Act as a proper exercise of the police power was a strong one, and it was anything but certain that they could convince the U. S. Supreme Court to overturn it.

Conversely, the Crescent City Company's slaughterhouse and stockyard had not resulted in the historic financial windfall imagined by some, nor were there signs that it would soon do so. And with the Fourteenth Amendment being played by the butchers as a sort of "wild card" in the game, a victory by the company in the U.S. Supreme Court could not be assumed. After all, Justice Bradley had already expressed his opinion that the act was an unconstitutional violation of the new amendment.

On March 2, 1871, only a week after the governor's veto of the repeal act had been sustained, Paul Esteben, president of the Live Stock Dealers and Butchers Association, laid before the association's board of directors the terms of a compromise that he had negotiated with the Crescent City Company. Subsequently, the proposal was unanimously endorsed by a mass meeting of the association's stockholders (and anyone else who cared to attend) held in the familiar venue above Fred Benst's saloon on Tchoupitoulas Street.

In keeping with this agreement, the Crescent City Company transferred 7,500 shares of its stock valued at $25.50 per share, or a total of $191,250, to the livestock dealers. The Crescent City Company's board of directors then resigned, and the stockholders elected a new board to serve until the regular election in March 1872. In this way, members of the board of directors of the Live Stock Dealers and Butchers Association became directors of the Crescent City Company, with Charles Cavaroc as president. The new board consisted of more stock dealers than butchers, but the *Times* declared them all to be "practical butchers."

To complete the compromise, on March 15, 1871, the newly elected board of the Crescent City Company resolved to purchase the slaughterhouse that the livestock dealers had constructed below the city on the east side of the river for $195,000, with $25,000 to be paid in cash and the remainder in promissory notes. Finally, the Live Stock Dealers and Butchers Association was dissolved and liquidated. The price of Crescent City Company stock responded very positively to these developments, rising to between $37 and $45 a share following the announcement of the compromise. It does not appear from the Crescent City Company's records that many of the original organizers ever came to regard the company as a long-term investment. An election of board members a year later brought several new faces to the board, including the controversial Charles A. Weed. But a list of the stockholders drawn up in 1873 did not include Weed or any of the other original organizers of the company, except for two: William Durbridge and Jonas Pickles, who were listed as owners of 80 and 100 shares, respectively.

A child of controversy since its inception, it was too much to expect that even the newly constituted Crescent City Company would stay out of court for long. Following the compromise, the company reopened the slaughterhouse on the left bank of the river that the Live Stock Dealers Association had built. This brought fears that the company would close its original, makeshift facility on the right bank. Several parties who had complied with the Slaughterhouse Act and gone to the expense of relocating their businesses filed suit in the Eighth District Court to enjoin both the closure of the original facility and the use of the new one. Judge Dibble had no difficulty ruling in every case that the Slaughterhouse Act did not require the company to maintain a facility on the right bank, provided that it maintained at least one facility and that it was located outside the limits proscribed by the statute.

In fact, the newly managed Crescent City Company maintained both its original west-bank slaughterhouse and the newly acquired one on the east bank for only a short time. Once the butchers were given a choice between the company's fairly makeshift original abattoir and the larger, better-equipped one located on the same side of the river as the city, the vast majority quickly abandoned the west-bank facility. With that, the company saw no need to maintain a second slaughterhouse, and on a Sunday morning in July 1871, with police in attendance and little or no notice to the butchers, the company dismantled its right-bank facility. Jean Bertin, a west-bank butcher, sued. He lost his case before Judge Dibble in the Eighth District Court in September 1871, but four years later in *Bertin et al. v. Crescent City Livestock Landing and Slaughterhouse Co.*, the state supreme court ruled in his favor. The state's high court held that after selecting a location for the new slaughterhouse and "compelling the butchers to repair to it, [the company] will not be permitted to compel them to discontinue their business at this place and follow the corporation to such other locality . . . as caprice may dictate."

The company was loath to comply with this judgment, and months passed before it finally reestablished its abattoir on the right bank. By this time, at least one private slaughterhouse had been set up on the right bank for the handful of butchers who remained there. Several legal actions followed, and it was not until April 1878 that the company won a ruling in the supreme court upholding its exclusive privileges. Even so, it is unclear whether all the west-bank competitors were ever persuaded to patronize the company's abattoir exclusively.

A final matter of conflict, and ultimately the most important, concerned the identity of the parties who had agreed to the compromise. It was generally assumed that the compromise signaled an end to all the *Slaughterhouse Cases*. On March 14, 1871, Paul Esteben, as president of both the Butchers Benevolent Association and the Live Stock Dealers and Butchers Association, and representatives of the William Fagan and Inbau firms agreed in writing "to discontinue, as part of the compromise . . . all suits of *every* kind now pending in the State and Federal courts against" the Crescent City Company. Seeing no further need for legal counsel, the directors of the Butchers Benevolent Association authorized fees to be paid to the firms of Campbell, Spofford and Campbell, Cotton and Levy, and Fellows and Mills in the amount of $3,000 each.

But in the fall of 1871, when J. Q. A. Fellows appeared before the U.S. Supreme Court, he moved only for the dismissal of the writs of error in three of the *Slaughterhouse Cases:* the two cases brought against the company by the Live Stock Dealers and Butchers Association and the firm of Inbau, Aycock and Company, and the one filed by the Crescent City Company against the steamship *B. L. Hodge.* This left three cases still standing in the high court: the suit filed by the Butchers Benevolent Association against the company in the Sixth District Court, the first of all the cases; the suit filed almost simultaneously by the company against the Butchers Benevolent Association in the Fifth District Court; and the action brought by the attorney general against William Fagan and his fellow stock dealers and butchers in the Fifth District Court. Company attorney Joseph P. Hornor admitted that this action "took the Slaughter-House Company by surprise, as they believed the whole litigation closed and settled."

As historian Charles Fairman wrote, "Some of the 'Gascon butchers' still wanted to fight." In a letter to the *New Orleans Bee*, Sylvain Verges, the new president of the Butchers Benevolent Association, explained why. Although the company was under new management, it remained a monopoly and was still charging all the fees authorized by the statute. Further, he claimed that only one of the company's directors was a butcher (the others were livestock dealers). "The butchers have no interest in the Company and can have none." His comments are evidence of an economic and social rift between many of the individual butchers and the stock dealers.

This unexpected turn of events led to an elaborate motion to dismiss filed in the U.S. Supreme Court on behalf of the company and the state by Matthew Carpenter and Thomas J. Durant on December 14, 1871. Company president Charles Cavaroc, a number of major stock dealers, and both Paul Esteben and Franklin J. Pratt all provided affidavits affirming their understanding that the compromise had brought an end to all slaughterhouse litigation. Individual butchers attested to their impression that the compromise had been popularly approved at the mass meeting at the Benst saloon.

In reply, members of the Butchers Benevolent Association, including its current president, Sylvain Verges, and other members of its board protested that the issue of compromise had never been put before their board or their membership. Esteben had never been authorized by the association to negotiate a compromise. The March public meeting at which the compromise had been approved had been called by the Live Stock Dealers and Butchers Association for its own members, and the Butchers Benevolent Association was not bound by resolutions taken there.

The Supreme Court agreed. It heard the argument on the motion to dismiss along with the arguments on all the other issues, and according to Justice Miller in his opinion for the Court, it was "much pressed by counsel." But Miller pointed out, "there are parties now before the court in each of the three cases . . . who have not consented to their dismissal. . . . They have a right to be heard." With that issue resolved, the *Slaughterhouse Cases* were at last in a position to be decided on the merits by the nation's highest court. The question now was whether the dispute could be resolved as a simple matter of the police power without it being transformed by John Campbell's innovative resort to the Fourteenth Amendment into a major constitutional case. As far as Campbell was concerned, the Civil War was over as a military encounter, but the fighting raged on.

CHAPTER 7

The Chase Court

In 1872, when John Campbell appeared before the U.S. Supreme Court for the first of two arguments on the merits in the *Slaughterhouse Cases*, the Court was no longer the Democratic stronghold it had been ten years before. The Judiciary Act of 1862 provided for an important restructuring of the federal judiciary. The act designated five circuits in the North and four in the South, and to a large extent, it redressed a long-standing population imbalance among the circuits that had worked in favor of the selection of Democrats to the Supreme Court. Historian Stanley Kutler has described the act as the first of the Republicans' Reconstruction measures because its aim was "to make national institutions more responsive to the needs of the dominant section." Another act, passed the following year, created a tenth circuit on the West Coast. These measures made it possible for Lincoln and Grant to remake the Supreme Court.

The Court that decided the *Slaughterhouse Cases* was nearing the end of the so-called Chase era. The term refers to Salmon P. Chase, who served as chief justice from 1864 to 1873. In 1872, only one of the justices, Nathan Clifford, had been in office since before the Civil War. Five justices, Noah Swayne, Samuel Miller, David Davis, Stephen Field, and Chase himself, had been placed on the Court by President Lincoln between 1862 and 1864. The remaining three justices had been chosen by Ulysses Grant. William Strong and Joseph Bradley took their oaths in 1870. Grant's third selection, Ward Hunt, was seated early in 1873. Only two of the nine justices were Democrats, Clifford and Field; the remainder were Republicans.

Members of the Chase Court shared several traits common among Supreme Court justices: all were male, white, and Protestant and had been active in politics. They were exceptional, however, in the extent to which their political activity continued after appointment to the

Court. The chief justice, whose presidential ambitions were as considerable as his legal acumen, had sought the presidency in 1860 and 1864. He even solicited Democratic interest in his availability as a candidate in 1868. Four years later, and in very precarious health, Chase allowed his name to be floated for yet another presidential candidacy. In 1872, Chase's colleague David Davis accepted the presidential nomination of the National Labor Union Reform party, although he prudently declined to resign from the Court in advance of his most improbable election. As late as 1884, Stephen Field hoped for favorable consideration as the Democratic presidential nominee, and even Samuel Miller flirted with a possible run in 1880 and 1884.

The justices also shared an important experience. They had all seen the Civil War transform their country. If asked, they might have been unable to articulate exactly how this had happened and to what extent it had affected them. But the bloodiest war in American history, a conflict that ended with more than 620,000 dead and 4 million human beings newly free, and that had destroyed cities and villages alike and released new and unpredictable economic forces, had reshaped the legal environment in which they operated. They did not explicitly refer to this transformation, but some of their opinions reflect it, and one cannot comprehend the ultimate decision in *Slaughterhouse* without a sense of the transformed context in which the Court operated from 1865 to 1873.

Some brief biographical information about the justices is important in understanding the decisions they ultimately reached. Nathan Clifford, the ranking member of the Court in terms of seniority, was born in New Hampshire in 1803 and was admitted to the bar before his twenty-fifth birthday. He moved to Maine, where he established both a large family and a successful law practice. By age twenty-seven, he had been elected to the Maine house of representatives as a Jacksonian Democrat, and his fidelity to that party lasted until his death. Clifford consistently opposed, for example, both high tariffs and a national banking system. After three terms in the Maine legislature (one as speaker of the house), he served two terms in Congress. In 1846, President James Polk selected Clifford as his attorney general, but Clifford later resigned from that position to participate in the final peace negotiations with Mexico. In 1858, Clifford's old friend James

Buchanan appointed him to the high court, where he did not hesitate to exercise his political predilections.

Clifford can accurately be described as a real doughface, a Northerner with Southern sympathies, and his nomination to the Court was clouded by the ongoing slavery-abolition crises in the Kansas territory. He received Senate approval by the narrow margin of twenty-six to twenty-three. His biases were predictable and consistent. He favored strict constitutional construction, objected to the abolitionists, and opposed expanded federal power — even as events moved steadily in that direction. Not unlike many Southerners, Clifford could denounce secession but fault Lincoln's imposition of a naval blockade in the *Prize Cases*. In the postwar period, he agreed with his fellow Democrat Stephen J. Field in rejecting both state and federal imposition of test oaths as a means of reserving public office and the professions for "loyal" citizens. But in the *Legal Tender Cases*, he endorsed a ban on the continued use of paper money (greenbacks) as legal tender and angrily dissented when a new majority reversed this holding. In his later years, he demonstrated consistent concern with the extension of federal authority during and beyond the era of Reconstruction.

Noah Swayne was the first of Lincoln's five appointments to the high court. Born in 1804 in Virginia to strict Quaker parents, Swayne was introduced to antislavery views at a very early age. He was admitted to the Virginia bar while still a teenager. Swayne moved to Ohio, where in 1829 he was elected to the state legislature as a Jacksonian Democrat. Indeed, in 1830, Jackson appointed him a U.S. attorney, a post Swayne retained for the next eleven years. Unlike Clifford, he grew increasingly uncomfortable with the Democratic position on slavery, and by 1854, he had joined the new Republican party. A strong Lincoln supporter, he enjoyed unanimous support from the Ohio congressional delegation in 1862 as he solicited a Supreme Court appointment, even though he had no judicial experience.

Swayne's efforts to lobby on his own behalf included a trip to Washington, and in the end, he proved successful. As a justice, Swayne tended to support business and industrial expansion. In 1864, for example, he upheld the contractual rights of railroad bondholders, even in the face of repudiation sanctioned by both the Iowa legislature and the state supreme court. Obligations sacred to law, he intoned, cannot be discarded simply because "a state tribunal has erected the altar and decreed the sacrifice." Remaining on the bench until 1881, Swayne eagerly schemed to become chief justice whenever a vacancy occurred, as it did in 1864 and 1873.

Lincoln's second appointment followed the passage of the Judiciary Act of 1862, by which Congress created a new federal judicial circuit consisting only of states west of the Mississippi. It made good political sense that he select a justice from this area and, like Swayne, one who enjoyed overwhelming support from its congressional delegation. Samuel F. Miller was born in 1816 in Richmond, Kentucky. Ironically, he shared a personal characteristic — one that was rare among Supreme Court justices — with Justice Bradley, with whom he often disagreed. Both men were the sons of farmers and the products of families of modest means. Miller had no formal legal training and, again like Swayne, no prior judicial experience. Indeed, in 1838, at age twenty-two, he had received an M.D. degree from Transylvania University. He practiced medicine in Kentucky for almost ten years but taught himself the law; in 1847, having abandoned his medical career, he was admitted to the bar on the motion of his office mate. Two years later, Miller moved to Iowa, where he established a successful practice and turned to local politics. A staunch Republican and Lincoln supporter with numerous contacts in Congress, Miller became the right man in the right place at the right time with the right credentials once the new western circuit was created. He was the first justice who lived west of the Mississippi River at the time of his appointment.

Possibly because he lacked judicial experience, Miller's opinions reflected a pragmatic approach to problems rather than a strictly logical application of legal doctrine. His legal insights were based more on experience than on formal training. He also had a tendency toward moderation when he rendered his decisions, a trait that his brethren seem to have appreciated. By the time of Miller's death in October 1890, he had spoken for the Court more than 600 times. In this he went far beyond the legendary Chief Justice John Marshall. Miller also demonstrated both a consistent reluctance to see his Court act as a censor of legislative policy and a tendency to seek a balance between federal and state lines of authority.

Lincoln's third appointment went to one of two personal acquaintances he named to the high court. David Davis was born in 1815 and was a graduate of Kenyon College in Ohio, which he had entered at age thirteen. By 1840, he had settled in Illinois as a young attorney with an interest in local politics. Indulging a talent for land speculation, which he practiced in Illinois and several other states, Davis developed valuable and lifelong business interests. He ran (unsuccessfully) for the state senate in 1840, but by 1844, he had gained a seat in the Illinois house of representatives. Davis spent the early part of his professional life as an itinerant lawyer, often in the company of another Illinois attorney, self-educated and self-taught Abraham Lincoln. In 1848, Davis was elected to a seat on the state circuit. Over the years, Davis and Lincoln became fast friends. Davis supported Lincoln's losing effort in 1858 to defeat Stephen Douglas as Illinois senator and managed his successful presidential campaign two years later.

Of all Lincoln's high court selections, Davis, appointed in 1862, appears to have enjoyed his tenure least, apparently finding the work tiresome and dull. In common with Lincoln's other appointees, Davis sustained various wartime measures the administration employed between 1861 and 1865, with one notable exception. This exception, however, was one of the landmark cases arising from the Civil War, and it provided Davis with the opportunity to write his most enduring and significant opinion.

Ex Parte Milligan concerned an appeal by a prominent antiwar politician in Indiana who had been arrested by the military for alleged treasonous activities and sentenced to death by a military commission. The Court decided unanimously in Milligan's favor, holding that a military commission lacked constitutional authority to try a civilian when and where civil courts were in operation. Although the Court announced its decision in early April 1866, it did not release the justices' opinions until December 1866, months after President Johnson had declared the insurrection at an end and shortly after he had criticized the continued substitution of military for civil authority. The time had come, Justice Davis wrote, when existing conditions permitted "that calmness in deliberation and discussion so necessary to a correct conclusion of a purely judicial question." In other words, there was now little likelihood that the Union army might ignore the holding.

Lincoln's fourth appointment to the Court reflected, once again, his dual concerns that the nominee be committed to the Union cause and that he represent a part of the country of major importance in terms of growth — both geographical and legal. A member of the California Supreme Court, Stephen J. Field filled these needs very well. Born in Connecticut in 1816, he was the sixth of nine children and was raised in Massachusetts in a strict Puritan environment by his father, David Dudley Field, a Congregationalist minister. Indeed, portraits of Justice Stephen Field seem to radiate a sense of rigid self-righteousness and certainty. Field spent a number of his teenage years abroad, returning to Massachusetts to enter Williams College at the age of seventeen. He graduated at the top of his class in 1837 and promptly entered the New York law firm of his older brother, David Field Jr., under whom he read law. The elder Field brother was well on his way to becoming one of the outstanding legal practitioners in the eastern United States. But the younger sibling may have found working with his brother a bit confining, because in 1849, he moved to California where he could build a legal career on his own.

By 1857, Field had been elected to the California Supreme Court, and he became its chief justice two years later. A close friend of influential Republicans such as Leland Stanford and well versed in land and mining law, Field seemed the right choice for Lincoln as he sought to bind California closer to the Union cause. Moreover, Field was a Democrat, and by selecting him, Lincoln emphasized his desire to place national priorities above partisan political interests.

As a justice, Field's major opinions tended to reflect his values, which included a veneration for property rights and a hostility toward state regulation, whether or not he could find a clear basis for them in either the Constitution or judicial precedent. In his majority opinion in the 1867 *Test Oath Cases*, for example, Field held that "the theory upon which our political institutions rest is, that all men have certain and inalienable rights — that among these are life, liberty, and the pursuit of happiness; and that in the pursuit of happiness all avocations, all honors, all positions, are alike open to everyone, and that in protection of these rights all are equal before the law." Even as Field wrote his opinion, a new constitutional provision, the Fourteenth Amendment, was awaiting state ratification. Later, it would serve Field well as a foundation for his basic assumptions concerning government and society.

Lincoln's final high court appointment, made only a few months before his assassination, was also his most unusual. Salmon P. Chase was born in New Hampshire in 1808. Before he reached the age of twenty-one, he had graduated Phi Beta Kappa from Dartmouth. Apprenticed for a time to Attorney General William Wirt, by the mid-1840s, Chase had established a successful practice in Ohio, where he also became interested in several worthy causes, especially temperance and abolition. Earnest and eloquent, he found himself drawn to a political career. In 1849, he was elected to the U.S. Senate from Ohio, and upon completion of his term, he served as Ohio's governor from 1855 to 1859. In 1860, he was again elected to the Senate. Known as an experienced politician and able administrator, Chase was one of the early favorites, along with New York senator William Seward, to win the Republican presidential nomination. But the convention turned instead to Abraham Lincoln, who was considered more moderate on the issue of abolition. Political realities required that both Chase and Seward be named to Lincoln's cabinet, as indeed they were.

But Chase could find no remedy to bring down his presidential fervor. Although he administered the Treasury with skill and successfully financed the vast expenses of the war, he connived against Lincoln on several occasions, seeking to bolster his own political fortunes at the expense of his president. Whenever Lincoln called him on it, Chase would threaten to resign, knowing that Lincoln valued his abilities. By mid-1864, however, the party was unified behind Lincoln in the wake of an ultimately successful campaign for renomination; this, along with increasingly favorable reports from the military front, meant that Lincoln no longer needed to put up with Chase's tactics. So when Chase tendered his resignation over a minor question of patronage concerning his department, Lincoln quickly accepted it. Samuel Miller recalled that Chase's considerable strengths were "warped, perverted and shrivelled by the selfishness generated by ambition." After his reelection, Lincoln began to focus increasingly on the issues of Reconstruction, and when the ailing and aged Chief Justice Roger Taney died, he appointed Chase. It was a shrewd decision, for in one stroke, Lincoln raised to the high court an able lawyer, a staunch supporter of the Union, and a perennial political nuisance, albeit one with strong supporters in Lincoln's party

For a time, Chase presided over a ten-member Court. Congress — seeking to ensure that Lincoln would have ample opportunity to appoint pro-Union justices — had added a tenth seat by the 1863 act. This was filled by Stephen Field. By 1867, however, two justices had died, and the struggle between Andrew Johnson and Congress resulted in Johnson's being unable to make any appointments to the high court, a fate shared by only one other president since William Harrison in 1841 — Jimmy Carter. With President Ulysses Grant inaugurated in 1869, Congress restored the Court membership to nine, where it has remained ever since.

Grant had moved promptly to fill the two Court vacancies by nominating his attorney general E. Rockwood Hoar and the former secretary of war Edwin Stanton. But Hoar fell victim to partisan wrangling in the Senate, and Stanton — although appointed and immediately confirmed — died before he could take the oath of office. Again, Grant had two vacancies to fill. He moved to fill them on February 7, 1870, the same day the Court handed down its decision in the first of the *Legal Tender Cases*, in which it held by a four-to-three vote that the continued use of paper money (greenbacks) was unconstitutional. In his opinion for the majority, Chief Justice Chase disavowed as unconstitutional a policy that, as secretary of the treasury, he had earlier endorsed and helped implement. Invariably, the question of a rehearing became linked to the question of where Grant's two nominees might stand on the issue of paper specie.

There was no doubt where one of them stood. William Strong, a native of Connecticut, had enrolled in Yale before he turned sixteen. He later received a master's degree from Yale Law School and was admitted to both the Connecticut and Pennsylvania bars in 1832, at the age of twenty-four. He settled in Reading, Pennsylvania, became fluent in both German and local dialects, and built a very lucrative practice. By 1846, he had been elected to Congress as an antislavery Democrat and served two terms. Having returned to his law practice, and still a Democrat, Strong was elected to the Pennsylvania Supreme Court in 1857 for a fifteen-year term. His antislavery views and strong support of the Union resulted in his shift to the new Republican party. Strong remained on the Pennsylvania bench until 1868.

One of his most important votes as a member of the Pennsylvania Supreme Court came when he joined his colleagues in affirming the constitutionality of the Legal Tender Act of 1862. A number of state courts had already so held, and by 1870, at least sixty state justices had considered this issue, with only one Republican jurist opposing the use of paper money as legal tender. The initial decision of the U.S. Supreme Court on the Legal Tender Act, declaring the measure *un*constitutional, came in February 1870, the same day that Grant sent Strong's name to the Senate. This led some to accuse the president of seeking to pack the Court in order to gain a rehearing and a reversal of its holding. Although there is no convincing evidence that Grant had so conspired, there is no doubt that Strong's view on legal tender was well known. Indeed, within a year, he would write for the new five-member majority in overruling Chase's decision.

Grant's other nominee, Republican Joseph P. Bradley, graduated from Rutgers College in New Jersey and taught himself sufficient law to be admitted to the bar at the age of twenty six. A voracious reader who was proficient in several languages and also well versed in mathematics, the young attorney built a successful career in Newark. Along the way, he married the daughter of New Jersey Chief Justice William Hornblower. Given Bradley's later hostility to railroads, it is interesting to note that as a lawyer, one of his most important clients was the notoriously corrupt Camden and Perth Amboy Railroad. By 1868, he had become a strong supporter of Grant for the presidency and was one of New Jersey's presidential electors pledged to him, specifically supporting the Legal Tender Act.

As mentioned in an earlier chapter, Bradley was the only justice to have considered and ruled on the merits of the Louisiana slaughterhouse controversy before it reached the Supreme Court. In 1870, while presiding over the circuit court in New Orleans, he had held the Slaughterhouse Act unconstitutional, although he declined on jurisdictional grounds to implement his decision fully. Yet his opinion had revealed a conservative trait in Bradley's thought, even as he focused on the innovative nature of the new Fourteenth Amendment. During the early stages of the Civil War, he had emphasized that the overriding duty was to "put down the rebellion cost what it may. . . . The rebellion must be put down. Nothing else must be thought of." The issue was not slavery. Rather, it was obedience to the Constitution, which should "stand just as it is, word for word and letter for letter." Bradley added that as far as the South was concerned, "the Constitution gives us no power to meddle with them, no more than it gives them power to meddle with us."

Like several of his colleagues, Ward Hunt, Grant's third appointment, had been a Jacksonian Democrat. A native of Utica, New York, he was born in 1810, and for a time he studied law at the famous Tapping Reeve School in Litchfield, Connecticut. By 1832, he had returned to Utica and established a successful law practice. Six years later, he was elected to the state legislature, and in 1844, he became Utica's mayor. Again, like some of his judicial brethren, Hunt found the Democratic party's position on slavery increasingly unacceptable, and in 1856, he joined in establishing the Republican party in New York State. In doing so, Hunt became well acquainted with a leading power in state politics, Roscoe Conkling. This friendship would ultimately lead Hunt to the U.S. Supreme Court.

In the meantime, Hunt had sought state judicial office, running unsuccessfully for a seat on the New York Court of Appeals. In 1853, he tried again and was defeated again. After the war, and now well established as a Republican, Hunt tried for a third time and at last met with success. In 1865, he succeeded his mentor and former partner Hiram Denio on the state high court. In 1868, Hunt became chief justice, and in this capacity he wrote the majority opinion in *Metropolitan Board of Health v. Heister*, discussed in a previous chapter.

In November 1872, Supreme Court Justice Samuel Nelson retired. Eighty years old and in poor health, Nelson had missed much of the Court's 1871–1872 term, including the first *Slaughterhouse* argument. That case remained undecided when President Grant — responding to an enthusiastic endorsement from now New York senator Roscoe Conkling — named Hunt to succeed Nelson. Nominated on December 3, 1871, Hunt took his seat early in January 1872, just in time to listen to the re-arguments in *Slaughterhouse* barely one month later. The Court's decision came down within three months.

The Supreme Court was called on to decide a number of constitutional issues arising out of the Civil War and Reconstruction. Indeed, between 1865 and 1873, it played an important role in the process by which the nation adjusted to the postwar era, and these decisions affected both its role and its image. Prior to 1865, the Court had exercised judicial review to pronounce the unconstitutionality of acts of Congress in only two cases. By 1873, however, no fewer than twelve acts of Congress had been invalidated by the Court, seven of these since 1869. When it handed down the *Slaughterhouse* decision in April 1873, the Court enjoyed virtual equality with the other branches of the national government and was capable of aggressively reviewing both state and federal legislation.

Although it is difficult to make generalizations concerning the Chase Court, a few points can be offered. As Lincoln expected, all were united on ensuring the survival of the Union, but this goal had already been assured by the time Chief Justice Chase took his seat on December 15, 1864. Further, it soon became evident that the justices tended to be more conservative than Congress, especially after the radical wing of the Republican party gained dominance between 1866 and 1869. As the era of Reconstruction ran its course, the justices navigated a sort of judicial minefield of explosive issues. As historian David Bondenhamer has shown, their docket required them to mediate in the struggle between President Andrew Johnson and Congress, to monitor the "changed nature of federal-state relations," to ensure the "rights of all citizens as promised by the Union victory," to confront if not resolve "constitutional problems posed by the new industrial economy," and, finally, to reach decisions in all these areas within a new judicial context, one that frowned on judicial and legislative instrumentalism and emphasized concern for the limits of legislative authority and for the means of protecting an expanded category of property rights.

In *Ex Parte Milligan*, for example, the entire Court agreed that Milligan's trial by military commission was unconstitutional. But only two of Lincoln's appointees accepted the conclusion that Congress lacked the authority, under any circumstances, to establish tribunals to prosecute civilians who were U.S. citizens. In the *Test Oath Cases* one year later, all four Lincoln Republican justices disagreed with Democrat Field's rejection of loyalty oaths as unconstitutional. As tensions between Congress and President Johnson were exacerbated, and as Congress enacted a number of Reconstruction measures, the political instincts of Chief Justice Chase contributed to an avoidance of outright confrontation between Congress and the Court while retaining, to a great extent, its traditional judicial authority.

Thus, in cases such as *Georgia v. Stanton* (1868) and *Mississippi v. Johnson* (1867), a unanimous Court declined to get into a judicial evaluation of congressional Reconstruction statutes. Similarly, in the case of *Texas v. White* (1869), Chief Justice Chase described the United States as "an indestructible Union composed of indestructible states." Although the case concerned a dispute over the payment of certain state securities, in fact, it involved serious issues such as the nature of the Union and the legitimacy of federal Reconstruction. By holding that the Union was permanent and indissoluble and that secession had been unlawful, Chase made it clear that Congress possessed plenary authority to deal with Reconstruction as a political process. Finally, in a case involving the use of habeas corpus, Chase's Court demonstrated what might be described as an exercise in aggressive caution.

Coming at the height of the conflict between Congress and Johnson, the case of *Ex Parte McCardle* involved a Southern editor's challenge to a newly enacted Reconstruction statute based on another recent federal law authorizing "federal courts to issue writs of habeas corpus" when the plaintiff was confined in violation of his constitutional rights. Fearful that the Court might use this habeas corpus appeal to reject congressional Reconstruction, Congress simply revoked the Court's authority, later restored, to hear such appeals. Although the Court had not yet decided the case, it had already heard oral arguments. Yet by a unanimous vote, the justices acquiesced in this action and dismissed McCardle's appeal for want of jurisdiction. But Chase, sensitive to the claim that the Court was simply "caving in," insisted that the Court's constitutional jurisdiction remained unchanged, as did the authority granted to it by the 1789 Judiciary Act.

By 1872, when the justices first considered the constitutional issues in *Slaughterhouse*, they were at the end of an era. The half dozen years between 1866 and 1872 represented a unique period of tension in American legal history, involving all three branches of the federal government, to say nothing of the Southern states undergoing Reconstruction. Certainly the Court had contributed to this situation with its decisions in *Milligan* and the *Test Oath Cases*, its standoff with Congress concerning habeas corpus appeals, and its flip-flop over the validity of paper as legal tender. But by the time it took up *Slaughterhouse*, much of this tension had eased. New issues concerning expansion and regulation of the market were on the docket, and both the Court's jurisdiction and the output of decisions were expanding. The Court was in a period of transition, with an instrumentalist approach to law giving way to a more formalistic emphasis on procedures, precedent (both old and new), and property rights. It was at this juncture that the justices confronted the complex issues of the *Slaughterhouse Cases*. And, as will be seen, its outcome revealed a divided Court, with some justices looking back to what had been and others looking forward to what lay ahead.

CHAPTER 8

The Arguments

By the time the Supreme Court heard the final arguments in the *Slaughterhouse Cases* between February 3 and 5, 1873, the lawyers had had ample time to perfect their positions. They had clashed over this controversy for more than three years — in the Louisiana district courts, the Louisiana Supreme Court, and the federal courts as well. Moreover, the high court had already disposed of the ill-fated supersedeas issue. Indeed, in January 1872, the merits had been debated before eight of the justices, in the absence of the aged and ailing Justice Samuel Nelson. It may well be that these earlier arguments had resulted in a four-to-four division among the eight sitting justices. In any event, the justices carried the argument over to the Court's next term (December 1872), without specifying any new issues on which counsel were to focus. The next step was a re-argument before a full bench, now available with the newly appointed Justice Ward Hunt seated on the Court.

As lead counsel for the butchers, John Campbell appears to have had a dual agenda. Like most in his profession, his first goal was victory for his clients. But the former Supreme Court justice was also engaged in another more far-reaching campaign. It was to employ the Constitution's new Reconstruction amendments as legal weapons to bring about Reconstruction's ultimate demise. Separated from his family while he practiced law in New Orleans, Campbell observed the progress of Reconstruction with dismay. In an 1871 letter to his daughter in Baltimore, he brooded, "the people have ascertained that they have been plundered, but they do not know how to find a remedy. We have the African in place all about us. . . . Corruption is the rule." In his racial attitudes and political preferences, Campbell embodied the "old" white South. The *Slaughterhouse* dispute was only one of a series in which Campbell represented and encouraged white businessmen in

New Orleans in resisting one Reconstruction measure after another. Indeed, through his professional efforts, he contributed significantly to the eventual failure of Reconstruction. And ultimately, one suspects that this was much more important to Campbell than the ultimate fate of his butchers. Thus his briefs and arguments must be considered for their duality of purpose.

In the opening pages of his first brief, Campbell reiterated his basic and often repeated contentions: first, that the Louisiana statute of 1869 had been enacted by "legislative caprice, partiality, ignorance or corruption," and second, that it was *wrong* to allow such a law to stand. Here he appealed, albeit somewhat vaguely, to natural rights philosophy, a position later embraced by two justices in their dissenting opinions. Although the Court had never accepted this line of reasoning as a test of constitutionality, there was no reason not to use it. An appeal to righteousness had popular appeal. Further, new amendments had been added to the Constitution that had yet to be authoritatively interpreted by the high court.

As an initial step in this argument, Campbell had to demonstrate that the concept of involuntary servitude, now outlawed by the Thirteenth Amendment, embraced much more than American Negro chattel slavery and thus could be applied to protect the rights of white butchers. This was an important first step because it was a given, not challenged by either side, that in the U.S. experience, the concept of slavery had been inseparable from the African American race. "We have never supposed," claimed the former slave owner, "that these Constitutional Enactments had any particular or limited reference to Negro slavery. The words employed do not describe that form of slavery and that only. They are absolute, universal." In fact, "the prohibition of slavery and involuntary servitude in every form and degree . . . comprises much more than the abolition or prohibition of African slavery." Thus, to be a freeman possessing privileges and immunities under the Constitution implied a number of rights:

1st. An immunity from compulsory work at the will, or for the profit of another. 2nd. No kind of occupation, employment or trade can be imposed upon him, or prohibited to him, as to avoid all choice or election on his part. 3d. He may engage in any lawful pursuit for which he may have the requisite capacity, skill, material or capital. 4th. He is entitled to the full enjoyment of the fruits of his labor or industry without constraint, subject only to legal taxation or contribution.

But this lawyer realized that comparing the lot of white butchers compelled to slaughter at the Crescent City abattoir with that of African American slaves might be somewhat extravagant. "We do not contend," he admitted, "that . . . plaintiffs . . . have been placed in handcuffs and carried to the houses, pens and yards of this corporation, with violence, to labor for this corporation of seventeen as African slaves might have been." Nor could it be said that they have "been imprisoned or confined to compel them to labor." Campbell insisted, however, that "all of them have been prohibited from doing their usual or customary work, except upon the property and for the compensation and profit of these parties." Further, "they have been compelled to close up the houses and other conveniences of business." Based on these facts, Campbell concluded that "the common rights of men have been taken away and have become the *sole and exclusive privilege* of a single corporation."

Here, Campbell combined a summary of the central terms of the statute with a wild yet powerful distortion of the statute's application to his clients. The 1869 enactment in no way forbade anyone to earn a living as either a stock dealer or a butcher. Stock dealers remained free to buy and sell stock. Butchers could still slaughter cattle, dress the meat, and offer it for sale in their shops. What it did require was that the slaughtering of animals be done in one central facility. The butchers' trade remained open to anyone who wished to pursue it, and individual butchers remained free either to slaughter their stock themselves in the company's abattoir upon payment of the fees stipulated in the statute or to employ journeymen at the slaughterhouse for this task, a course of action that many of them quickly adopted.

But, as he had done throughout the litigation, Campbell repeatedly asserted that the Slaughterhouse Act barred the butchers from practicing their chosen occupation. "The daily avocation and employment, the means by which, perhaps, a thousand persons have earned their daily bread have been jeoparded [*sic*] and impaired." As Campbell saw it, to defend the statute was to assert the company's "sole and exclusive privilege to conduct and carry on an important business in which hundreds had been engaged." And again, "The butcher is compelled to abandon his trade." Yet to say that the statute barred a butcher from a chosen occupation was to argue that a butcher could not pursue his calling without owning or operating a slaughterhouse of his own. And this was simply not true.

The former slave owner emphasized that the basic motive for both the Thirteenth and Fourteenth Amendments "is that as man has a right to labor for himself, and not at the will, or under the constraint of another, [so] he should have the profits of his own industry." Hinting again at his greater objective, Campbell reminded the justices that the Fourteenth Amendment, as well as the Civil Rights Act that preceded it, "guaranteed its protection against sordid interests, selfish aims and ambitious usurpations, or greedy appetites." Like them or not, the postwar amendments reflected "a great and weighty significance." Although Campbell would not admit that the amendments had brought about "a radical change in the government of the United States," he held that "they go very far to determine that the Constitution of the United States creates a national government and is not a federal compact." Here, the former Supreme Court justice took a position far from the doctrine of states' rights — in support of which he had followed his state out of the Union a decade before. But he did so not because he criticized its rationale as much as he condemned its results as expressed in the Slaughterhouse Act.

Probably thinking of the effects of Reconstruction and the abolition of slavery, Campbell claimed that "it may have been forseen [*sic*] that disorder would follow from . . . the introduction of a more relaxed system of social life and manners. . . . It was to have been expected," he added, "that there would be more corruption in the state governments, and that the rights of individuals would be insecure. It was to have been expected that in the existing state of society, monopolies would be asked for and easily obtained." The Constitution had always sought to protect certain rights from abuse by Congress. Thus the intent of the new amendments was to guarantee that the citizens' "privileges and immunities shall never be abridged by *State laws*, nor shall the *State* deny them equal protection." The same law that protects freedom of religion, speech, or publication from violation by a state now "protects the personal right to labor." Campbell readily admitted that "the sovereignty of the State government is reduced — and wisely reduced by the Constitution — to a very limited extent." Now, "life, liberty, property, privilege, immunity, civil, political and public rights have been placed upon a foundation that the [state legislatures] cannot subvert or destroy. Their superstruction [*sic*] of law must be made on this foundation, or it will fall of itself."

One of several fatal constitutional flaws in the Slaughterhouse Act, as Campbell viewed it, was its creation of a monopoly. Much of his first brief is devoted to a detailed account of the abuses caused by monopolies throughout history and the efforts to alleviate them, beginning with the great sixteenth-century *Case of Monopolies* in England. A similar aversion to monopolies was evident in American law. Indeed, Campbell contended that every essential point in the *Case of Monopolies* was reflected in the provisions of the new amendments to the Constitution.

In support of his anti-monopoly attack on the statute, Campbell was able to cite one recent state decision that seemed particularly relevant, if not decisive. The case deserves some attention because it helps elucidate the extralegal aspects of Campbell's reasoning and the ultimate weakness of his position. *City of Chicago v. Rumpff* involved an 1865 municipal ordinance by which the city, in effect, had entered into a contract granting a single private firm the exclusive right to have all slaughtering in the city done on its premises, in return for the company's agreement to erect and maintain the buildings and stockyards necessary to accommodate the needs of all the butchers. The ordinance went on to forbid slaughtering to take place elsewhere (packinghouses excepted). The measure had been enacted under the council's express legislative authority to regulate and direct the location of slaughtering within the city.

The Illinois Supreme Court saw a monopoly in this arrangement and declared it "unreasonable." It then held the ordinance invalid on the spurious grounds that it was not a regulatory measure at all, but a mere offer to contract. Unlike a regulatory measure, said the court, the ordinance "did not speak the language of command," and "it did not declare . . . the business of slaughtering animals in the city a nuisance." Not even a separate legislative act confirming the city's authority to enact such an ordinance was sufficient to dissuade the court from its finding of invalidity. Ever mindful of its political flank, in a related case the same court refused to award damages to a butcher whose slaughterhouse had been closed by city officials, pursuant to the ordinance. Since the measure was invalid, reasoned the court, actions of city officials to enforce it were ultra vires (outside their authority) and also void — and thus could not be used as a basis for a suit! The Illinois justices had managed both to side with Chicago's butchers against regulation and to shield the city's taxpayers from any liability for damages.

The *Rumpff* decision was particularly apt for Campbell's purposes. It was a case in which an appellate court had somehow found legal grounds for declaring invalid an act that it considered unreasonable. It was also a decision based on notably bogus reasoning in which the justices of the Illinois Supreme Court professed their inability to discern the regulatory aspects of a measure addressing the horrific urban blight caused by Chicago's slaughterhouses and ignored the ample police power available to deal with such problems. In that sense, too, it was precisely the sort of precedent on which Campbell and his fellow counsel needed to rely.

To vindicate his emphasis on the anti-monopoly theme in both European and American history, Campbell quoted and distorted a famous statement from Thomas Jefferson's first inaugural address. The new president had called for "a wise and frugal government which shall . . . not take from the mouth of industry the bread that it has earned." In his brief, however, Campbell went on to attribute to Jefferson a denunciation of monopolies (possibly from John Stuart Mill), which, "at the expense of the interests and rights of the public," had "depressed industry and public prosperity."

Campbell's denunciation of monopolies echoed an aversion to monopolies deeply rooted in both English and American jurisprudence. However, it was far from clear that the statute was in fact an invidious aberration of both common right and common law. The statute prevented no man from earning a living, with the possible exception of a man who sought to earn a living solely by operating a slaughterhouse, and even in this instance, nothing prevented this individual from seeking to work at the facility.

Having assailed the evils of monopolies, in the last part of his brief, Campbell turned his attention to the Louisiana statute of 1869. Here again, however, his accuracy left something to be desired. Campbell claimed, falsely, that in the case before the Louisiana Supreme Court, there had been "no question of the health of the city, or the location of the landings for stock." He added, again falsely, that "the waters of the river Mississippi are never mentioned in any connection with . . . [efforts] to spare the waters of that muddy and nasty stream from further pollution." Finally, Campbell argued, "We do not find any material inquiry regarding the water supply of New Orleans, nor how the Mississippi waters could be made pure." As previous chapters have indicated, a great deal of evidence concerning the effect of slaughterhouse practices on the city's water supply had been presented to the legislature over a period of about twenty-five years. It would be one thing to confront and rebut such evidence in these three instances, but to dismiss it as nonexistent is questionable.

In his conclusion, Campbell tempered his anger with sarcasm as he offered his interpretation of Reconstruction, which "furnished a broad field of labor for a class of philanthropic adventurers, who desire to do good and grow rich by administering the affairs of the poor." Their number "is legion. State, county and city improvements; the education of the young, the care of the poor; the purification of air and water; the building of roads, canals, railroads; sewerage, drainage, streets, pavements, gas, levees, lotteries, gambling houses, slaughterhouses have severally attracted their benignant observation. . . . Give to any one of them a sufficient fulcrum of State or city bonds, or of sole and exclusive privilege, and they will undertake to move the city to a very extraordinary elevation." Here was Campbell's perception of Reconstruction.

In the brief he submitted in support of the 1873 re-argument, Campbell further developed his views on the implications of the aftermath of the Civil War, and here the Fourteenth Amendment assumed greater importance in his analysis. Though a Jacksonian Democrat, Campbell the Southerner was no friend of universal suffrage. He was alarmed by the "large and growing population who came to this country without education, under the laws and constitution of the country, and who had begun to exert a perceptible influence over government and administration." Even worse was the fact that emancipation and the franchise had been linked together. Since the war, "nearly four millions of emancipated slaves, without education, capacity, and generally with the habits and ignorance that belonged to a savage condition — 'the heathen of the country' — . . . have become free citizens." The possible enfranchisement of the freemen disturbed him even more than the alleged abuse of his butcher-clients.

Campbell gave full range to his ideas about the evils of universal suffrage. "The force of universal suffrage in politics is like that of gun powder in war, or steam in industry. In the hands of power, and where the population is incapable or servile power will not fail to control it, it is irresistible. Whatever ambition, avarice, usurpation, servility, licentiousness, or pusillanimity needs a shelter will find it under its protecting influence." To make matters worse in the South, "the flower of the virile population had perished in an inter-states war," and "a large portion of the dominant population had been disfranchised" by the Fourteenth Amendment.

In the South, he lamented, the result "had been a subversion of all the relations in society and a change in social order and conditions." Elsewhere, "there had been a great accumulation of capital and credit; shameful malfeasance had become very common, and there had been an effusion over the whole land of an alert, active, aspiring, overreaching, unscrupulous class, the foulest offspring of the war, who sought money, place and influence in the worst manner and for purposes entirely mischievous. Their associations were formed not for such mutual advantage as is consistent with law, but for the execution of rapines that the laws prohibited." How could order be imposed in such a state of affairs? Campbell had an answer readily available.

"The 14th Amendment embodies all that the statesmanship of the country has ordained for accommodating the Constitution and the institutions of the country, to the vast additions of territory, increase of the population, multiplication of state and territorial governments, the annual influx of aliens, and the mighty changes produced by revolutionary events, and by social, industrial, commercial development." Campbell saw the amendment as having worked a vast change in the relationship between the national government and the states, and in the way that liberty was to be safeguarded. The amendment's purpose is "to establish through the whole jurisdiction of the United States one people, and that every member of the empire shall understand and appreciate the constitutional fact that his privileges and immunities cannot be abridged by state authority." This meant that the Constitution now protected any fundamental right from violation by a state. It was the new authority that Campbell sought to apply on behalf of his butcher-clients.

Having described the benefits of the Fourteenth Amendment, Campbell pointed out that it "is not confined to any race or class. It comprehends all within the scope of its provisions. The vast number of laborers in mines, manufactories, commerce, as well as the laborers on the plantations are defended against the unequal legislation of the States. Nor is the amendment confined in its application to the laboring men. The mandate is universal in its application to persons of every class and every condition of persons. . . . Labor under the 14th Amendment is placed under the same protection. The signs of the time very plainly show that the protection has not been extended too soon."

In the final section of his brief, Campbell returned to his case for the butchers. Again he denounced the motives and goals of the Crescent City proprietors. "This corporation stalked and strutted through the land as a seignoral power." Despite such rhetoric, there is merit in one writer's comment that Campbell's goal "seems to have been neither the defense nor the overthrow of monopolies in general, but the undoing of the outcome of the Civil War." With no indication of any inconsistency, he could insist on a very broad conception of the Fourteenth Amendment, even as he insisted on a very narrow view of the rights of the ex-slave in Louisiana. The new enactment protected butchers, as well as, according to Campbell, "the right of a New Orleans theatre to segregate Negro operagoers, despite a [Louisiana statute] which forbade that form of racial discrimination." Finally, it might be noted that even as he attacked the slaughterhouse statute, Campbell had no difficulty defending another Louisiana monopoly granted by the legislature to a New Orleans gas company. The ultimate issue at hand for Campbell appeared to be very simple. "Freedom. Free action, free enterprise — free competition." This was a clever and possibly intentional paraphrase of the catchy Republican motto for the 1860 presidential campaign.

John Campbell's co-counsel, J. Q. A. Fellows, also submitted a brief for the re-argument on behalf of the butchers. Like Campbell, he did not attempt to resist the effects of the postwar amendments but rather tried to turn them against Louisiana's reconstructed legislature. He noted that after 1789, two political parties arose with opposite interpretations of the Constitution. One contended for a preponderance of power in the national government, and the other regarded the states as the primary governments in the new arrangement. According to Fellows, the "party which contended for a narrowly restricted National Government . . . so prevailed that the judiciary had, to a considerable extent, coincided with these views." Further, "a large majority in one section of the country had imbibed these doctrines and come to consider them as fundamental." Here, Fellows apparently referred to the Taney Court's record on the issues of slavery and national power and conveniently ignored both the nationalist jurisprudence of Chief Justice John Marshall and the debates over slavery between 1820 and 1861. In any event, for him, it was this fundamental disagreement that had led to the Civil War.

According to Fellows, the postwar amendments had to be read as a piece. The Thirteenth Amendment proclaimed that "slavery and involuntary servitude . . . should cease; that the rights of every man to the fruits of his own labor should be guaranteed." Yet something more was needed, and this was provided by the Fourteenth Amendment. "The same spirit . . . still prevailed which, before the rebellion, had deprived many of the fruits of their industry." Thus the Fourteenth Amendment defined the citizens, and "over them, in all their rights of labor, was thrown the protecting aegis of the national government." Finally, Fellows stated, "that each citizen might have the power to aid in the vindication of his rights, the Fifteenth Amendment was also passed . . . giving to him the right of suffrage."

Fellows did not ask the Court to accept his interpretation of the amendments at face value. Alone among the lawyers who submitted briefs, he explored the intentions of the amendments' framers. He cited Senator Lyman Trumbull, who had emphasized that the 1866 statute "applies to white men as well as black men. It declares that all persons in the United States shall be entitled to the same civil rights; the right to the fruit of their own labor; the right to make contracts; the right to buy and sell, and enjoy liberty and happiness." The reason for the new amendment was to ensure the constitutionality of the new Civil Rights Act. "The leading statesmen . . . determined to put the question beyond dispute . . . and beyond its repeal." He quoted Charles Sumner's assertion that the Thirteenth and Fourteenth Amendments had abolished "oligarchy, aristocracy, caste, or monopoly with peculiar privileges or powers."

Fellows also invoked the words of John Bingham, the primary author of the Fourteenth Amendment's first section, who had stated "that the protection given by the laws of the States shall be equal in respect to life, liberty and property to all persons." He further quoted future president and then congressman James Garfield, who argued that the Fourteenth Amendment "proposes to hold over every American citizen, without regard to color, the protecting shield of law." Putting all his citations together, Fellows summarized the intentions of the enactments: "in other words, that the aim, object and intent was to make sure to all men those rights of life, of liberty, and of property, of the right to labor freely, and the enjoyment of the fruit of their own industry."

Although the case was argued before the high court over a two-day period in February 1873, only one of the oral arguments appears to have been recorded — that of John Campbell. There was little original material in it, as he summarized and synthesized what he had presented in the earlier briefs. Campbell contended anew that the definition of chattel slavery had to be broadened far beyond its traditional American context. Even more important, he emphasized his interpretation of the phrase "involuntary servitude." He stated, "there are many conditions of servitude in the world in which there is no requirement upon the labor of the slave; in which the slave yielded nothing to the master." One could be subject to involuntary servitude and yet not be a slave.

To drive home his point, Campbell exaggerated yet again the effect of the statute on his clients' profession. Insofar as the 1869 statute required of any butcher, "in order to prosecute his industry, that he must do it by force of law in the houses of this Company," such "is a personal servitude affecting the person." When "you tell me that I cannot use a portion of my property at my home; that I cannot protect, preserve, or control it there; that I must for the profit of a company lately incorporated, place it in their possession and under their control, under a tariff of prices fixed, not by me, but by a corporation, I say that it imposes upon me a servitude."

If the Court did not accept his point concerning involuntary servitude — and Campbell was too experienced an advocate not to sense that some of the justices might find it unconvincing — the former Supreme Court justice had a second objection to the 1869 statute, which was that it nurtured a monopoly. Finally, Campbell turned back to the Fourteenth Amendment, with which he tried to bind his two previous points. "I contend, that this Constitution . . . has placed every citizen of the United States, within or without a State, equally under the [its] protection . . . ; that this Constitution was designed to make in respect to certain rights one people; one compact body of people, deriving their protection to those rights from the Constitution . . . itself, and that it has taken every citizen of the United States, in respect to their privileges and immunities, immediately under the protecting care of the Federal Government."

Certainly Campbell had cast a broad net in structuring his arguments. He had railed against monopolies and ignored the possibility that in some circumstances a prudent exercise of the police power might justify a resort to exclusive privileges. He had deliberately distorted and oversimplified facts in the record, especially as pertained to the effect of the 1869 statute. His motives may well have sprung from a desire for the South, his section, to reconstruct a return in some instances to the status quo ante. His short-range target was, of course, a specific statute. But his long-range objectives, again, were the conditions and circumstances that had enabled a Louisiana legislature to convene and enact such offensive legislation in the first place.

In his first brief on behalf of the company, Thomas Durant relied heavily on leading precedents set by the Court regarding the reserved powers of the states, particularly their power to regulate persons and property for the common good. He cited, for example, *Prigg v. Pennsylvania* to justify his claim that "the police power of the State extends over all subjects within the territorial limits of the State, and has never been conceded to the United States." He drew on the decision in *Gibbons v. Ogden*, in which Chief Justice John Marshall had pointed out that the validity of police power laws "has never been denied" and that they "are considered as flowing from the acknowledged power of a State to protect the health of its citizens." Finally, Durant referred to *Briscoe v. Bank of Commonwealth of Kentucky* for his insistence that "a State may grant acts of incorporation for the attainment of those objects which are essential to the interests of society. This power is incident to sovereignty."

Thus Durant placed the 1869 Louisiana statute squarely within what he considered a well-established and well-defined, if not plenary, state police power. What the legislature had enacted obviously involved the "health, comfort, and prosperity of the population." Moreover, "it is manifest that to carry out successfully the policy of the state as displayed in the act . . . no rival establishments could be permitted for such would defeat the very object and design of the act." Taking issue with Campbell, he concluded: "if it can be said with truth that any man has a common law — natural — right to keep a stock landing or a slaughterhouse, so it may be equally said that every man has such a right to build and carry on a railroad, to be a banker, have a ferry, carry letters for pay." Yet "if the sovereign power judges that the interests of society will be better promoted by making such rights the exclusive privilege of a few, or of the State itself, this private right must yield to the public good." Only in the final paragraph of his brief did Durant dismiss Campbell's "erroneous impression that [his clients] are prohibited by the act . . . from carrying on the trade of butchers." "This is not so, their trade is left free. All they are required to do is to have their animals slaughtered at the place provided by the State, and they, the butchers, may slaughter their animals there themselves." Both Durant and his co-counsel, Charles Allen, went much further and reflected a more vigorous tone in the additional briefs they submitted for the re-argument. In the short run, at least, they would be persuasive.

Durant began his second brief with a reference to the title of the 1869 statute, "to protect the health of the city on New Orleans," as well as to "locate the stock landings and slaughter-houses." These objects, he insisted, "are all of the highest importance to the welfare of the people of the State; they are, beyond all possibility of dispute, matters entirely within State control . . . such, in short, as are necessary to the very existence of the State." Further, "none of these objects have been surrendered to the United States by the Federal Constitution, and so far as the purposes aimed at are concerned, the Federal judiciary has no more authority to interfere with them than with similar measures adopted in any European State." What of the Fourteenth Amendment and Campbell's insistence that the statute interfered with the right to labor in the vocation of a butcher? Durant confronted the second issue first. He readily conceded that the plaintiffs were indeed butchers, livestock landing owners, or slaughterhouse keepers, working "in their vocations" after the bill was enacted, just as they had been before it was introduced.

He defined a butcher as one who either "slaughter[s] animals for food" or "sell[s] the flesh of the slaughtered animals." In the latter sense, the statute "does not interfere with the right . . . to labor in their vocation at all, nor does it seek in any way to regulate the exercise of that right." In truth, "every butcher can labor in his vocation of sell-ing meat since the act just as he could before its adoption." As to those who slaughter, "the act does not deny to any citizen or person the right, privilege, or title to labor in such a vocation." Nor was it in-tended to do so. The statute simply "provides only for regulating the mode in which such vocation shall be exercised." Pointing to the requirements that the animals be inspected prior to slaughtering, Durant added that once approved by this official, the owner of the ani-mal may slaughter "either with his own hands, or by those of his ser-vants." Further, the statute "does not compel the owner of the animal to employ any State agent or corporation servant to slaughter. . . . All the act does is to say where the animal must be slaughtered."

In a real sense, it was the proprietors of the Crescent City Com-pany, more than the butchers, who faced compulsion. If the butchers were compelled to bring their animals to a central point for inspection and ultimate slaughter, the proprietors were compelled to provide at their expense "a grand slaughterhouse of sufficient capacity to accom-modate all butchers." Further, the statute imposed a substantial penalty on them if they refused to allow certified animals to be slaughtered there. In short, Durant argued, "every butcher may slaughter his own cattle, and his right to labor in his vocation is not taken away."

Durant also conceded that the statute did indeed give an exclusive privilege to a chosen set of proprietors. Yet he insisted that English law had long provided for monopolies intended "for the public benefit." Indeed, "there can be nothing better known to the court that the legislative power does constantly, and with undoubted right, grant exclusive privilege to corporations, by which the latter make a profit certainly, but which are intended for the public benefit." The issue of whether such action served the public interest "is not a judiciary ques-tion at all, but purely political."

What, then, of the Fourteenth Amendment? The lawyer for the Crescent City Company linked passage of the Civil Rights Act in April 1866 with the submission of the Fourteenth Amendment to the states a few months later. These two acts "explain one another," and they "both have the same object in view." The constitutional amendment "was designed to do nothing more than embody what the [earlier] law had enacted." It was to ensure that the states could not evade or ignore the civil rights statute. Since Durant and Campbell obviously disagreed about the "true meaning" of the amendment, Durant suggested consideration of "the reason and spirit of it," or "the occasion and necessity which moved the legislature to enact it." In other words, Durant insisted that the reasons for adopting the amendment in the first place were vital to understanding its intended scope.

He asserted there could be neither doubt nor debate on why the new amendment had been needed. Durant quoted from the now discredited Supreme Court decision in *Dred Scott*, written by Chief Justice Roger Taney and concurred in by then Associate Justice John Campbell. Taney had emphasized the fact that persons of African descent "had no rights which the white man was bound to respect." Hence, "to confer upon the disinherited people the rights, privileges, and immunities they never had possessed [and to place these beyond state interference] was the sole purpose of, as it was the sole necessity for, amending the Constitution." The basic issue was "the constitutional status of the people of African descent, and if there had been no such people in the country, no such amendment would have been proposed. It was adopted for them." Moreover, without any citation, Durant stated that "contemporaneous discussions and debates at the time . . . show that no other object was in view, nor can it be made to embrace any other without sacrificing its spirit."

The all-embracing language of the amendment, he added, was understandable. "When it says that *all* persons born or naturalized in the United States are citizens . . . it can mean by [*all*] only the people of African descent, because all other people were already citizens of the United States." Durant even pointed to several earlier constitutional references to "such persons" or "no person" or "three fifths of all other persons" and insisted that, as used, the term "persons" is "a form of expression usual in the language of the Constitution, where people of African descent are always spoken of in similar terms."

Clearly, the attorney for the company was as adept as Campbell in letting his conclusions gallop far ahead of his premises. Durant emphasized that the privileges and immunities clause of the new amendment "can have no meaning except as to persons of African descent, for in no State were any *citizens* ever subjected to any of the injuries, outrages, and disabilities denounced by the amendment." In contrast, as Michael Curtis has shown, prior to the Fourteenth Amendment, there were instances of state denial of equal protection not to slaves but to white citizens caught up in disputes involving slavery and abolition. Further, it is beyond debate that a few members of Congress had spoken of the proposed amendment in the broad terms later claimed for it by Campbell. Whether these few individuals echoed the general consensus of their colleagues, however, probably cannot be definitively ascertained.

Durant also took note of the well-established judicial doctrine that legislative motive was not a proper subject for judicial inquiry, a position that Chief Justice John Marshall had articulated more than half a century before in *Fletcher v. Peck*. Hence, "it is a matter beyond investigation here" that the 1869 statute "was really adopted in good faith by the Louisiana legislature to enforce its inspection laws, and to promote the health of its capital city. . . . All these are matters beyond controversy." The only possible ground for federal intervention, then, was the new Fourteenth Amendment. And if this enactment "forbids such legislation, it annuls all that is past and prohibits all such in [the] future."

Indulging in an early example of "slippery slope" analysis, counsel for the Crescent City Company listed all those legislative grants that would henceforth be barred: "canal charters, turnpike charters, bridge charters, railroad charters, gaslight company charters." Further, he cited regulatory measures for the manufacture and storage of "nitroglycerine, gunpowder, petroleum, and other dangerous substances . . . laws imposing licenses and taxes on trades, occupations and professions; laws forbidding labor on the first day of the week." All these and more must be invalid if the amendment "means to constitute individual rights absolutely superior to the public welfare of the States in matters not political." But it was not designed to bring about such a result.

On the contrary, "it is most manifest [that] the design of the amendment was limited to the investiture of blacks with all the rights and immunities of whites, whatever these may be, and to protect them in their lives, liberties and properties just as whites are protected. That is all that was and is necessary." To extend the amendment, as proposed by Campbell, "would break down the whole system of confederated State government, centralize the beautiful and harmonious system we enjoy into a consolidated and unlimited government, and render the Constitution of the United States, now the object of our love and veneration, as odious and insupportable as its enemies would wish to make it."

In addition to Durant's brief, the defendants filed a similar document prepared by co-counsel Charles Allen, who had served as the attorney general of Massachusetts from 1867 to 1872. Allen reiterated the applicability of police power precedents to the Louisiana statute and affirmed anew the equally well-established practices of awarding exclusive franchises. Moreover, he pointed to the fact that in such instances, these enactments invariably resulted in unequal restrictions on some segments of the citizenry By 1873, "the validity of such legislation, under similar constitutional provisions, is recognized in the general treatises, and is hardly open to question." Although there is no doubt that the 1869 statute did indeed confer an exclusive franchise on the Crescent City Company, "it was upon the consideration of moneys to be expended and duties to be performed by the corporation for the public benefit." This point was important for Allen, because it undercut the plaintiffs' claim of a monopoly, a foundation on which much of Campbell's brief had been constructed.

It is apparent, he claimed, that "these sums to be expended, and these duties to be performed, furnished a substantial consideration for the granting of the charter." They were, in other words, compulsory obligations imposed on the company by the legislature. This fact distinguished this corporation from a monopoly. According to Allen, a monopoly "is an exclusive privilege, *granted without consideration.*" But the charter granted to the Crescent City Company "was for a consideration." To be sure, "certain persons cannot carry on the business of butchering as advantageously to themselves as they did before." But "other persons can carry on the business more advantageously to themselves than they did before."

Allen emphasized how much easier it now was to become a butcher in New Orleans. "There is no longer any necessity of a butcher providing a slaughterhouse for himself. Any man with capital or credit enough to procure the necessary animals may now be a butcher." Echoing Durant, Allen claimed that far from creating a monopoly, the 1869 statute "makes it easier to be a butcher than it was before." Thus, the only question at issue was whether the Fourteenth Amendment "involves the surrender, on the part of all the States, to the general Government, of all rights of legislation of this character." Again, Allen detailed all the existing classes of regulatory legislation that would be invalidated if the answer was positive. He insisted that "it was certainly never intended or contemplated that this amendment should receive such a construction." Will this Court, inquired Allen, "sit in judgement to determine whether, as an act of municipal legislation, [the Louisiana statute] is reasonable in all its provisions?" How, he added, shall the Court "judicially know the exigency which will require the granting of such a charter . . . ? How shall the court inform itself judicially of the facts," as may be ascertained through the legislative process? To ask such a question, he implied, was to answer it.

All that remained was for Allen to confront the uncomfortable issue of wording, the broad language employed in the Fourteenth Amendment. Here, he reminded the Court that "the object to be accomplished by the amendment, and the mischief designed to be remedied or guarded against, may also be considered." The amendment must be seen in relation "to the state of things in which it had its origin." Reliance on the actual wording of the enactment outside of such a context would be a mistake. "The letter killeth." Further, Allen cited a number of examples in which actual judicial interpretation departed from "a literal construction of constitutional provisions." He pointed, for example, to the limiting of ex post facto laws only to crimes, although there is no such limitation in the Constitution. He noted, also, that the constitutional right of a trial by jury had been held not to apply in admiralty proceedings, even though this limitation does not appear in the Constitution.

In fact, Allen concluded, what Campbell had sought was to clothe an old term, "privileges and immunities," in a raiment "different from that put upon similar language by this court heretofore; different from that put by State courts upon provisions as comprehensive, and different from that put upon this amendment by Congress or by the people of the nation." There was neither reason nor justification for such a step. Did the argument of white butchers over where they might slaughter beef within a crowded municipality rise to the level of a "fundamental privilege or immunity"? Although he never stated this query in his brief, one suspects that Allen had no doubt about the answer. "The design in establishing this amendment . . . was simple and well known. It was to assure to all citizens and persons the same rights enjoyed by white citizens and persons. Every citizen should enjoy the same rights as white citizens. Every person should enjoy the same protection of the laws as white persons."

Depending on which brief the justices found most convincing, these attorneys had given the high court a clear choice. They might move in the direction discussed by Campbell and later endorsed by Justice Bradley, accepting the proposal that the language in the amendment was universal in its scope and that its presence in the Constitution indicated a new role for the federal government and, of course, the Court. Or they could follow Durant and Allen, agreeing that context was more important than content, that what had changed were the now legitimate expectations of the former slaves, for whom the amendment was clearly intended. Whatever route they took, the results promised to be important and controversial. The arguments were concluded early in February 1873. For a little more than two months, the lawyers and their clients waited. On April 14, the high court handed down its decision, and the Fourteenth Amendment received its first interpretation from the justices. More than a century later, reverberations from this decision continue to affect constitutional law.

CHAPTER 9

Decision and Dissents

On April 14, 1873, the country observed the eighth anniversary of Lincoln's assassination, President Ulysses Grant had just begun his second term, and in a "practically empty" courtroom, Justice Samuel F. Miller delivered the decision of the Court in the *Slaughterhouse Cases*. Although not the senior justice (that title was held by Justice Clifford), Miller was the logical jurist to speak for the majority. In his eleven years on the bench, he had already served as spokesman of choice in a number of cases involving constitutional issues. He was also at home with issues of public health. In his earlier career as a physician, he had written on the danger of cholera from polluted water. By the time of his appointment to the Court, he had resided for a decade in Keokuk, Iowa, a town on the Mississippi River that had once been the sixth busiest pork-packing center in the nation. Justice Miller was all too familiar with the noxious nature of the slaughtering industry, and he had witnessed a successful regulatory effort in Keokuk.

After a brief summary of the 1869 statute, Miller took note of Campbell's argument that the act had created a monopoly and conferred "odious and exclusive privileges upon a small number of persons at the expense of the great body of the community of New Orleans." Even worse, however, the law deprived "the whole of the butchers of the city of the right to exercise their trade, the business to which they have been trained and on which they depend for the support of themselves and their families." Indeed, Campbell contended that the whole community was affected because "the unrestricted exercise of . . . butchering is necessary to the daily subsistence of the [city] population." Having thus condensed several pages of Campbell's prose into a short paragraph, Miller dismissed his entire thesis in one sentence: "But a critical examination of the act hardly justifies these assertions."

No one denied that the statute granted exclusive privileges to a specified group for twenty-five years. Further, Miller was prepared to discuss "whether those privileges" had been granted "at the expense of the community in the sense of a curtailment of any of their fundamental rights, or even in the sense of doing them an injury." But "it is not true," he held, "that it deprives the butchers of their right to exercise their trade or imposes upon them any restrictions incompatible with its successful pursuit, [or their ability to furnish] the people of the city with the necessary daily supply of animal food." Thus, early in his opinion, Miller sustained a key point that had been asserted in support of the act throughout the litigation and carefully rehearsed by Durant and Allen in their briefs: the act determined the places where stock was to be landed and slaughtered, but it did not prevent anyone from plying the trade of a butcher. He also recognized that it was the company's exclusive privilege to operate a slaughterhouse (which affected individual butchers), rather than its control of the stock landing and stockyards (which affected mainly livestock dealers), that lay at the heart of the charges of "gross injustice to the public, and invasion of private right." All the Louisiana statute did, according to Miller, was to define "these localities and [forbid] slaughtering in any other." Having established this important distinction, he returned to Campbell's main argument.

The 1869 enactment "does not, contrary to [Campbell] prevent the butcher from doing his own slaughtering." In point of fact, "the Slaughterhouse Company is required, under a heavy penalty, to permit any person who wishes to do so, to slaughter in their houses." Further, it is "bound to make ample provision for the convenience of all the slaughtering for the entire city." Thus, the butcher "is still permitted to slaughter, to prepare, and to sell his own meats; but he is required to slaughter at a specified place and to pay a reasonable compensation for the use of the accommodations furnished him at that place." Under such conditions, it was "difficult" for Miller to see how Campbell could insist that his clients "are deprived of the right to labor in their occupation, or the people of their daily service in preparing food, or how this statute, with the duties and guards imposed upon the company, can be said to destroy the business of the butcher" or even "seriously interfere with its pursuit." Having located a legitimate legislative prerogative, Miller had no difficulty identifying its source.

It was, of course, the police power. This power "must be from its very nature, incapable of any very exact definition or limitation." But Miller emphasized that "the regulation of the place and manner of conducting the slaughtering of animals, and the business of butchering within a city . . . are among the most necessary and frequent exercises of this power." In affirming its special relevance for these cases, Miller cited authorities already set forth by Durant and Allen. He invoked the names of famous jurists such as Lemuel Shaw, John Marshall, and James Kent, all of whom had applied or endorsed the police power. The 1869 statute was "aptly framed to remove from the more densely populated parts of the city, the noxious slaughter-houses, and large and offensive collections of animals necessarily incident to the slaughtering business of a large city, and to locate them where the convenience, health, and comfort of the people require" it. And "it must be conceded that the means adopted by the act for this purpose are appropriate, stringent, and effectual."

Justice Miller then turned to the question of whether the legislature could ever validly grant exclusive privileges to a citizen or corporation. Although he paid tribute to Campbell's research concerning monopolies and to his eloquence in denouncing them, Miller rejected his argument out of hand. "We think it may be safely affirmed that . . . the legislative bodies of this country have from time immemorial to the present day, continued to grant to persons and corporations exclusive privileges." He conceded that in such instances, the same privileges are "denied to other citizens," and indeed, they "come within any just definition of the word monopoly, as much as those now under consideration." Nevertheless, "the power to do this has never been questioned or denied. Nor can it be truthfully denied that some of the most useful and beneficial enterprises set on foot for the general good, have been made successful by means of these exclusive rights, and could only have [gained] success in that way."

Here Miller might have ended his opinion. He had made the case for the Slaughterhouse Act as a valid, even routine exercise of the state's police power by reference to well-established state and federal precedents. The only remaining question was whether the act violated provisions of the Fourteenth Amendment, and this could have been decided without even entering into an exegesis of its provisions. It would have been sufficient to say simply that whatever the amendment meant, it did not mean to prevent the state from passing a sanitary measure like this one. Indeed, counsel for the company had argued strenuously that such a contrary ruling would be at odds with a wide range of licensing and other regulatory measures.

Some sixty years later, in *Ashwander v. Tennessee Valley Authority*, Justice Louis Brandeis would pen a classic dictum in which he cataloged a number of canons ordinarily observed by the Court as a means of limiting its constitutional pronouncements to cases in which they are unavoidable. But these canons were less well recognized in 1873, as was the adage that "hard cases make bad law." Besides, the scope of the case had already been framed by the briefs of counsel. All of them had considered and interpreted the Reconstruction amendments. And Miller was well aware that four of his brethren were prepared to consider and, to a large extent, accept Campbell's constitutional arguments. Moreover, the dissenting justices were readying opinions that would rely heavily on the amendments. These positions could not easily be ignored. Thus, even though the case may not have been an appropriate context in which to confront Campbell's arguments, one can understand why Miller felt it essential to consider them.

As the Court undertook to interpret the Thirteenth and Fourteenth Amendments for the first time, Miller confessed to an awareness of "the great responsibility which this duty devolves upon us. No questions so far reaching . . . in their consequences . . . and so important in their bearing upon the relations of the United States, and of the several States to each other and to the citizens of the States and of the United States, have been before this court during the official life of any of its present members." Further, he emphasized the lengthy judicial examination these questions had received. "We have given every opportunity for a full hearing at the bar; we have discussed it freely and compared views among ourselves; we have taken ample time for careful consideration, and now we propose to announce the judgments we have formed in the construction of those articles, so far as we have found them necessary to the decision of these cases before us, and beyond that we have neither the inclination nor the right to go." As the last part of this sentence reveals, Miller made it clear that his holding would be a narrow one. He had already upheld the 1869 statute by a broad reading of the police power. Here, he indicated that he would consider the amendments in as narrow a context as possible, possibly reflecting his conclusion that *this* case might not be the most appropriate vehicle for an original judicial exegesis of the enactments. Yet Miller felt compelled to offer such an exegesis, and as will be seen, with mixed results.

Miller considered it imperative to begin his analysis with a consideration of the historical events leading up to adoption of the three Reconstruction amendments. "Fortunately, that history is fresh within the memory of us all, and its leading features as they bear upon the matter before us, free from doubt." Issues related either to the curtailment of slavery or to its security and perpetuation had culminated in an effort by the slave states to leave the Union. "This constituted the war of the rebellion, and whatever auxiliary causes may have contributed to bring about this war, undoubtedly the overshadowing and efficient cause was African slavery." With the reestablishment of federal authority, it was clear that the "great act of emancipation" could not rest on Lincoln's proclamation or on "the actual results of the contest . . . both of which might have been questioned in after times." Hence, the Thirteenth Amendment was enacted. African slavery had caused the war, and it was the underlying cause of the new enactment.

Here, Miller dismissed Campbell's contention that the Slaughterhouse Act imposed on the butchers a "servitude" in violation of the Thirteenth Amendment. To put aside the obvious purpose of the amendment, Miller wrote, and "with a microscopic search endeavor to find in it a reference to servitudes, which may have been attached to property in certain localities requires an effort, to say the least of it." Miller insisted that all involved in the amendment had understood that, in the American context, involuntary servitude was virtually identical to African slavery. One can only ponder what the outcome of the *Slaughterhouse Cases* might have been if some of Campbell's clients had been black.

Just as the quest for freedom linked American slaves to the Thirteenth Amendment, so their treatment in freedom's aftermath linked them to the Fourteenth Amendment. Miller described in some detail conditions under the black codes for the ex-slaves. Without further protection from federal authorities, the "condition of the slave race" would "be almost as bad as it was before." By 1866, "something more was necessary in the way of constitutional protection to the unfortunate race who had suffered so much." Not only was the Fourteenth

Amendment enacted, but congressional leaders "declined to treat as restored to their full participation in the government . . . the States which had been in insurrection, until they ratified that article by a formal vote of their legislative bodies." Finally, with the enactment of the Fifteenth Amendment, "the Negro having, by the 14th Amendment, been declared to be a citizen of the United States, is thus made a voter in every State of the Union." Miller thus found common chains of causation for all three Reconstruction amendments, and the importance of this fact became clear in the next paragraph of his opinion:

> We repeat, then, in the light of this recapitulation of events, almost too recent to be called history, but which are familiar to us all; and on the most casual examination of the language of these amendments, no one can fail to be impressed with the one pervading purpose found in them all, lying at the foundation of each, and without which none of them would have been even suggested; we mean the freedom of the slave race, the security and firm establishment of that freedom, and the protection of the newly-made freeman and citizen from the oppressions of those who had formerly exercised unlimited dominion over him.

But Miller was careful to explicitly reject the idea that only the ex-slave was entitled to the protection of the amendment. Indeed, "if other rights are assailed by the States which properly and necessarily fall within the protection of these articles, that protection will apply, though the party interested may not be of African descent." Here, Miller was at pains to accept the argument of Durant and Allen that to discern the meaning of the amendment, one had to look beyond its words to the purpose that had inspired it. "What we do say, and what we wish to be understood is, that in any fair and just construction of any section or phrase of these amendments, it is necessary to look to the purpose which we have said was the pervading spirit of them all, the evil which they were designed to remedy."

Against this background, Justice Miller launched into the Court's first exegesis of the Fourteenth Amendment, beginning with the definition of citizenship found in Section 1. He noted that "no such definition was previously found in the Constitution" and added, "nor had any attempt been made to define it by act of Congress." (Actually, this was not accurate. In the Civil Rights Act of 1866, which was enacted before the Fourteenth Amendment was submitted to the states for ratification, Congress had provided a similar definition of federal citizenship: "All persons born in the United States, and not subject to any foreign power, excluding Indians not taxed, are hereby declared to be citizens of the United States.") Miller observed that the absence of a citizenship clause in the original Constitution had made it possible for the Court to decide in the *Dred Scott* case that a Negro could not become a citizen either of the United States or of a state. This famous (or infamous) decision had never been overruled, and as matters then stood, "all the Negro race who had recently been made freemen, were still, not only not citizens, but were incapable of becoming so by anything short of an amendment to the Constitution."

The "main purpose" of Section 1, then, according to Miller "was to establish the citizenship of the Negro." This was accomplished by providing that "all persons born or naturalized in the United States and subject to the jurisdiction thereof are citizens of the United States and of the state wherein they reside." To Miller, the wording of the amendment was all-important. In this section, he saw a "distinction between citizenship of the United States and citizenship of a state . . . clearly recognized and established." It is obvious, he wrote, "that there is a citizenship of the United States and a citizenship of a State, which are distinct from each other, and which depend upon different characteristics or circumstances in the individual."

This distinction between citizenship in the United States and citizenship in a state was a pivotal element in Miller's analysis, because in its next section, the amendment forbids the states to make or enforce "any law which shall abridge the privileges and immunities *of citizens of the United States.*" From this, Miller inferred that the amendment intended to protect only such privileges and immunities possessed by a person in his or her capacity as a citizen of the United States. "It is a little remarkable," wrote Miller, that "if this clause was intended as a protection to the citizen of a State against the legislative power of his own State, that the word[s] 'citizen of the State' should be left out. . . . It is too clear for argument that the change in phraseology was adopted understandingly and with a purpose." Here, Miller essentially argued that if *A* refers to one and two, but *B* specifies only one, therefore two is assumed to be excluded from *B*'s frame of reference. *A* sets forth dual citizenship of state and nation, but *B* refers only to privileges and immunities of American citizenship. Therefore, asserted Miller, there must be separate categories of privileges and immunities — some protected only by the federal government under the new amendment, and others protected as they always had been *only* by the states.

Based on this line of reasoning, Miller concluded for the majority that the amendment applies to only those federal privileges and immunities "which are placed by this clause under the protection of the Federal Constitution and that the latter [meaning privileges and immunities protected by the state constitutions], whatever they may be, are not intended to have any additional protection by this paragraph of the amendment." The privileges and immunities of a state citizen, Miller insisted, "must rest for their security and protection where they have heretofore rested," within the hands of the state. It was not difficult for Miller to conclude that whatever the privileges and immunities of U.S. citizens may be, the rights claimed by the butchers were not among them.

Modern scholars have argued that, ironically, this interpretation of the privileges and immunities clause would later deprive the freedmen of any of its protections — in spite of Miller's earlier insistence that a concern for their freedom had pervaded all the Reconstruction amendments. But there is no evidence to support the claim that such was Miller's intention. He did not attempt an exhaustive definition of "the privileges and immunities of citizens of the United States." He simply assumed that whatever they were, they did not encompass the rights being asserted by the New Orleans butchers. Specifically, he ventured no opinion on the implications for the freed slaves. No such claim was before the Court. He also may have assumed that a future case would permit the Court to explore exactly what the clause meant. Yet, in the remaining seventeen years of Miller's tenure, the justices apparently never reconsidered Miller's doctrines. That the Court failed to do so reflects less on Miller's 1873 holding and more on developments in American law after the end of Reconstruction. Miller is not exempt from criticism, however, because, by his silence, he facilitated subsequent developments.

Miller noted further that before the adoption of the new amendments, neither the federal government nor the Constitution had been looked to as a protector of the fundamental privileges and immunities of the citizen. With the exception of a few limitations imposed on the states directly by the Constitution, such as the prohibitions against ex post facto laws, bills of attainder, and laws impairing the obligation of contracts, "the entire domain of privileges and immunities . . . lay within the constitutional and legislative power of the States, and without that of the Federal government."

Against this background, Miller forcefully confronted the implications of Campbell's argument and asked, "Was it the purpose of the 14th Amendment, by the simple declaration that no state should make or enforce any law which shall abridge the privileges and immunities of citizens of the United States, to transfer the security and protection of all the civil rights which we have mentioned, from the States to the Federal government?" And since the amendment empowered Congress to enforce the amendment, "was it intended to bring within the power of Congress the entire domain of civil rights heretofore belonging exclusively to the States? . . . All this and more must follow, if the proposition of the plaintiffs . . . be sound." Echoing Durant and Allen once again, Miller added that sustaining Campbell's position "would constitute this court a perpetual censor upon all legislation of the States, on the civil rights of their own citizens." He candidly acknowledged that, in its prediction of dire consequences, his "slippery slope" analogy carried certain risks. "The argument we admit is not always the most conclusive which is drawn from the consequences urged against the adoption of a particular construction." In *this* case, however:

> these consequences are so serious, so far-reaching and pervading, so great a departure from the structure and spirit of our institutions; when the effect is to fetter and degrade the State governments by subjecting them to the control of Congress, in the exercise of powers heretofore universally conceded to them of the most ordinary and fundamental character; when in fact it radically changes the whole theory of the relations of the State and Federal governments to each other and of both . . . to the people; the argument has a force that is irresistible, in the absence of language which expresses such a purpose too clearly to admit of doubt.

Without any reference to either the congressional debates or the excerpts cited by Fellows, Miller put the point very simply: "We are convinced that no such results were intended by the Congress which proposed these amendments, nor by the States which ratified them." This single sentence is as close as Miller got to the sticky question of congressional intent. Debate over whether he accurately read or misread such intent, or indeed, whether any clear intention of Congress as a whole concerning the scope of the Fourteenth Amendment can be determined, has raged ever since.

There is no reason to doubt Miller's sincerity in articulating a limited view of the amendment's scope. The amendment presented him with a serious problem concerning the extent of its impact on the federal system. Further, he found no persuasive evidence that the amendment's framers had intended to make a fundamental change in the federal system, and nothing in its language to require such an interpretation. Speaking for a majority of the justices, Miller had already held that the police power provided a sufficient basis for the Slaughterhouse Act. Therefore, the case did not require the justices to go further and explore ways to reconcile the amendment's guarantee of fundamental rights with the values of the federal system.

Having found that only the privileges and immunities of citizens of the United States were protected against state action by the amendment, and that the rights being claimed by the New Orleans butchers were not among them, Miller concluded that "we may hold ourselves excused from defining the privileges and immunities of Citizens of the United States which no State can abridge, until some case involving those privileges may make it necessary to do so." Nonetheless, it may have occurred to Justice Miller that defining such rights would not only strengthen his opinion but also anticipate the arguments that would certainly be made by the dissenting justices. Hence, he did precisely what he had said it was unnecessary to do. As dicta, he offered some examples of privileges and immunities "which owe their existence to the Federal government, its National character, its Constitution, or its laws."

He included, for example, the right to become a citizen of any state of one's choosing, guaranteed by the very amendment under consideration, as well as the other provisions of the Fourteenth Amendment and the rights guaranteed by the Thirteenth and Fifteenth Amendments. There was no need to attempt an exhaustive list. The rights listed, he implied, were far above those claimed by the butchers. "We are of the opinion that the rights claimed by these plaintiffs in error, if they have any existence, are not privileges and immunities of citizens of the United States within the meaning of the clause of the 14th Amendment under consideration."

Miller then turned to the arguments that the Slaughterhouse Act deprived the butchers "of their property without due process or law, or that it denies to them the equal protection of the law." The due process clause was destined to become the focus of attention for generations to come, but in its first review by the Court, Miller dismissed its relevance in a single sentence: "It is sufficient to say that under no construction of that provision that we have ever seen, or any that we deem admissible, can the restraint imposed by the State of Louisiana upon the exercise of their trade by the butchers of New Orleans be held to be a deprivation of property within the meaning of that provision."

Only Campbell's resort to the equal protection clause remained to be dealt with. If, Miller noted, the states failed to adjust their laws to conform to the equal protection clause, then under Section 5 of the amendment, Congress was authorized to pass legislation to enforce the amendment. But "we doubt very much whether any action of a State not directed by way of discrimination against the Negroes as a class, or on account of their race, will ever be held to come within the purview of that provision. It is so clearly a provision for that race and that emergency, that a strong case would be necessary for its application to any other." This judicial aside has been considered by many scholars to be particularly regrettable. It unnecessarily limited the broad implications of the equal protection clause. Moreover, it could be used to narrow the scope of Congress's enforcement power under the amendment's last section. That the statement was dicta and nothing more has done little to exculpate Miller.

The former physician concluded his opinion with a brief description of the federal system, as his majority envisaged it. The threat to the Union posed by the Civil War had served as a powerful reminder of the importance of maintaining a strong national government. And undoubtedly, this sentiment had contributed to the adoption of the recent amendments. Nonetheless, he insisted that there was no reason to believe that they had been intended to bring about a fundamental change in the federal system. "We do not see in these amendments any purpose to destroy the main features of the general system. . . . Our statesmen have still believed that the existence of the States with powers for domestic and local government, including the regulation of civil rights — the rights of person and of property — was essential to the perfect working of our complex form of government, though they have thought proper to impose additional limitations on the States, and to confer additional power on that of the Nation." Thus Miller ultimately affirmed Louisiana's Slaughterhouse Act. What started out as a narrow holding endorsing the police power had become — despite the broad and controversial provisions of the Fourteenth Amendment — a commitment to the proposition that, *except* for the ex-slave, the Union is as the Union was.

Although Chief Justice Chase was the senior justice among the four dissenters, by the middle of April 1873, his health had deteriorated to the point that he could only indicate his concurrence. Indeed, less than a month after the case was decided, he died. It fell to Stephen Field to speak for his brethren, and if there was any sense of hesitation or tentativeness in Miller's opinion, the same cannot be said of Field's. Now in his tenth year on the Court, he had already fashioned a judicial activism based on both his Jacksonian heritage and his own economic conservatism.

Field reviewed the various complaints that Campbell had leveled against the Slaughterhouse Act on behalf of the butchers and concluded, "No one will deny the abstract justice which lies in the position of the plaintiffs." He then launched into an opinion aimed at showing that the butchers' position was well grounded in the Constitution. Field made short work of Miller's efforts to defend the 1869 statute as a valid exercise of the police power. He readily recognized the power of the state to make regulations for the health, safety, and well-being of the community. But even the police power had to be exercised in a way that was consistent with constitutionally protected rights. "Under the pretense of prescribing a police regulation, the State cannot be permitted to encroach upon any of the just rights of the citizen, which the Constitution intended to insure against abridgement."

In Field's view, only the provisions of the act requiring the inspection, landing, and slaughtering of animals below the city of New Orleans could properly be called police regulations. He ridiculed the claim that it was legitimate to award to a single company exclusive privileges over all stock landing, yarding, and slaughtering in an area encompassing three Louisiana parishes and 1,154 square miles. Nor could Field accept the 1869 statute as an example of an exclusive franchise such as the state might award for the construction and maintenance of a road, ferry, or bridge. Such grants are given for the accomplishment of some purpose falling within the purview of the government, he said. "The grant, with exclusive privileges of a right thus appertaining to the government, is a very different thing from a grant, with exclusive privileges, of a right to pursue one of the ordinary trades or callings of life, which is a right appertaining solely to the individual." Here, without question, Field accepted Campbell's dubious linkage of slaughtering beef with the trade of the butcher. In his eyes, the 1869 statute represented "a naked case . . . where a right to pursue a lawful and necessary calling, previously enjoyed by every citizen, and in connection with which a thousand persons were daily employed, is taken away and vested exclusively . . . in a single corporation . . . and there allowed only upon onerous conditions."

To drive home his point, Field allowed himself to exaggerate and employed some slippery slope reasoning of his own. Ignoring the notorious problems caused in an urban area by a system of distributed stockyards and slaughterhouses, as well as several limitations written into the act, he argued that if the Louisiana legislature could give exclusive privileges to a seventeen-person corporation, such privileges may

> be equally granted to a single individual. If they may be granted for twenty five years, they may equally be granted for a century, and in perpetuity. If they may be granted for the landing and keeping of animals . . . they may be equally granted for the landing and storage of grain . . . or for any article of commerce. . . . Indeed, upon the theory on which the exclusive privileges granted by the act in question are sustained, there is no monopoly, in the most odious form, which may not be upheld.

The dissenting justice insisted that "the question presented is, therefore, one of the gravest importance. . . . It is nothing less than the question whether the recent Amendments to the Federal Constitution protect the citizens of the United States against the deprivation of their common rights by state legislation. In my judgment the 14th Amendment does afford such protection, and was so intended by the Congress which framed and the states which adopted it."

Campbell had argued forcefully that the Slaughterhouse Act subjected his clients to a kind of involuntary servitude in violation of the terms of the Thirteenth Amendment. Field admitted that he was so accustomed to thinking of the amendment in terms of Negro slavery that he was not prepared to give it "the extent and force ascribed by counsel." But having said that, he went on to make several observations that seemed to support the very point he had disavowed. For all this, Field concluded, "it is not necessary . . . for the disposition of the present case in favor of the plaintiffs . . . to accept [Campbell's position] as entirely correct."

Field insisted that the Fourteenth Amendment held the key to the case. Without exploring the amendment's history, as Miller had, he rejected Miller's finding that the amendment established a separate citizenship in the United States and in the states, each imbued with its own privileges and immunities. Yet Field asserted that the amendment "does not attempt to confer any new privileges or immunities upon citizens or to enumerate or define those already existing." The amendment assumes that U.S. citizens are endowed as a matter of right with certain privileges and immunities "and ordains that they shall not be abridged by state legislation." Then, taking aim at the narrow definition of the privileges and immunities of *U.S.* citizens espoused by Miller, Field argued that "if this inhibition . . . only refers . . . to such privileges and immunities as were before its adoption specially designated in the Constitution or necessarily implied . . . it was a vain and idle enactment, which accomplished nothing, and most unnecessarily excited Congress and the people on its passage." (In spite of Field's aggressive rhetoric, it is far from clear to what extent the first section of the Fourteenth Amendment had in fact "excited" either Congress or the people upon its passage.) However, he added, "if the amendment refers to the natural and inalienable rights which belong to all citizens," as Field insisted it did, then "the inhibition has a profound significance and consequence."

At the heart of Justice Field's argument is the idea that the Fourteenth Amendment obligated the states to exercise their power in a way that did not interfere with the equal enjoyment by citizens of the United States of their privileges and immunities. This concept was central to Article IV, which had to do with the equal enjoyment of the privileges and immunities of state citizens. Now, according to Field, "under the 14th Amendment the same equality is secured between citizens of the United States." It was this equality that the Slaughterhouse Act had butchered in 1869 when it gave a monopoly over slaughtering to a single concern. In terms of this analysis, even the Illinois Supreme Court's decision in *Chicago v. Rumpff*, so heavily relied on by counsel for the butchers, took on renewed strength. Field cited it with approval. Counsel for the company had chosen not to attack the decision frontally as a betrayal of Chicago's legislatively granted police power. Instead, they sought to distinguish the case on the spurious grounds that it involved an allegedly unauthorized city ordinance, whereas the Slaughterhouse Act was the product of a fully empowered state legislature. Field summarily dismissed the rebuttal. "A legislative body is no more entitled to destroy the equality of rights of citizens, nor less to fetter the industry of a city, than a municipal government."

Field concluded his dissent with the declaration that "this equality of right, with exemption from all disparaging and partial enactments, in the lawful pursuits of life . . . is the distinguishing privilege of citizens of the United States. To them, everywhere, all pursuits, all professions, all avocations are open without other restrictions than such as are imposed equally upon all others of the same age, sex, and condition." This, he insisted, "is the fundamental idea upon which our institutions rest, and unless adhered to in the legislation of the country our government will be a republic only in name." Field's mention of restrictions should be kept in mind. In the celebrated case of *Bradwell v. Illinois*, decided one day after *Slaughterhouse*, Miller held that the Fourteenth Amendment did not give Myra Bradwell a constitutional right to follow a particular profession, presumably because Illinois law forbade *all* women to practice law (see 83 U.S. 130 [1873]). Field joined with Bradley, who wrote a concurring opinion that today could only be described as blatantly sexist.

Moreover, Field's heavy reliance on equality of right can be seen as a weakness in his rationale. As a justice of the Supreme Court, he was not in the position of a municipal official in a large city to observe that some pursuits — the privilege of operating a slaughterhouse, for example — could *not* be allowed to all, consistent with public health and good order. As constitutional scholar Thomas Cooley had observed in 1868, "there are unquestionably cases in which the State may grant privileges to specified individuals without violating any constitutional principle, because, from the nature of the case, it is impossible they should be possessed and enjoyed by all." Cooley believed that, for the most part, protection of fundamental rights remained with the states, as that is "where it naturally and properly belongs."

Justice Bradley supplemented Field's massive dissent with a "few observations" of his own. He was the only member of the Court who had had some prior experience with the *Slaughterhouse Cases*. New Orleans was part of his federal circuit, and in 1871, he had expressed the opinion that the Slaughterhouse Act was unconstitutional. Bradley considered the 1869 act to be "one of those arbitrary and unjust laws made in the interest of a few scheming individuals, by which some of the Southern States have, within the past few years, been so deplorably oppressed and impoverished." Justice Miller's opinion had been informed from the start by his finding that the amendment had been written first and foremost on behalf of the newly freed slaves. Bradley found a serious flaw in this conclusion.

"It is futile," he emphasized, "to argue that none but persons of the African race are intended to be benefited by this amendment." They may indeed have been "the primary cause" for it, but the language "is general, embracing all citizens, and I think it was purposely so expressed." Alone among his brethren, Bradley argued that far more was involved. "The mischief to be remedied," he said,

> was not merely slavery and its incidents and consequences; but that spirit of insubordination and disloyalty to the National government which had troubled the country for so many years in some of the States, and that intolerance of free speech and free discussion which often rendered life and property insecure, and led to much unequal legislation. The amendment was an attempt to give voice to the strong National yearning for that time and that condition of things . . . in which every citizen of the United States might stand erect on every portion of its soil, in the full enjoyment of every right and privilege belonging to a freeman.

Finally, Bradley confronted Miller's "great fears" that an expansive interpretation of the amendment would lead to interference from Congress, as well as excessive involvement from his own Court. He predicted that "no such practical inconveniences would arise." And if they did? "Even if the business of the National courts should be increased, Congress could easily supply the remedy by increasing their number and efficiency." In focusing on what Bradley believed were simply chimerical fears, Miller missed the point. The "great question" that he failed to answer, according to Bradley, was "what is the true construction of the Amendment?" It was to reflect the "National will and National interest."

In the final dissent, Justice Swayne outdid even Bradley in his hostile reaction to the 1869 statute. "A more flagrant and indefensible invasion of the rights of many for the benefit of a few has not occurred in the legislative history of the country." He further argued that the language of Section 1 meant just what it said. "By the language 'Citizens of the United States' was meant *all* such citizens; and by 'any person' was meant *all* persons within the jurisdiction of the State." There was no intimation of a distinction "on account of race or color," and "this court has no authority to interpolate a limitation that is neither expressed nor implied." Further, Swayne described Miller's construction as "much too narrow." Although he cited no evidence, he insisted that "it defeats, by a limitation not anticipated, the intent of those by whom the instrument was framed and of those by whom it was adopted."

———

Press reaction to the decision needs to be understood in the context of a broader reaction to the events of Reconstruction, still unfolding even as the opinions became public. Those that were concerned either by a claim of monopoly or by the course of Reconstruction in the Southern states were critical of the Court's decision. The *Cincinnati Enquirer* noted that Miller's majority opinion displayed "the degeneracy of the Court" in a holding based on a statute from a legislature "elected by the bayonet and through the agency of the most degraded and ignorant portion of the population." Truly, this was "the monopolists' decision."

Conversely, those journals that tended to oppose the federal role in Reconstruction were encouraged by Miller's conclusions. Thus, the *Nation* stated that "the Court is recovering from the war fever and is getting ready to abandon sentimental canons of construction." The

Chicago Tribune argued that although the Court had indirectly sustained a monopoly, its decision "does not turn upon this point." The real issue, according to the *New York World*, was "whether those amendments had changed the previous relations of the States to the Federal Government. The Court very properly decided that they had not."

A similar conclusion appeared in the *New York Times*, which emphasized the great importance of the decision "for several reasons. It is calculated to throw the immense moral force of the Court on the side of rational and careful interpretation" concerning rights of both the states and the federal government. Further, Miller's opinion was intended to maintain and increase "the respect felt for the Court, as being at once scrupulous in its regard for the Constitution, and unambitious of extending its own jurisdiction." Finally, the decision dealt "a severe and, we might almost hope, a fatal blow to that school of constitutional lawyers who have been engaged, ever since the adoption of the Fourteenth Amendment, in inventing impossible consequences for that addition to the Constitution." The writer added that its coverage "was not and could not be that subordination in matters of business and profit which it is not in the province of the National Constitution to regulate, and which the people did not intend to bring within" national jurisdiction.

The editorial conceded that the amendment's provisions were general. But they had been framed for the freedmen, and if the condition of that portion of the American people had not required it, the amendment would never have been passed. There could be little doubt, the editorial concluded, that the amendment "was not a piece of abstract declaration, meant to establish a general definition of rights for Congress to legislate for, and the Supreme Court to adjudicate on." Rather, "it was a piece of practical legislation, meant to remove certain obvious evils, and to establish certain results which were the logical outgrowth of the war."

At least one senator who had participated in the actual framing of the amendment's language claimed that, somehow, the Court "radically differed in respect both to the intention of the framers and the construction of the language used by them." In contrast, according to the Washington correspondent for the *Boston Daily Advertiser*, "the opinion of Mr. Justice Miller is held by the Bar to be exceedingly able, while passages in it were regarded as striking examples of judicial eloquence." And even John Campbell later admitted that it was probably "best for the country that the case so turned out."

Perhaps. But before placing this retrospective reflection in a broader contemporary context, some brief comments on the conclusion of the slaughterhouse controversy should be noted. By no means did it end with Miller's decision.

CHAPTER 10

The Legacy

By April 14, 1873, when Justice Samuel Miller announced the Supreme Court's decision in the *Slaughterhouse Cases*, the process of Reconstruction in Louisiana was showing signs of utter disintegration. Bloody race riots in both New Orleans and Colfax in central Louisiana, the latter only days before the Court announced its *Slaughterhouse* decision, made it evident that Louisiana's Republican administration was not in firm control of the state. Indeed, change was sweeping across the political landscape. National and state elections in November 1876 signaled an end to Reconstruction in Louisiana. The Democratic party quickly regained control of the state with Francis T. Nicholls as governor. Federal troops were withdrawn from Louisiana in 1877. The 1878 elections put Democrats into more than three-quarters of the seats in the state legislature. The *Daily Picayune* pointed out that they were united in their determination to effect reform by restoring "white home rule" and taking steps to ensure that "the reign of robbery will never be restored."

To that end, a constitutional convention met in New Orleans in April 1879. It consisted of 134 delegates, only 30 of whom were Republicans. The 104 Democratic delegates included a small but influential group of highly reactionary and racist Bourbons who were bent on revenge and the removal of every vestige of Republican rule. The Louisiana Constitution of 1879 was a far cry from the liberal document of 1868, and blacks did not fare well in a number of vital areas. For present purposes, however, it is sufficient to draw attention to just a few instances in which the constitution of 1879 sought to address what the drafters saw as a legacy of legislative irresponsibility. High among these priorities was the 1869 slaughterhouse statute. The new constitution prohibited special legislation "creating corporations" or "granting to any corporation . . . any special or exclusive right, privilege or immunity." Further, Article 248 gave parish and city governments exclusive authority to regulate slaughtering and the keeping of livestock, subject to two provisos: first, they could not do so by means of a monopoly or exclusive privileges, and second, any ordinances designating areas where slaughtering was to take place had to be approved by the board of health. Finally, Article 258 abrogated the Crescent City Company's exclusive franchise by providing that "the monopoly features in the charter of any corporation now existing in the State [railroads excepted], are hereby abolished."

These provisions of the new constitution opened the door to the reestablishment of private slaughterhouses within New Orleans city limits, and it was not long before individual butchers began petitioning the city council for permission to do just that. Some of these requests sought to return slaughterhouses to the very part of the city from which they had been removed by the 1869 act. Officials of the waterworks were quick to express strong opposition. On March 5, 1880, incorporators created a new slaughterhouse corporation for New Orleans, the Butchers Union Slaughterhouse and Livestock Landing Company. For its part, the city council began considering an ordinance for the board of health's approval that would regulate slaughtering and designate the area in the city where it could take place.

The Crescent City Company recognized that these developments threatened both its exclusive franchise and an investment that was now estimated at half a million dollars, and it wasted no time in initiating a series of defensive actions. On February 5, 1880, just two months after the new constitution was ratified, the company filed suit in Fifth District Court to enjoin the city of New Orleans from exercising any authority under Article 248. In this new litigation, entitled *Crescent City Livestock Landing and Slaughterhouse Company v. New Orleans*, the company contended that the Slaughterhouse Act had created a contract between it and the state whereby the company was given an exclusive twenty-five-year franchise to operate a slaughterhouse in return for its agreement to construct and maintain facilities adequate to meet the needs of the stock dealers and butchers of New Orleans. It argued that in abrogating this arrangement, Article 258 of the new constitution violated Article I, Section 10 of the U.S. Constitution, which prohibited a state from passing any "law impairing the obligation of contracts." The lower court granted a preliminary injunction but refused to make it permanent, and the company appealed.

The state supreme court rejected the company's argument and upheld the anti-monopoly provisions of the new constitution. The court recognized that the Slaughterhouse Act had been passed in the exercise of the state's police power — its power to legislate for the health, safety, and well-being of the community. It was a power, the court said, that was central to the functions of state government and one that a state could never relinquish or permanently contract away. Consequently, the nature of the act was not so much a contract as a mere *license* authorizing the company to act for the state. In short, what the legislature had formerly granted in the exercise of its police power, it could now take away in the exercise of the same power.

Authority for this ruling was not hard to find. Only a year before, in *Stone v. Mississippi*, the U.S. Supreme Court had held that the contract clause was not violated by a provision of the Mississippi Constitution of 1868 that had the effect of abrogating a twenty-five-year charter to conduct a lottery. The Court had explained that the "Legislature cannot bargain away the police power of a State. Irrevocable grants of property and franchises may be made, if they do not impair the supreme authorities [*sic*] to make laws for the right government of the State, but no legislature can curtail the power of its successors to make such laws as they deem proper in matters of police."

Never one to take no for an answer, the Crescent City Company returned to court in the person of Stoddard Howell, a butcher and an ally. With construction of the new Butchers Union Company abattoir well advanced, Howell sued that company in his capacity as a private citizen, allegedly seeking to abate a nuisance. He argued that the privilege of setting up a slaughterhouse belonged exclusively to the Crescent City Company. The action was a ruse sponsored and funded by the Crescent City Company to prevent the Butchers Union Company from going into business. The state supreme court ruled against Howell, but an angry Butchers Union Company retaliated by suing the Crescent City Company for damages as a result of malicious prosecution — an action it eventually lost in the state supreme court.

On November 28, 1891, an undeterred Crescent City Company initiated still another effort to defeat Article 258. For the first time, it filed suit directly against the Butchers Union Company, calling it to account before the U.S. Circuit Court in New Orleans. The result there was quite the opposite of the one reached by the Louisiana Supreme Court.

In the view of the judges of the circuit court, Article 258 could *not* be upheld as an exercise of the police power when the Crescent City Company's operations were already located where they could not endanger the health of the city.

On appeal, however, the U.S. Supreme Court reversed this decision in *Butchers Union Slaughterhouse and Live Stock Landing Co. v. Crescent City Livestock Landing and Slaughterhouse Co.* Here the Court was presented with a rare second opportunity to adjudicate the validity of the Crescent City Company's slaughterhouse monopoly, albeit in this instance in terms of the "contract clause." Writing once again for the majority, Justice Miller restated the first and central point of his previous *Slaughterhouse* opinion, but in doing so he took pains to emphasize the limited scope of his original opinion. He conceded that as a result of the Slaughterhouse Act, a contract existed between the state and the Crescent City Company, and that the provisions of the constitution of 1879 and the recent city ordinances did indeed abrogate that contract. But he rejected the idea that the state's contract was irrepealable. In creating a corporation and providing it with the exclusive privilege to operate a slaughterhouse, the legislature had simply acted in the exercise of its *police power.* As such, Miller wrote, it "*is a valid law, and must be obeyed, which is all that was decided by this court in the Slaughter-House Cases.*"

This sentence offers an intriguing insight into Miller's position. Now, ten years after the original *Slaughterhouse* opinion, he appeared to have relegated his earlier pronouncements concerning the Fourteenth Amendment to the realm of dicta. It is significant that he saw no need to repeat any of the points he had previously made concerning the meaning of the amendment's various provisions. This leads to the unmistakable suggestion that Miller ultimately considered the Fourteenth Amendment to be irrelevant to the decision in the *Slaughterhouse Cases.* It may be, said Justice Miller, that a state could enter into an irrepealable contract with regard to some aspects of the police power. But "a wise policy forbids the legislative body to divest itself of the power to enact laws for the preservation of health and the repression of crime."

The Court's decision in the *Butchers Union* case was unanimous, but both Justices Field and Bradley chose to write separate concurring opinions. Their desire to see an end to the slaughterhouse monopoly had been vindicated, yet they still felt a need to elaborate their position that the first Slaughterhouse Act had *never* been a valid exercise of the police power. In so doing, they elaborated on the volatile ideas they had expressed earlier in dissent about *fundamental* rights and their protection by the Fourteenth Amendment.

Field began by agreeing that the legislature could not permanently contract away its authority to provide for the health and morals of the public. But he went on to deny that health conditions could ever justify the creation of "a monopoly of an ordinary employment and business." He held that monopolies are against common right. As in his original dissent, Field's argument combined an appeal to higher law with a reliance on the Constitution's new textual guarantee of equality. He noted that the maintenance of "free institutions" required the recognition of "certain inherent rights." Among these rights is the right of men "to pursue any lawful business or vocation, in any manner not inconsistent with the equal rights of others." If textual support were needed for this right of labor, it could be found in the first section of the Fourteenth Amendment, which was, he said, "designed to prevent all discriminating legislation for the benefit of some to the disparagement of others." Field recognized that congressional efforts to enforce the terms of the amendment were controversial, but no one could complain if the amendment was used to support a resort to the *courts* in the defense of truly fundamental rights. He concluded "that the act, in creating the monopoly in an ordinary employment and business, was to that extent against common right and void."

In spite of his rhetoric, Field was less a foe of monopoly than he had indicated. Apparently, it depended on *what* the monopoly affected. Barely four years later, when Florida granted a monopoly to a local telegraph company, Field had no objection, and upon the high court's rejection of such a legislative grant, he dissented. Given his position in *Slaughterhouse*, his comments are of interest. "There can be no serious question that . . . Florida possessed the absolute right to confer upon a corporation created by it the exclusive privilege for a limited period." Indeed, Field added, "the exclusiveness of a privilege often constitutes the only inducement for undertakings holding out little prospect of immediate returns." This, of course, was the exact position taken by Miller in 1873. Again, Field failed to confront the fact that no one had been prevented from earning his living by the Slaughterhouse Act.

In the second concurring opinion, Justice Bradley (joined by Justices Harlan and Woods) reiterated his view that the regulatory aspects of the 1869 Slaughterhouse Act were "hitched on to the charter as a pretext." Still unable to detect any public benefit in a consolidated slaughterhouse, he held it as "an incontrovertible proposition of both English and American public law, that all *mere* monopolies are odious and against common right." Like Field, he resorted to principles enshrined in the Declaration of Independence and the Fourteenth Amendment for authority. "The right to follow any of the common occupations of life is an inalienable right" recognized in the Declaration's guarantee concerning the rights life, liberty, and the *pursuit of happiness.*

Not content to rely on constitutional theory for authority, Bradley held that the Slaughterhouse Act contravened the specific prohibitions of the Fourteenth Amendment's first section. "I hold that a legislative grant, such as that given to the appellees in this case is an infringement of each of these prohibitions. It abridges the privileges of citizens of the United States; it deprives them of a portion of their liberty and property without due process of law; and it denies to them the equal protection of the laws."

With its right to do business confirmed at last by the highest court in the land, the Butchers Union Company returned to court to recover damages from the Crescent City Company for malicious prosecution, just as it had done after the Stoddard Howell decision, and with equally little effect. A jury in the lower court awarded the Butchers Union Company monetary damages amounting to $19,000 and an additional $2,500 in attorneys' fees; this verdict was affirmed by the Louisiana Supreme Court, but on appeal, the U.S. Supreme Court reversed this finding. It pointed out that the Crescent City Company's rights vis-à-vis those of the Butchers Union Company had never been formally adjudicated. Consequently, the Crescent City Company was entitled, on the advice of counsel, to test its rights in the federal courts.

In fact, the Butchers Union Company did not remain in business for very long, and given the city's reluctance to license other slaughtering establishments, the Crescent City Company eventually became the city's sole abattoir once again. But the New Orleans livestock industry continued to attract the attention of speculators, and the old ways of winning the support of political bodies, though sometimes bitterly criticized, proved to have a staying power of their own. In 1891, for example, the city council approved an ordinance permitting a three-person "syndicate" to construct a new slaughterhouse in the city. The *New Orleans Item* dubbed the scheme "one of the periodic speculative moves for the erection of a new slaughterhouse" and opposed the venture on grounds that "one slaughterhouse is nuisance enough." The mayor vetoed the ordinance for sanitation reasons, but the city council overrode the veto. The board of health ratified the ordinance and then, in the face of a growing furor, withdrew its approval.

The dispute quickly widened into a major scandal. Indeed, twenty-two years after passage of the original Slaughterhouse Act, history seemed to be repeating itself. The press reported that the incorporators had made three-eighths of the stock of the proposed company and a sum of money available to B. B. Pringle, a broker, for his help in guaranteeing approval by the council and the board. Members of the board of health were reportedly bribed to support the ordinance and were said to have profited from sales of stock in the old slaughterhouse, "to the intense disgust of the public." Three members of the board resigned.

The attorney general was called in and a grand jury investigated, but no charges were pressed against anyone. In October, the board of health unexpectedly reversed itself and voted to ratify the city ordinance and license an additional slaughterhouse after all. Perhaps as a result of its long experience with the ways of New Orleans, the *Daily Picayune* seemed to view the affair with a degree of resignation. "There is talk of bribery just as there was the same sort of talk in the case of the Board of Health, but nothing will be proved. There was some speculating in slaughterhouse stock; but it appears to be a common thing for officials to speculate in stocks when they have official knowledge which can affect their value, but there is nothing unlawful in that. But the report of the investigation makes good reading."

In 1893, a year before the Crescent City Company's twenty-five-year charter expired, its stockholders rechartered themselves as the Crescent City Livestock Yard and Slaughter House Company. In one corporate form or another, the company continued in operation in the same location until about the 1920s. On June 6, 1963, the *New Orleans Times Picayune* reported the closing of the New Orleans Butchers Cooperative Abattoir owing to "labor difficulties and a dwindling supply of cattle due to residential expansion into former pasture area." In operation for sixty-years, it was the last slaughterhouse in the New Orleans area.

One can still visit the original site of the Crescent City Company's slaughterhouse and stockyards, as we did, located a short drive east of downtown New Orleans and not far from the site of the 1815 Battle of New Orleans. Most of the vast slaughterhouse tract is now occupied by solid middle-class neighborhoods. But near the Mississippi River, evidence of the slaughterhouse plant proper can still be found. Street signs in the neighborhood still bear the names of some of the butchers and stock dealers who initiated the *Slaughterhouse Cases* — Esteben, Aycock, Mehle. Wandering in the area, it is not difficult to imagine what it must have been like in 1873, when the stock landing and stockyards were bustling, buyers and sellers went about their business, and the slaughterhouse itself carried on its noxious activities. As our study concludes, it is appropriate to place the controversy in some sort of historical perspective.

The *Slaughterhouse Cases* involved the grant of an exclusive franchise to a private company for the operation of a centralized slaughterhouse in a rapidly growing urban area. The act can be defended as a routine exercise of the regulatory power of the state. Similar reforms had already been implemented in other metropolitan areas — though seldom without a political or legal fight from the butchers and stock dealers affected. In New Orleans, however, the struggle was all the more intense because the franchise had been awarded in the era of Reconstruction, and then to a hastily gathered group of investors, most of whom were newcomers.

In their efforts to defeat the 1869 statute, attorneys for the New Orleans butchers and stock dealers relied most notably on the Fourteenth Amendment's guarantees of "privileges and immunities" of citizenship, "due process of law," and the "equal protection of the law." As a factual matter, however, the case brought by white New Orleans butchers did not readily lend itself to the exploration, let alone the resolution, of the questions raised by the Fourteenth Amendment. Indeed, it was an especially inappropriate and unfortunate controversy in which to attempt a resolution. It did not grow out of circumstances akin to those that had led to the amendment, and none of the parties supposedly affected by it were involved.

Seldom has the Supreme Court been presented with a case so rich in irony. A Reconstruction amendment intended to secure the civil rights of black Americans was first utilized on behalf of the property rights of white butchers. It was employed in an effort to defeat an act passed by a reconstructed, racially integrated legislature. Counsel for the butchers, John A. Campbell, had a well-earned reputation as an advocate of states' rights. Yet now he called for an expansive interpretation of rights, privileges, and immunities to be protected as never before by the federal courts.

Campbell's opponents, including Matthew Carpenter, a lawyer who had participated in the congressional deliberations leading to the Fourteenth Amendment, and Thomas Durant, whose positive efforts to help the liberated blacks in Louisiana had resulted in his self-imposed exile from that state, found themselves in a similarly ironic position. To win their case, they had to argue for a most narrow interpretation of an amendment cast in very broad language. They had to deny its application to all except blacks, who were in no way party to the case. Thus John Campbell — no reconstructionist — pleaded for a liberal interpretation of privileges and immunities, while counsel for the Reconstruction government in Louisiana called for a restrictive reading of its terms.

The arguments they crafted presented the Supreme Court with a uniquely delicate task. Campbell asked the Court to hold that the right to earn one's living at a chosen calling was a fundamental right protected by the Fourteenth Amendment. But the Court could accept this contention only with unpredictable results. Using the amendment to protect this newly claimed "right to labor," for example, might lead to a call for the Court to discover other fundamental rights within the amendment. In short, the justices had to resolve this dispute without revolutionizing the federal system in a single decision, while at the same time not damaging the potency of the new constitutional provisions guaranteeing the rights of blacks. It could be argued that there was little reason to suppose that the Fourteenth Amendment had been intended to bring about a fundamental change in the federal system as it had traditionally been understood. Like the Civil Rights Act of 1866, the thrust of the amendment was to provide for federal intervention when the states either failed to do so or were guilty of such infringement themselves. As Michael Les Benedict put it, the "primary responsibility for . . . protecting their rights from infringement would remain with the states."

In deciding the case, the Court readily found that the police power of the state was ample to support the statute. But in reply to the constitutional arguments, Justice Miller's interpretation of the privileges and immunities clause of the Fourteenth Amendment held that it protected only the rights of national citizenship, which he found to be few indeed. Further, the majority opinion defined the due process clause as exclusively a guarantee of fundamentally fair procedure, and it held that the equal protection clause had relevance only for blacks and not for the white butchers of New Orleans. This was a restriction that would not stand the test of time. There was nothing in this provision, nor indeed in the entire amendment, that limited its application to blacks. In a supreme irony, Justice Miller, who had specifically singled out the ex-slave as the primary cause for the new amendment, apparently left the ex-slave's privileges and immunities, for the most part, at the mercy of the state. And this was done, as Philip Paludan has argued, not because the black man "was hated, but because constitutionally established federalism was loved."

There was no reason to doubt Miller's credentials as a Republican who consistently supported the goals of the war and of Reconstruction. It should be remembered that in sustaining the 1869 statute, he affirmed the work of a Reconstruction legislature, elected in part by black votes. It may be that Miller did not intend the 1873 decision to be a broad and definitive exegesis of the Fourteenth Amendment's full scope. He suggested as much in his opinion in the *Butchers Union* case, the 1884 sequel to *Slaughterhouse*, when he seemed to relegate his interpretation of the Fourteenth Amendment to the realm of dicta. But by choosing not to couch his decision exclusively in terms of the police power, he undercut his intention. He could have found the statute within the police power and gone no further. But he did go further, motivated perhaps by a desire to rebut Campbell's expansive vision of the amendment, as well as the vigorous comments of the dissenters. Not long after the *Slaughterhouse* decision, Miller wrote to his brother-in-law that few cases had ever given him such difficulty in making up his mind, but he strongly believed that the case had been decided rightly. Though he remained on the bench for seventeen years, he never found an opportunity to expand on the scope of the privileges and immunities clause.

In one sense, the Court's decision in favor of the Crescent City Company was short-lived. Within three years, the Louisiana legislature returned to Democratic control. One year later, Reconstruction ended, and by 1879, the 1869 statute was a thing of the past. Yet in a different sense, *Slaughterhouse* has had a transforming effect on modern constitutional law. In interpreting the privileges and immunities clause in a way that seemed consistent with American federalism as he knew it, Justice Miller rendered the clause ineffectual — or at least it is widely assumed so. There is no doubt, however, that in the years after *Slaughterhouse*, other portions of the amendment received much greater emphasis.

Justices Field and Bradley dissented in *Slaughterhouse* because they had failed to persuade their colleagues to apply the Fourteenth Amendment on behalf of New Orleans butchers and thus rescue them from what appeared to be a violation of their right to pursue a lawful calling. Their argument resonated with the amendment's equal protection clause. Yet it would not be until 1880 that the high court applied this clause in *Strauder v. West Virginia*, where it struck down a state statute that expressly barred African Americans from jury service. Thirteen years after *Slaughterhouse*, in *Yick Wo v. Hopkins*, a unanimous Court again applied the clause, this time to a group of Chinese laundrymen seeking to work at their trade in California. Here is yet another example of the irony that permeates the *Slaughterhouse* story. In 1886 the Court applied the Fourteenth Amendment's equal protection clause to these Chinese plaintiffs, endorsing their right to practice their trade or calling — exactly what it had declined to do for Campbell's white butchers in 1873.

The Civil War was followed by great industrial expansion and a consequent demand that the police power be applied to regulate various aspects of the burgeoning market economy. John Campbell's idea of property as a fundamental right entitled to protection under the provisions of the first section of the Fourteenth Amendment, although put aside in *Slaughterhouse*, had never been defeated. In fact, Justices

Field and Bradley had trumpeted it anew in their dissents in the *Butchers Union* case. Now, in their search for legal weapons against various business regulations in the postwar period, corporate lawyers made it their own, and they found a basis for it in the due process clause. In *Slaughterhouse*, due process had been defined as strictly a guarantee of fair procedure. But now it took on a substantive meaning. It became a measure of the legality not only of *how* government exercised its powers but also of *what* actions the government initiated.

It took until the end of the century to perfect this theory of substantive due process, but one of the first steps was taken only three years after *Slaughterhouse* when, in *Munn v. Illinois*, the Court upheld an act regulating storage rates at grain elevators against a challenge based on the due process clause. In his opinion for the majority, Justice Morrison Waite accepted the due process argument, but he reasoned that the private property involved in this case had been dedicated to "the public interest." To that extent, it was subject to regulation. Both Miller and Bradley concurred in Waite's opinion. If Miller realized how far his brethren had moved from his narrow holding in *Slaughterhouse*, he did not indicate it. In dissent, Justice Field, joined by Strong, took a hard substantive due process stand and disputed the distinction based on property vested with a public interest.

Due process was shaping a new judicial doctrine that would enable the courts to second-guess actions of the legislature, and Justice Miller bristled at this development. The next year, writing for the majority in *Davidson v. New Orleans*, he called counsel to task for their novel use of due process. He found in the growing body of due process litigation "abundant evidence that there exists some strong misconception of the scope of this provision" and lamented its use to test "the merits" of legislation. But substantive due process continued to evolve as a potent weapon against the regulation of business. Indeed, in 1890, in an opinion authored within ten months of his death, Justice Miller himself concurred in a decision that saw his brethren doing exactly what he had warned against in 1873— deciding that the reasonableness of a state police power regulation was a matter within judicial purview. It was another twist of *Slaughterhouse* irony.

The pinnacle in the development of substantive due process was reached in 1897 in the case of *Allgeyer v. Louisiana*. With his opinion for a unanimous court, Justice Rufus W. Peckham, in an apparent effort to write the economic theory of laissez-faire into the law, resorted to the arguments of Field, Bradley, and Campbell in the *Slaughterhouse Cases* to find that the due process clause protected a fundamental freedom to contract. The *Allgeyer* decision gave employers a way to challenge legislation regulating various aspects of the employer-employee relationship, and not a few used this line of attack successfully.

With the arrival of laissez-faire thinking, the justices' predilections concerning the reasonableness of regulation came into full play. Less than ten years after the *Allgeyer* decision, in *Lochner v. New York*, a majority of the Court, in another opinion authored by Justice Peckham, rejected a New York statute regulating working hours in bakeries, claiming that it interfered with the laborer's freedom of contract. Unlike the legislature, the Court found no reasonable grounds to justify the law. The shadow of *Slaughterhouse* hovered over this case, with the arguments advanced by Field and Bradley forming the basis for Justice Peckham's majority opinion; Miller's earlier holding, forcefully expanded by Holmes, shaped the dissent. The majority and dissenting opinions in *Lochner* stand today as landmarks in the literature of judicial activism and restraint. For the next thirty years, the high court fulfilled Miller's fear that the justices would make themselves the overseers of all kinds of state regulatory legislation.

The Supreme Court was much slower to employ the due process clause as protection against state infringement of the great substantive rights enshrined in the First Amendment or the procedural rights guaranteed elsewhere in the Bill of Rights. In 1897, the justices ruled that the Fifth Amendment's guarantee of just compensation applied to the states through the due process clause of the Fourteenth Amendment. In 1925, in *Gitlow v. New York*, the justices read the First Amendment guarantee of free speech into the due process clause, and with that, they began a long process of applying the Bill of Rights to the states.

By the late 1960s, the justices had read virtually all the elements of the Bill of Rights into the due process clause, thereby making them applicable to the states. From 1873 to the present, a majority of the Court steadfastly refused to accept the doctrine of total incorporation, which was the idea that the Bill of Rights had been made applicable to the states, ipso facto, by the Fourteenth Amendment. Instead, the revolution that Miller had resisted in *Slaughterhouse* was brought about on a case-by-case, amendment-by-amendment basis, over the course of nearly a century. Today the Bill of Rights limits the exercise of power by both the national government and the states.

It remains only to note that Justice Miller's declaration in *Slaugherhouse* that the equal protection clause applied primarily to blacks proved remarkably shortsighted. Indeed, Miller himself had joined the Court's decisions in *Strauder v. West Virginia* and *Yick Wo v. Hopkins*, mentioned earlier. But the Court was slow to utilize the amendment further on behalf of blacks. However, beginning in the twentieth century especially, the equal protection clause has been employed with historic significance to remove racial barriers to the political, economic, and social development of Americans, including but by no means limited to blacks. This provision has been successfully applied to cases involving criminal justice, legislative apportionment, and issues of gender relationships within the law. And the list goes on.

Today, as a result of its response to a century of litigation in all these areas of the Fourteenth Amendment, the Court has achieved for itself and the other federal courts an all-important role in the system of checks and balances and in the formulation of important national policies as well. In case after case, it has identified fundamental rights and placed them under constitutional protection. In doing so, it has vindicated John Campbell's expansive view of the Fourteenth Amendment far beyond his original conception and, indeed, with far more positive benefits.

The Fourteenth Amendment is still among the most frequently litigated amendments in the Constitution. Throughout it all, the 1873 *Slaughterhouse* holding has survived; though it is now most often ignored, it has never been overruled, not even *sub silentio*. The staying power of Miller's opinion cannot be explained merely by the rule of precedent. Miller himself enthusiastically participated as the Court reversed itself in the *Legal Tender Cases*, and this occurred less than two years after its initial decision. Nor is it fair to say that Miller's analysis permanently gutted the effectiveness of the privileges and immunities clause; rather, cultural and constitutional predilections have caused its desuetude. But expressions of anguish over its supposed demise are premature. Like its sister the contracts clause, the privileges and immunities clause of the Fourteenth Amendment remains part of the living constitution, readily available whenever the Court wishes to employ it. And indeed, in a number of cases the justices have done just that.

More than a century later, blaming Miller for current judicial disinclination to apply the clause is unwarranted. When the Court desires to utilize it, the clause is there.

A variety of factors, some obvious and others much more subtle, come into play when the Supreme Court decides to change its mind. If and when it decides to reexamine *Slaughterhouse*, the Court will only be acting on a basic tenet of our legal history: that the process of accommodating law to change, as legal historian Lawrence Friedman noted so well, "is never signed, sealed and delivered; it is always incomplete, always inchoate, always a work in progress, a work that is never done."

1718	New Orleans established as a settlement.
1803	Early in the American period, butchers begin locating slaughterhouses within inhabited areas.
1813	Louisiana Governor Claiborne complains of widespread city "pollution" and "filth."
1833	New Orleans waterworks granted an exclusive franchise by the city.
1848	The eighth city board of health since 1804 is established. It aggressively asserts the need for sanitary reform.
1850	Dr. J. C. Simonds publishes statistics showing an inordinately high death rate in New Orleans compared with other American cities.
1853	The worst yellow fever epidemic in New Orleans history decimates the city's population.
1854	A sanitary commission chaired by Dr. Edward Barton singles out slaughterhouses as long-standing nuisances and urges reform through regulation.
1855	Louisiana legislature establishes a state board of health in New Orleans.
1862 (April)	Exclusive franchise for a municipal slaughterhouse is awarded to Hepp, Rochereau, and Pochelu by the city council of Jefferson City, Louisiana.
	Union forces occupy New Orleans; General Benjamin Butler orders a citywide sanitation program.
1866	Long-sought health ordinance fails to prohibit slaughtering above the waterworks but creates a corps of health officers.
1867 (February)	Special legislative committee recommends relocation of the slaughterhouses.
1867 (March)	Legislature scuttles a slaughterhouse removal bill; requires instead that the city pass an ordinance forbidding slaughterhouses to dump their waste into the river.

	Congressional Reconstruction is implemented in Louisiana.
1867	In *City of Chicago v. Rumpff*, the Illinois Supreme Court invalidates an ordinance establishing a municipal slaughterhouse on grounds of monopoly.
1868 (April)	Reconstructed Louisiana legislature is elected.
1868 (July)	Fourteenth Amendment is ratified.
1868	In *Metropolitan Board of Health v. Heister*, New York City's power to confine slaughtering to a designated area is upheld by a state court of appeals.
1869 (March)	Slaughterhouse statute is enacted; Crescent City Livestock Landing and Slaughterhouse Company is established.
1869 (May, June)	Numerous state lawsuits are filed concerning the slaughterhouse statute; six suits are selected for appeal.
1869 (September)	Live Stock Dealers and Butchers Association begins construction of a consolidated slaughterhouse of its own.
1870 (March)	Legislature creates new district court in New Orleans with exclusive jurisdiction over suits for injunction.
1870 (April)	Louisiana Supreme Court sustains the Slaughterhouse Act.
1870 (June)	In federal circuit court, Justice Joseph Bradley expresses his opinion that the Slaughterhouse Act is unconstitutional but declines to enjoin its execution.
	The newly created district court orders the closure of the livestock dealers' slaughterhouse.
1871 (February)	A legislative act repealing the Slaughterhouse Act is successfully vetoed by Governor Warmoth.
1871 (March)	Livestock dealers compromise and become owners of the Crescent City Company; the company's original organizers bow out of the litigation. Three of the six slaughterhouse cases are discontinued.
1872	Remaining *Slaughterhouse Cases* are argued before the high court.
1872 (November)	Justice Samuel Nelson retires; New York Court of Appeals Justice Ward Hunt is appointed to replace him.
1873 (February)	Re-argument.
1873 (April)	Supreme Court sustains the statute by a five-to-four

margin, with Justice Samuel Miller writing for the majority; Justices Chase, Field, Bradley, and Swayne dissent.

1876   National and state elections signal the end of Reconstruction in Louisiana.

1879   New Louisiana Constitution prohibits monopolies, abrogates the Crescent City Company's exclusive privileges.

1880   In *Strauder v. West Virginia*, the Supreme Court employs the equal protection clause of the Fourteenth Amendment to invalidate a statute that barred African Americans from jury service.

1881   In *Crescent City Company v. New Orleans*, the Louisiana Supreme Court holds that the contract implied by the company's charter is not impaired by the anti-monopoly provisions of the new constitution.

1884   In *Butchers Union v. Crescent City Company*, a unanimous Supreme Court also rejects the argument that the anti-monopoly provisions of the new state constitution impair the company's contractual rights under its charter. Justices Field and Bradley again argue that the Fourteenth Amendment should be used to protect property rights.

1886   In *Yick Wo v. Hopkins*, the Supreme Court uses the Fourteenth Amendment to defend the right of Chinese laundrymen in California to earn their living on an equal footing with other tradesmen.

1897   In *Allgeyer v. Louisiana*, a unanimous Court holds that the Fourteenth Amendment's due process clause protects the freedom to contract and that restrictions of this right need to be justified. This decision positioned the Supreme Court to enforce laissez-faire economic theory as constitutional doctrine.

BIBLIOGRAPHICAL ESSAY

Note from the series editors: The following bibliographical essay contains the primary and secondary sources the authors consulted for this volume. We have asked all authors in the series to omit formal citations in order to make their volumes more readable, inexpensive, and appealing for students and general readers.

A complete bibliography of the materials on which this case study is based is included in the original, hardback edition of this book. This brief essay provides a sample of works that shed light on the various aspects of the *Slaughterhouse* controversy. They have been selected partly because of their availability in university libraries.

A careful reading of the records and briefs of a case on appeal is a necessary step in any case study. The appellate records contain a copy of the lower court's entire record, including the testimony of witnesses, and they are a rich source of information. The official compilation of these materials for cases decided by the U.S. Supreme Court is *United States Supreme Court Records and Briefs*, available only in the Legal Division of the Library of Congress and very few other libraries. Fortunately, this collection is widely available in a privately published microfilm edition: *Scholarly Resources Microfilm Edition of the Records and Briefs of the United States Supreme Court* (Scholarly Resources, 1975). The briefs and arguments in the *Slaughterhouse Cases* in the Supreme Court (though not the lower court records) are also available in Phillip B. Kurland and Gerhard Casper, eds., *Landmark Briefs and Arguments of the Supreme Court of the United States: Constitutional Law* (University Publications of America, 1975). For the whereabouts of the extant *Slaughterhouse* briefs and oral arguments used in the state courts, refer to the original bibliography.

The Reconstruction era of American history has provoked a vast and still-growing body of scholarship. The best modern and comprehensive treatment is Eric Foner, *Reconstruction: America's Unfinished Revolution: 1863–1877* (Harper and Row, 1988). Works focusing on the Louisiana experience include Joe Gray Taylor, *Louisiana Reconstructed, 1863–1877* (Louisiana State University Press, 1974), and Ted Tunnel, *Crucible of Reconstruction: War, Radicalism and Race in Louisiana* (Louisiana State University Press, 1984). For an example of a much earlier and now largely discredited interpretation, but one that influenced work touching on the *Slaughterhouse Cases*, see Ella Lonn, *Reconstruction in Louisiana* (G. P. Putnam's Sons, 1918).

There are a number of studies that deal with constitutional and legal history during the era of the *Slaughterhouse Cases*. Among them are Harold M. Hyman, *The Reconstruction Justice of Salmon P. Chase* (University Press of Kansas, 1997), and Stanley I. Kutler, *Judicial Power and Reconstruction Politics* (University of Chicago Press, 1968). Other topical treatments of the Reconstruction era include Michael Les Benedict, *A Compromise of Principle: Congressional Republicans and Reconstruction* (W. W. Norton, 1974); Richard N. Current, *Those Terrible Carpetbaggers* (Oxford University Press, 1988); Robert M. Goldman, *Reconstruction and Black Suffrage* (University Press of Kansas, 2001); and Charles Vincent, *Black Legislators in Louisiana during Reconstruction* (Louisiana State University Press, 1976).

The legislative act that led to the *Slaughterhouse* controversy is rooted in New Orleans's woeful nineteenth-century experience with public health, its unregulated livestock industry, and its volatile economic history. The need for sanitary reform is evident in relevant chapters of John Duffy, ed., *Rudolph Matas History of Medicine in Louisiana* (Louisiana State University Press, 1958). The role played by epidemic disease in overcoming resistance to reform can be gleaned from works such as Duffy's highly readable *Sword of Pestilence: The New Orleans Yellow Fever Epidemic of 1853* (Louisiana State University Press, 1966); Jo Ann Carrigan, *The Saffron Scourge: A History of Yellow Fever in Louisiana, 1796–1905* (University of Southwestern Louisiana, 1994); and Charles E. Rosenberg, *The Cholera Years: The United States in 1832, 1849, and 1866* (University of Chicago Press, 1979). The travails of the board of health in New Orleans are chronicled in Gordon E. Gillson, *Louisiana State Board of Health* (Louisiana State Board of Health, 1967). That the course of reform in New Orleans paralleled developments in other cities and, indeed, reflected a national trend toward sanitary reform is evident in such works as John Duffy, *A History of Public Health in New York City, 1625–1866* (Russell Sage Foundation, 1968); Louise Carroll Wade, *Chicago's Pride: The Stockyards, Packingtown and Environs in the Nineteenth Century* (University of Illinois Press, 1987); Duffy, *The Sanitarians: A History of American Public Health* (University of Illinois Press, 1990); and Wilson G. Smillie, *Public Health: Its Promise for the Future* (Macmillan, 1955).

Works covering the rise and fall of New Orleans as a great commercial center in the nineteenth century include Steven Caldwell, *A Banking History of Louisiana* (Louisiana State University Press, 1935), and George D. Green, *Finance and Economic Development in the Old South: Louisiana Banking, 1804–1861* (Stanford University Press, 1972). The New Orleans experience with railroad construction is the subject of James C. Baughman, *Charles Morgan and the Development of Southern Transportation* (Vanderbilt University Press, 1968), and Merl E. Reed, *New Orleans and the Railroads: The Struggle for American Commercial Empire, 1830–1860* (Louisiana State University Press, 1966). For a useful history of the national economy, see Douglass C. North, *The Economic Growth of the United States, 1790–1860* (Prentice-Hall, 1961).

There were those in New Orleans who hoped to capitalize on the post–Civil War transformation of the livestock industry. The standard history of the industry is Rudolf A. Clemen, *The American Livestock and Meat*

Industry (Ronald Press, 1923). Related works include Edward E. Dale, *The Range Cattle Industry: Ranching on the Great Plains from 1865 to 1925* (University of Oklahoma Press, 1960), and Charles W. Towne and Edward N. Wentworth, *Cattle and Men* (University of Oklahoma Press, 1955).

The Slaughterhouse Act survived its encounter with the Fourteenth Amendment because the Supreme Court found that it was a valid exercise of the regulatory power of the state, known technically as the police power. The history and scope of this important power are exhaustively explored in William J. Novak, *The People's Welfare: Law and Regulation in Nineteenth Century America* (University of North Carolina Press, 1996).

Biographies of the justices of the Supreme Court, including those who participated in the *Slaughterhouse* decision, can be found in Claire Cushman, ed., *The Supreme Court Justices* (Congressional Quarterly, 1983); Melvin Urofsky, ed., *The Supreme Court Justices: A Biographical Dictionary* (Garland, 1994); and Kermit Hall, ed., *The Oxford Companion to the Supreme Court of the United States* (Oxford University Press, 1992). Hall's book also includes brief accounts of salient Supreme Court cases. Samuel F. Miller, the author of the *Slaughterhouse* majority opinion, is the subject of two biographies: Charles Fairman's *Mr. Justice Miller and the Supreme Court, 1862–1890* (Harvard University Press, 1939) reflects the influence of early interpretations of Reconstruction as a misguided national venture. It has been superseded by the recent and very readable work by Michael A. Ross, *Justice of Shattered Dreams: Samuel Freeman Miller and the Supreme Court during the Civil War Era* (Louisiana State University Press, 2003). Justices Stephen Field and Joseph Bradley, the two principal *Slaughterhouse* dissenters, are the focus of Paul Kens, *Justice Stephen J. Field: Shaping Liberty from the Gold Rush to the Gilded Age* (University Press of Kansas, 1977), and Jonathan Lurie, "Mr. Justice Bradley: A Reassessment," *Seton Hall Law Review* 16 (1986): 343–75.

Two early efforts to trace the dispute from its origins in the New Orleans lower courts to the U.S. Supreme Court are Mitchell Franklin, "The Foundations and Meaning of the Slaughterhouse Cases," *Tulane Law Review* 18 (October 1942): 1–88 and (December 1943): 218–62, and Charles Fairman, *Reconstruction and Reunion, 1864–88* (Macmillan, 1971). The *Slaughterhouse* decision is a pivotal one, and it is discussed in every comprehensive account of American constitutional development. See, for example, Alfred H. Kelly, Winfred A. Harbison, and Herman Belz, *The American Constitution: Its Origins and Development* (7th ed., Norton, 1991). Some early constitutional histories took a decidedly negative view of the Reconstruction experience and of the Slaughterhouse Act. An example is Charles A. Warren, *The Supreme Court in United States History* (Little, Brown, 1926). A more objective treatment of the factors that led to the adoption of the Slaughterhouse Act is provided in Herbert Hovenkamp, *Enterprise and American Law: 1836–1937* (Harvard

University Press, 1991). See also the thoughtful study by Harold Hyman and William Wiecek, *Equal Justice under Law: Constitutional Developments, 1835–1875* (Harper and Row, 1982). Alternative resolutions of the *Slaughterhouse* controversy that were available to Justice Miller are discussed by Loren Beth in "The Slaughterhouse Cases Revisited," *Louisiana Law Review* 23 (1963): 487–505. See also Pamela Brandwein, *Reconstructing Reconstruction: The Supreme Court and the Production of Historical Truth* (Duke University Press, 1999), and David Bogen, "Slaughterhouse Five: Views of the Case," *Hastings Law Journal* 55 (2003): 333.

Historians continue to debate the meaning of the Fourteenth Amendment and the impact that the *Slaughterhouse* decision had on its development in the ensuing years. A recent treatment of the amendment is William Nelson, *The Fourteenth Amendment: From Political Principle to Judicial Doctrine* (Harvard University Press, 1988). The reluctance to interpret the amendment in a way that would disturb the existing balance of power between the national government and the states is explored in Phillip Paludan, *A Covenant with Death: The Constitution, Law and Equality in the Civil War Era* (University of Illinois Press, 1975). The question of whether the rights protected by the Fourteenth Amendment include those enshrined in the Bill of Rights is thoroughly considered in such works as Michael K. Curtis, *No State Shall Abridge: The Fourteenth Amendment and the Bill of Rights* (Duke University Press, 1986), and Akhil Reed Amar, *The Bill of Rights: Creation and Reconstruction* (Yale University Press, 1998). Curtis further explores the future potential of the privileges and immunities clause in two articles: "Historical Linguistics, Inkblots, and Life after Death: The Privileges and Immunities of Citizens of the United States," *North Carolina Law Review* 78 (2000): 1071–151, and "Resurrecting the Privileges and Immunities Clause and Revising the *Slaughterhouse Cases* without Exhuming *Lochner:* Individual Rights and the Fourteenth Amendment," *Boston College Law Review* 38 (1996): 1–106. The unlikely career of the Fourteenth Amendment's concept of due process of law that was inadvertently launched by the *Slaughterhouse* decision is briefly outlined in Walton H. Hamilton's still delightful gem "The Path of Due Process of Law," *Ethics* 48 (April 1938): 269–96.

Lincoln, Abraham, *continued*
Reconstruction and, 43
Supreme Court appointments by,
113
Live Stock Dealers and Butchers Ass'n
of New Orleans v. Crescent City
Live Stock Landing and
Slaughter House Co., 111
District Court decision, 82–83
initiated, 79
Louisiana Supreme Court
decision, 83–90
Live Stock Dealers and Butchers
Association of New Orleans
slaughterhouse
closing of, 108
compromise agreement and,
108–111, 111–112
District Court suits, 79–80,
102
injunctions against, 102
Louisiana Supreme Court on, 87
reopening of, 110
Livestock industry
cattle drives, 50
Charles Weed and, 57
Chicago and, 51
postwar beef supply, 49
Texas cattle trade, 49–51
Lochner v. New York, 10, 176
Lockwood, John, 55
Longhorns, 48, 49
Louisiana Code of Practice, 1867
Article 304, 76
Article 566, 76
Article 575, 76
Louisiana blacks in, 43–45
constitutional convention of
1864, 37, 43–46
constitutional convention of
1879, 164–65
population of, 43

Reconstruction and, 43, 44–45,
164
Louisiana. See Allgeyer v.
Louisiana ex rel Belden v. Fagan, 103
District Court decision, 83
initiated, 79
Louisiana Supreme Court
decision, 83–90
See also Slaughterhouse Cases
Louisiana House
blacks in, 46
Carter and, 105
House Bill 88, 58–60
House Bill 187, 105–6
House Bill 209, 106–8
party division in, 45
Louisiana legislature
blacks in, 45, 47
Campbell on, 133, 137
Crescent City Company stock
and, 64
of 1865–1867, 44–45
of 1868–1869, 5–6, 9, 45, 46–47
of 1869–1871, 46–47, 105–6
Eighth District Court and, 93
elections of 1873 and 1876, 164
grand jury recommendation to,
37
informality of, 137
on monopolies, 68, 106
motives of, 141
oath of office for, 45
party division in, 45
race and, 5–6, 46–47
on slaughterhouse relocation,
37–41
Louisiana Lottery Company, 76,
164
Louisiana Senate
blacks in, 47
party division in, 45
Senate Bill 142 and, 61